10649971

Paul the Traveller

Paul the Traveller

ERNLE BRADFORD

This edition published by Barnes & Noble, Inc.,
by arrangement with Brandt & Brandt.

1993 Barnes & Noble Books

ISBN 1-56619-377-X

Printed and bound in the United States of America

M 9 8 7 6 5 4 3 2

Contents

[1]

The Traveller

In the autumn of A.D. 59 a small coaster came alongside in the port of Myra. She was bound up north to Adramyttion, a town at the head of a long gulf near the island of Lesbos. She had left the famous city of Sidon about two weeks before, but because of the prevailing northerlies that sweep this section of the Mediterranean had been forced to creep around the southern coastline of Asia Minor, seeking a lee. Now she had found her way into a comfortable river-mouth where she could discharge local cargo and wait for a favourable wind to boost her on her way through the island-studded Aegean to her home port.

Myra was one of the most important towns in southern Asia Minor. It lay a few miles inland, in the delta between two rivers, one of which, Andracus, flowed through a busy port some three miles away. It was a place like many others at that time, where the worlds of Greece and Rome met with those of Asia, Syria and the Near East. Nothing now, an obscure village in Turkey, Myra in the first century A.D. was a thriving little city. Coastal traders running between the Levant, the Aegean, Byzantium and the Black Sea thronged the quays. Large grain-carrying vessels also waited here before taking the long route that led past Crete, up the eastern coast of Sicily, through the Messina Straits and on to Puteoli in the Bay of Naples.

Aboard this coaster there was, apart from travellers and traders taking passage to Myra, Adramyttion, and other ports of call, a Roman Lieutenant of the Augustan Regiment named Julius. He was in charge of a group of prisoners on their way to Rome, either to be tried or – as men who had already been condemned to death – to serve as part of the spectacle in the arenas. (Criminals were constantly dispatched from different areas of the empire to satisfy the never-ending taste for blood that was part and parcel of 'The Grandeur that was Rome'.) The regiment to which Julius belonged acted as a kind of imperial messenger force. Apart from escorting prisoners to the capital city, they served as guards on grain ships, and as a general police force working with provincial garrisons in the maintenance of the imperial peace. A man like Julius was probably commissioned from the ranks. As such he was even more probably a devotee of Mithras, the Persian Sun-God whose cult, with its advocacy of manliness and the military virtues, had been widely adopted throughout the army. He had no doubt been called Julius after the great Julius Caesar, as a sign that his parents honoured the Julian House, whose current ruling descendant was the Emperor Nero.

The Lieutenant was looking for a passage to Rome for himself, his soldiers, and his prisoners. The coaster had only been an intermediate method of transport until he reached Myra. It was near the end of the traditional sailing season, for few deep-sea vessels ventured out after mid-September. Some three hundred years later a Roman expert on military affairs, Vegetius, was to write that 'From mid-September until the 3rd day before the Ides of November [10 November] navigation is uncertain.' He added that, after this date, 'the seas are closed'. Except for urgent troop movements, or the necessary use of dispatch vessels in case of emergency, the whole Mediterranean went to sleep until the end of May.

The Lieutenant was eager to get his prisoners safely delivered to Rome, and was counting on finding a late-sailing merchantman whose owner or master was set on catching the winter grain market. The reason he was fairly confident of finding a suitable ship at Myra was that the prevailing westerlies in this part of the sea often caused ships from Alexandria to make their way up north – as the coaster had just done – and wait at Myra for a favourable wind to boost them on to Rome.

He found his ship. She was an Alexandrian grain-carrier destined for Puteoli and carrying a number of passengers, some of them no doubt Romans who had been to Egypt on a sight-seeing tour, to marvel at the Great Pyramids (still faced in those days with marble), among other things. There were, as well, dancers, slaves and entertainers bound for the palaces of Rome. The ship was probably one of the imperial mercantile fleet. The Lieutenant's arrival with his prisoners would have occasioned little comment;

criminals under escort were a common enough sight on the imperial highways and seaways. One prisoner, however, might have commanded some attention, for it was clear that he was a man of consequence. The Lieutenant not only treated him with deference but listened with great interest to whatever he said. His manner, too, showed that he was used to people paying attention to him, and he would sometimes preface a remark with a rhetorical gesture, a wave of the hand that seemed to command silence. He had two travelling companions with him – slaves, it would be assumed. Both were Greek and, while one appeared to be a physician, the other attended him in the capacity of a body-servant.

There was something strangely compelling about the man, even though his physical appearance was scarcely attractive. Certainly he was neither young nor good-looking – probably in the middle or late fifties, a fellow voyager would have guessed. He was almost totally bald, but heavily bearded with a sprinkling of grey. His face was volatile, an alive and slightly smiling expression, the nose long and aquiline. A Levantine face – probably a Jew? There were enough of those scattered throughout the empire. The really compelling thing about the man was his eyes, very bright and grey, and framed under shaggy, overhanging eyebrows that met in the middle. He was slight in stature and stooped a little. His face, his manner and his whole appearance suggested a man of authority, one who perhaps had travelled widely and to whom this ship and this projected voyage were no more than repetitious experiences in a life that had known many of the same. But at this early moment, while the merchantman still lay at the quay, and while the passengers were concerned about themselves, their private affairs, keeping an eye on their goods and bedding, and buying additional stores to make sure that they were adequately fed on the voyage, few would bother to speculate much about one Levantine under escort. Time was getting on, they were late, and all, for their varying reasons, were eager to reach Puteoli and the gracious Bay of Naples. Business or pleasure called them. The customary affairs and concerns of the world – no different then from now – occupied their dreams as well as their waking life.

Quite apart from the crew, the master, the pilot and other officers, there were 276 passengers. It is probable that the ship could have accommodated a great many more – grain-carriers of her type sometimes carried as many as 600 passengers. But it was a late-season sailing and most travellers would have caught earlier transport to avoid the dangers of being caught at sea during the autumn, when the Mediterranean weather often becomes rapidly unstable. A grain-carrier of this type was likely to have been about 340 tons. This was the size that the Roman imperial government preferred, and ship-owners who built a vessel of this tonnage for use in government transport were automatically exempt from compulsory public service. It was, then, clearly to the advantage of wealthy ship-owners to contribute one ship of such a size to the government. Their design followed the basic pattern that had been evolved by those master-mariners the Phoenicians centuries before, in their *gauloi* or tubs. Somewhat like half a walnut in hull-shape, they were intended above all for carrying capacity and not for speed. Unlike the galley, they were sailing ships first and foremost, having a large longboat for giving them a pluck out of or into harbour. This could also be used in calms at sea to tow them in the direction of any whisper of wind. Under normal conditions the longboat would lie astern on a line, but if the weather grew rough it would be hoisted aboard.

Apollonius, philosopher, mystic, wonder-worker (like others of his day and age he is credited with having raised people from the dead), was a native of Asia Minor and a contemporary of these travellers. On one occasion, in an attempt to reconcile the quarrelling citizens of Smyrna, he had pointed to the departure of just such a ship as this from their harbour, and used it as an example of how they should run their city: 'Look at the crew of that ship,' he said. 'Do you see how some are embarked in the skiffs ready to take towing ropes? Look, too, how some are hoisting the anchors and securing them inboard, while others are readying the sails to spread them before the wind, and at the same time parties are busy about their duties on poop and prow. If a single member of the crew failed to do his own particular job, or did it in an inefficient or unseamanlike manner, all would have a bad passage and they would themselves be their own tempest. But if there is a healthy rivalry between them, and if each tries to be as efficient as his neighbour, then the ship will make a good landfall. . . .'

No doubt in just such a manner this merchantman put to sea from Myra. She headed first of all northward towards the port of Cnidus on the all-but-island of Triopion – 'all-but', since it was connected with the mainland by a causeway which had gradually converted into a sandy isthmus. This gave two good harbours, one to the north and one to the south. It was the southerly that the ship will have sought out at this time of the year.

It had been a slow passage, bucking the north-westerly head winds, anchoring at night, and hoping always for a favourable slant that would give them a chance to sheer off to the west and set their course for home. At Cnidus no doubt most of the passengers went ashore – some to admire the magnificent Aphrodite by Praxiteles in her temple – but most of them to enjoy good food and wine, and supplement their rations. There were few comforts aboard passenger-carrying merchantmen, although there were some vessels afloat which offered for the rich such accommodation as would not be seen again in this sea for many centuries after the fall of the Roman empire. In these, and in particular the royal pleasure barges of the emperors, there were baths and lounges, elegant cabins, exercise areas, covered promenades and chapels. Their floors were paved with mosaics, lamps and pitchers were of bronze, while silver or gold dishes and goblets graced the table. But in a standard ship such as this which had just left Myra there were no such luxuries. Since nearly all Mediterranean sailing was done during the indulgent summer months, people travelled as simply as peasants, most of them camping out on the upper deck with a roll of bedding and sleeping with their heads under the stars. Any slaves, condemned criminals, or steerage passengers would have been down below, hardly able, as the Greek writer Lucian put it, 'to stretch out their legs on the bare boards beside the bilge water'. Between the floor timbers limber-holes were cut to permit the bilge water to run freely to the pump-well where, either by an Archimedean screw or by leather buckets, the seamen on watch bailed the ship. A few passengers – certainly Julius and most probably his distinguished charge – would have shared in the modest comforts of the deckhouse at the stern, where the captain also had his cabin. The galley was also hard by, its stove smoking away in fair weather, with the smell of vegetable soup or hot bread to whet the appetite. Simple though it was, such a galley, with its hearth and oven raised on iron bars above a clay base, and sitting on a floor of tiles, was far more sophisticated than the open fireboxes used aboard the ships in which Columbus crossed the Atlantic 1,400 years later.

That year the northerlies which prevail over the Aegean throughout summer persisted well into the autumn. The captain, who had hoped to pick up a favourable slant off the mainland so as to run straight across the southern Aegean to Aphrodite's island, Cythera, was in something of a dilemma. With his awkward rig, dependent almost entirely upon one square-sail, he was naturally worried that the ship would make so much leeway that, instead of fetching up at Cythera, he would find himself on the iron-bound northern coast of Crete. And there were few enough harbours in that part of the world. He consulted with the pilot and both agreed that the sensible course was to drop down south of Crete where, in view of the steady northerlies, they would be able to find themselves in a lee. From here they could coast along and, if wind and weather permitted, could then make their way across Adria (the Ionian Sea) until they reached either Syracuse or Messina in Sicily.

Leaving the rocky islands of Karpathos and Kasos to port they dropped down the Aegean and came under the lee of Cape Salmone at the eastern end of Crete. Even now navigation was not easy. The northerly winds whipped down the mountains causing shuddering squalls over the foothills. The merchantman, with her heavy main-yard braced as far fore-and-aft as possible, made little progress. They worked slowly along the coast, always aware that if they got carried away they would be hurled southwards to Africa. About half way along the southern coast of Crete they found a sheltered anchorage in a small bay known as Fair Havens, a little east of Cape Matala. Here they waited, hoping for a favourable shift of the wind. With the northerlies still persisting they could not possibly beat up into the bay beyond the cape. It was now nearing the end of September and it seemed clear that, unless there was a considerable improvement in the weather, the ship would have to winter in Crete. It was not a very happy prospect. Certainly the anchorage where they lay – although it had a small town called Lasaea nearby – was far from suitable. All were eager to get on if possible, but even the captain, concerned about the delivery of his precious cargo, was aware that the winter weather had set in earlier than usual this year.

On 5 October, the Jewish Day of Atonement, the bald-headed man and one of his servants – though not the other who was a doctor – were observed to take no bread or wine. Jews, then, as had already been surmised. A few days later the captain called a conference in his cabin. Although the master of the ship, he was at the same time an employee of Rome, and the senior officer aboard was Julius. Roman practice made no distinction between service ashore or afloat. A lieutenant of the Augustan Regiment, even if not professionally a sailor, was nevertheless in command unless there was an army officer superior to him among the passengers. Among those who attended this conference at the invitation of the Lieutenant was the older Jew. He was said to be a very experienced traveller, a man who had been shipwrecked more than once, and who was conversant with the climate and the weather of the eastern Mediterranean.

The result of the shipboard conference was recorded by the medical and literary man. The decision taken was that the anchorage of Fair Havens was unsuitable for wintering in, and that as soon as possible the ship should make for a harbour called Phoenix. This lay to the north-west across the gulf beyond Cape Matala and was known to be the only really safe winter harbour in southern Crete. Although strong gusts might be expected to sweep across Phoenix when the wind was in the north, vessels could be safely secured by anchors laid out in good holding-ground, and with stern-lines doubled-up to the stone quays. Even when the wind went into the south it seldom 'blew home' against the precipitous mountains that surrounded the town and harbour. There was only one dissentient from the general opinion to winter in Phoenix and that was the elderly Jew. He said that, if they went on any further, he was quite sure they would lose the ship, the cargo and possibly their lives as well. Julius, following the opinion of the captain and the sailing-master, naturally elected to go on to Phoenix. It certainly seemed the best thing to do at the time.

While they were anchored in Fair Havens the passengers went ashore and traded with the locals for fresh vegetables, meat and wine. The Cretans were a dour and truculent race of people, and they disliked their Roman rulers. Certainly they made a bad impression upon one man. The bearded Jew was to remark of them later in a letter to a friend: 'All Cretans are liars, evil people, and lazy gluttons.' He was, it was true, quoting the Cretan poet Epimenides, but clearly something or other had stuck in his mind that caused him to write this way. No doubt, like many other travellers before and since, he had been fleeced by the locals while doing some shopping.

They waited for a southerly wind, something that would boost them gently along the coast and then, as they turned towards Phoenix, would enable them to get the benefit of the wind under their stern. In due course it came. Some of the people now went aft to the stone altar which most vessels of this size had on the poop and made a libation to the gods. They entrusted themselves to their care and implored a safe arrival. The Jew and his two attendants were conspicuous by their absence. But then, everyone knew that the Jews were a peculiar people. They were contemptuous of all others, worshipped some peculiar god of their own, and were inclined to believe that the rest of the races of the world were damned. They were troublemakers within the empire.

Taking advantage of the southerly the ship ran along the coast keeping close in to the shore. They had to round Cape Matala and then, if the wind remained favourable, it would be no more than a fifty-mile run to Phoenix. The danger about such coastal navigation in the lee of the mountains of Crete was that if the wind changed and swung into the north the most terrifying squalls hurled down the slopes; squalls sufficient to dismast even a well-found ship. They were known as 'white squalls', because their coming could be seen by the way the sea splintered into foam as they advanced. It was only by keeping a wary eye towards the coast that the sailor could immediately drop his canvas or, if there was no time for this, run the ship off in front of them. This was exactly what happened to the Roman grain-ship. A blast of wind hurled down on her from the north-east and the helmsman – struggling at the bar controlling the two long steering-paddles – turned before it. The sailors tore across the deck and began to lower the great yard so as to reduce the centre of pressure, while others manned the brailing ropes and began to shorten sail. But it was more than just a temporary squall. Euroclydon, the violent north-easter, the most dangerous wind in the eastern Mediterranean, had settled in to blow. There was nothing for it but to take the wind astern, just keeping sufficient steerage-way on the ship to prevent her broaching to.

Thirty miles away in a south-west direction lay the little island of Clauda, rising to a height of 1,000 feet, and providing limited shelter on its southern coast for a careful pilot. If they failed to round up and get in the lee of the island there was every likelihood that they would be swept away and find themselves on the sandbanks of North Africa. Meanwhile the longboat surged out on its tow behind them. Waves were breaking over it and it was in imminent danger of foundering. But the main danger was that, in the increasing violence of the wind and sea, the ship's timbers might start to open. Then, if the cargo of grain got wet it would start to swell, exerting intolerable pressure on the ship's sides. The captain was skilful. They cleared the coastal bank to the north of the island, passed the sunken reef with its two rocky islets, and came round into such shelter as Clauda afforded.

While the passengers lent a hand to get the longboat safely aboard, the sailors were busy in an all-important operation – frapping the ship. For a merchantmant of the period this meant passing large cable-laid ropes over the bows and walking them aft until they had reached the amidships section. They then hauled up the port and starboard eyes on the ropes until they met in the middle of the deck and, with the aid of tackles or a windlass, made them as taut as possible. The whole object of the operation was to bind the centre part of the hull with a strong belt of rope so as to take some of the strain off the planks and ribs.

With the mainsail completely furled, and the long mainyard lowered and lashed along the deck, the ship was now kept under a simple storm-sail. This was a small square of canvas set from a foremast, a highly steeved-up length of timber that in later centuries was to become known as a bowsprit. Under this limited canvas the vessel, while it could not properly heave to, had a controlled rate of drift. She could be made to lie with her head about forty-five degrees from the direction of the wind. The result was that, as the gale persisted from the east-north-east, the grain ship now drifted across the Mediterranean from Clauda in a direction slightly north of west. It was far from comfortable. The galley fire had long since been doused and, except for cold beans and bread, there was little to be eaten – even if the passengers had felt like it. Most of them by now were far beyond caring whether they ever saw another meal or not. Above or below, sprawled on their bedding, they had given themselves up to seasickness, dampness and despair.

The sky was heavily overcast, neither sun nor stars visible for many days', blown spume tearing over the gunwales, the monotonous clunk-clunk of blocks and tackle slapping against the mast, and the sour smell of wet corn and the even worse smell of the stirred-up bilges. The captain and his advisers knew little except that they were drifting far to the west of Crete. They had no compass, no log for measuring the distance run, and little except their knowledge of the ship and the drift she was likely to make under her stormsail. (She was in fact making something between one and two knots in a westerly direction.) After seeing the steep sides of Clauda disappear behind them, the captain, aware of the danger of his bulk cargo, set all hands to clearing out as much of it as possible and throwing it overboard. The dark sea became stained with corn. Then, as the sailors labouring at keeping the water under control cried out that they were in danger of foundering, he gave order for the furnishings and fittings of the ship – other than those necessary for her salvation – to be thrown overboard to lighten her.

They were way out in the central area of Adria, one of the stormiest parts of the Mediterranean. By now, after days of drifting, exhausted by lack of food and cold, the passengers and even the crew had lost all hope. It was noticeable that one man alone – not the captain, nor even the Lieutenant – seemed unperturbed. The old Jew with the piercing eyes came out on deck, gazed at the sky, passed a salt-stained hand along the gunwale-capping, and moved his lips as if talking to himself.

One day, when the huddled bundles of humans and bedding seemed to have exasperated him beyond measure, he shouted out to them. Everyone had been wrong, he said, they should have listened to his advice and not left Fair Havens. Any who had the slightest spirit left must have felt impelled to tell this self-opinionated fellow to jump over the side. He was now ranting away about some God whom he served who had spoken to him in a dream, and guaranteed all their lives. Apparently as a Roman citizen he had appealed to be tried under the supreme Roman court – Caesar himself – and this God of his had promised him that he should go there. In the meantime, if they understood him properly, they were all destined to be wrecked on some island, the ship was going to be lost, but they themselves would all survive. Another fanatic! The East was full of them....

Who was this man?

[2]

Boy in the East

He was a Jew by birth, a Roman by citizenship, and a revolutionary. He was bent upon establishing throughout the Roman empire a series of communities, whose allegiance was not to the state but to a supranational religious kingdom. He and his associates held the belief that the world was soon to end, and that they alone would survive in some transmogrified state.

He had been born in the city of Tarsus in southern Asia Minor, during the reign of the Emperor Augustus, in the early years of what is now called the Christian era. On the eighth day after his birth, according to Jewish custom, he was circumcized and given the name of Saul. He was called after the first king of Israel, that brave, impulsive and violent man, from the tribe of Benjamin. The Benjamites were noted for their ability as fighters and they always stood in the forefront of the battleline. They had earned this honour because they were the first to cross the Red Sea in the exodus of the Jews from Egypt. He was also given a Roman name, Paulus – Paul.

He was 'a Hebrew sprung from Hebrews' yet he was also proudly to boast later that as well as being a Jew he was 'Tarsian, a citizen of no mean city'. Not only his Jewishness but his Roman citizenship meant a great deal to him. If temperamentally the former prevailed in his nature he was always conscious of the dignity of having been born a Roman citizen. How this Jewish family had acquired citizenship is unknown, but it is just possible that Paul's father or his grandfather had been one of the many to whom Mark Antony had granted Roman citizenship during his riotous courtship of Cleopatra in their city.

To be a Roman citizen was no small honour. In A.D. 47 the Emperor Claudius had a census taken of the whole empire. The officials recorded that there were just under 6,000,000 citizens out of a total population of something like 80,000,000. Quite apart from the privilege of the vote, citizenship also guaranteed that the holder could not be flogged without a fair trial. He was also protected by Roman law and, in the event of a grave charge being brought against him, he might take his appeal to the highest court of all – the judgement of the emperor. The dignity and majesty of Roman law were the foundations upon which the whole fabric of the empire rested, and it was unique in the ancient world. As Cicero put it: 'Without the law the state would be like the body without a mind. . . .'

The city of Tarsus where this Roman Jew was born was the capital of the province of Cilicia. It stood on the river Cydnus, about twelve miles above its mouth. It may have originally been a Greek settlement but by this time it had become largely orientalized. (Indeed there was a tradition that it had been founded by the last great king of the Assyrian empire, Sardanapalus.) In any case, despite the influence of the Greeks, and the Roman face-lift imposed by Mark Antony, it had remained a meeting-place of nations and cultures; Jews, Asiatics, Syrians, Persians and Phoenicians as well as Greeks and Romans. Its importance was largely due to its excellent well-sheltered harbour formed by the lake on which the city stood, as well as the fact that it was on a great caravan route between east and west. This came through a road which had been cut across Mount Taurus through what were called the Cilician Gates; a narrow gorge about 100 yards long. It was in the harbour of Tarsus that the royal barge of Cleopatra, together with all its attendant escorts and supply ships, had seduced the simple hard-drinking Antony with the demonstration of the immeasurable wealth, luxury and refinement of the Egyptian queen. Tarsus, where Rome had met Alexandria, was a melting-pot of cultures, races and religions.

The river ran cold through the heart of the city – something that its citizens were prone to boast about – and it was, despite the large population, still clean and clear. The same could hardly be said of the citizens themselves. Apollonius of Tyana, a philosopher but no puritan, is said to have commented upon the perverted miasma that overhung Tarsus. Although educated in the city, he decided at an early age to withdraw to nearby Aegae where he embraced the ascetic way of life. Perhaps there was something about the overpowering and open sexuality of Tarsus that would have given any honest or scrupulous man a distaste for the pagan world. And this boy called Saul was not only brought up as a monotheistic Hebrew, with the belief that his race and his alone was chosen by God before all others; he was brought up as a Pharisee – the strictest sect of Judaism.

To be a Pharisee was to belong to a party which had first really emerged in the second century B.C., and which – though often divided within itself – was the dominant factor in the development of orthodox Judaism. As G. H. Box put it:

> Their general aim was to develop and deepen the work of the earlier *Hasidim* [the men of piety] in making the Torah the accepted rule of life for the mass of the Jewish people. Their work was

> astonishingly successful. They made the synagogue a permanent and widespread institution of Jewish life. Here in the weekly assemblages the lections were read and expounded to the people; the synagogue prayers were developed and made familiar. They also organized a system of elementary religious instruction.

It was to a school of this nature that the boy Paul would ultimately go. But in the meantime, even if his father and mother and the other stricter Jews shunned the world in which they lived, he was nevertheless growing up in a completely pagan city.

In Tarsus there was to be found every element of paganism from the simplest and crudest versions to the most refined levels. Tarsus was also a university city. This meant that the influence of Greek philosophy permeated the life of the thoughtful minority. At the time when Paul was still a small boy, the head of the university of Tarsus was a remarkable man, Athenodorus, who had been born in a nearby village. He had been the intimate adviser of the Emperor Augustus, who had also been his pupil for a time. His influence over the emperor was strong and lasting. He is said to have trained Augustus to curb the violence of his temper by reciting the Greek alphabet whenever he felt a fit of anger coming over him. Similarly he had also given Augustus an object lesson on the necessity of curbing his sexual passions. Augustus had the unattractive habit of commanding any woman whom he had seen and fancied to be brought to his palace in a closed litter (so that she would not be recognized en route), when he would take his pleasure with her. More often than not these would be the wives of his friends and close acquaintances. At no time in his life did Augustus have any scruples if he wanted something or somebody. Athenodorus was appraised of this characteristic of his pupil when one day he called on a friend of his and found him broken-hearted because his wife had received just such an imperial summons. Athenodorus, as in so much else, was not the man to be at a loss for appropriate action.

He comforted his friend and told him that there was no cause to worry; he would attend to matters. In due course the litter arrived at Augustus's palace in Rome and was set down in the imperial quarters. Augustus approached, greedy as a schoolboy for this new dish in his relentless banquet of women, when to his astonishment out leapt his mentor with a sword in his hand. 'Augustus!' the philosopher shouted, 'aren't you ever afraid that one day someone will assassinate you like this?'

Although nothing could cure the Emperor of constant adultery (his wife Livia often acting as his procuress), on this occasion he thanked Athenodorus for the lesson. In future he presumably ordered the women whom he fancied to come openly to the palace. Athenodorus finally grew tired of Rome and, despite the Emperor's protestations, insisted on returning to his native Tarsus. Here he found a totally corrupt administration which was plundering the city. Using the Emperor's favour, he had managed to break it and had restored good government to Tarsus. A practical man then, as well as a philosopher; his life is best summed up in his maxim: 'You are only free from passion when you ask God for nothing that you would not ask for openly.' It was not only the Jews who lived righteous and honourable lives.

But there was another face to the pagan world, and one of which Paul, growing up in this provincial capital, cannot have been unaware. Like most other oriental cities Tarsus was a centre of the fertility cults which had dominated this area of Asia since time immemorial. Through her streets went the processions in honour of the Great Earth Mother, she who had dominated the whole of the eastern Mediterranean in the days of Neolithic Man, and for long after in the civilizations of the Cyclades and Minoan Crete. Through her streets went the priests and pristesses of Isis, another goddess of the maternal principle who had held sway over Egypt long before the Jews had even been taken captive, let alone before the exodus. Dionysus, not just the father and promoter of the vine, but a god with a strong mystical element in his worship – promising resurrection into another and better world – was a major cult. Had not Antony, when he was master of the eastern half of the Roman empire, deliberately proclaimed himself 'The New Dionysus'? He had been hailed as such by the citizens of Tarsus, and Cleopatra had been acclaimed as Venus Anadyomene, Venus risen from the waves. 'Aphrodite had come to revel with Dionysus for the good of Asia,' the Tarsians had said.

There were other aspects of the city which could not have escaped even a Jewish schoolboy. He was later to write: 'There was a time once when I too lived outside the Law. But when the commandment came "thou shalt not lust" sin sprang to life, and I died.' The reference is ambiguous, but certainly suggests that at some time in his life, and presumably during his youth in Tarsus, Paul had succumbed to the sensual temptations by which he was surrounded. He was after all, as F. A. Spencer commented, 'a highly sensitive, strongly emotional Jewish boy living in a city of a thousand strumpets and sodomites'.

Tarsus like most eastern cities did not conceal its vices but paraded them. While the modest Jewish women only went outside their houses with their heads covered and faces veiled, the street-women were to be seen everywhere, with high-tiered hair and extravagant make-up soliciting for customers. Everywhere too there minced along their male counterparts, gesturing obscenely to one another, perfumed, and as elaborately coiffured and made-up as their sisters 'in trade'. In the East homosexuality was not regarded with any abhorrence. Indeed, since all marriageable as well as married women of respectable families lived an almost harem-like existence, homosexuality was as inevitable as it is to this day in many such countries. Apollonius, as has been seen, had withdrawn from the city because he disliked its whole atmosphere, commenting that its people were buffoons and that they cared more about extravagant clothes than anything else. Tarsus was indeed 'no mean city', but it was one where the lack of morality and the essential emptiness at the heart of the pagan world was only too clearly displayed.

The boy's parents seem to have been of the prosperous middle class. His father was a tent-maker – a trade which, though it means little or nothing today, would have been equivalent then to being a caravan manufacturer or a builder of working-class houses. All over the East millions of people lived in tents, permanent homes being largely the prerogative of city-dwellers. When he was six years old the boy would have started his studies in the House of the Book. This was the Jewish centre for instruction in reading, writing, and in the Law, and it was maintained in the synagogue. Its upkeep was paid for by a tax that was levied by the Jewish elders upon the whole of their community.

Instruction began with the first chapter of Leviticus: 'And the Lord called unto Moses and spake unto him out of the tabernacle of the congregation. . . .' Throughout the days, weeks, months and years of his education the boy and his fellow pupils would learn by heart the whole of the Law – in much the same manner as Greek bards committed the whole of Homer to heart. The scriptures that they studied would have been written in ancient Hebrew, but the instruction would have been given either in Aramaic (the spoken Hebrew of the day), or in the common demotic Greek which served as a *lingua franca* throughout the eastern Mediterranean. Although he was growing up in a strict Jewish family, he was living in a world ruled by Rome where the language was predominantly Greek – but interwoven with the racial and religious climate of the Orient.

However much Paul's family may have shunned the world in which they lived they could not ignore it. A Jew who was also a Roman citizen and a businessman like Paul's father could hardly avoid all his non-Jewish neighbours. Neither could the boy. And one as impressionable as Paul cannot have failed to absorb – along with his knowledge of the Law – something of the multi-coloured, multi-scented atmosphere of the city.

[3]

Stoics and Cynics

Peace and security were the two great blessings that Augustus had brought to the Mediterranean world. Whatever the faults of his regime, nearly everyone felt that the Pax Romana which he had imposed was a blessing, especially after the horrors of the Civil Wars. The whole of the known world had then been torn apart in the struggles between Caesar and Pompey, and later between Augustus, Antony and Pompey's son. The conclusive victory of Augustus and the establishment of a firm autocratic rule had brought an end to all this. From the Golden Milestone in the Forum at Rome some 3,000 miles of excellent roads spread out like arteries feeding the body of the empire. Along them marched the soldiers of Augustus, a visible sign to all the nations that Roman arms were never far away. Along them spurred his couriers carrying the imperial decrees, or returning to the capital with news and dispatches from the provinces and from their governors. Not until the late eighteenth century – and even then not throughout all Europe – was there to be so efficient a system, with a regular service of government post-stations supplying a change of horses at regular intervals. Throughout the 'Middle Sea', which had been largely pacified by Pompey, trade now flowed unmolested. The pirates who had haunted large areas of the Mediterranean, and particularly the eastern basin, had been eliminated, and the great grain ships and the smaller cargo-carriers sailed without fear of the raider sliding out suddenly from behind some island bluff.

Within the memory of Paul's father the Taurus mountains behind the city had been the home of countless brigands, and trade had been imperilled. Even the city itself had been at the mercy of spurious trade unions whose members went about armed and terrorized their fellow citizens. Augustus had dissolved all these throughout the empire, leaving only genuine registered unions susceptible to the rule of law. The boy's father, and later Paul himself, were members of one of them, the guild of tent-makers. Such guilds not only secured benefits for themselves by arbitration, or strike action if need be, but also fixed prices and standards of workmanship. They were a curious combination of a chamber of commerce, trade union in the modern sense, and something akin to an association like the Rotarians. Every trade, craft or profession had its guild – from flute-players and fruit-sellers to tailors and doctors. Encouraged throughout the empire, they served not only to protect themselves and the public but also to maintain internal stability in the many cities that now came within the all-powerful embrace of Rome. In the tradition which has survived in the Mediterranean into the twentieth century in the shape of fiestas, they each had their respective patron 'saint'. On the appropriate day the members of the guild would parade through the streets with the most important members leading the procession, followed by a band, and then all the other members carrying banners and flags. They also held conventions in exactly the same style as modern business associations, where prices and standards and trade problems would be discussed, after which the wine and the dancing girls would be brought on. Human nature has hardly changed.

Cosmopolitan tolerance was one of the main and best features of the Augustan world, with the Greek language binding the Mediterranean together in commerce, literature, philosophy and everyday communication. If the law was administered in Latin, and Latin was the language of the military rulers, it was in Greek that the citizens of this superb and sprawling empire went about their daily business. Most important of all was the religious tolerance that was practised; all gods and all creeds were equally accepted and, though some gods might be 'more equal than others', there was no discrimination between one religion and another. Only the Jews held aloof from their pagan neighbours, maintaining that they were the chosen people of the one and only god, and that all others were deluded idolators.

Many years before Paul's birth the Old Testament had been translated into Greek (he himself was later to quote it in this language). Known as the Septuagint, because it was said to have been translated at Alexandria by a committee of seventy rabbis, this was widely available throughout the ancient world. Any interested Gentile could easily become familiar with the beliefs and laws of the monotheistic Hebrews. Along with other Oriental religions like Isis-worship, the religion of Jehovah had its converts among Greeks and Romans. This was facilitated by the dissemination of the Jews throughout the empire; they immediately established synagogues in all the cities where there was a Jewish community.

On the surface the Roman world which Augustus had so successfully established might have seemed an astounding success – as indeed in many respects it was. Even so, it still had its critics and their view was voiced by Tacitus. Although writing a century later, he probably best summed up the disillusionment felt by free-thinking men who still clung to the old Republican persuasion.

> After he had seduced the army by gifts and the common people by the provision of cheap food he attracted everyone by the desired gift of peace. But then he gradually began to enlarge his powers, encroaching on the functions of the Senate, of the magistrates and then of the law itself. There was no opposition. Men of spirit had either died on the battlefield or been eliminated by judicial murder. Such of the aristocracy as survived were rewarded financially and politically in return for slavish obedience. Having done well out of the revolution they naturally liked the current security as compared with the dangers and vicissitudes of the former regime. . . .

Tacitus goes on to say, however, that the provinces definitely preferred the Augustan system as opposed to the previous dangers and uncertainties, and the complete absence of the rule of law during the death-throes of the republic.

Predominant among thinking men throughout the empire at this period was the philosophy of the Stoics whose noble and austere view of life, acknowledging the overall rule of one god, was in some respects not so dissimilar from the Judaic monotheism that young Paul was daily absorbing in his synagogue school. Stoicism had captured many of the best intellects in Rome. As R. D. Hicks put it:

> The introduction of Stoicism at Rome was the most momentous of the many changes that it saw. After the first sharp collision with the jealousy of the national authorities it found a ready acceptance, and made rapid progress amongst the noblest families. It has been well said that the old heroes of the republic were unconscious Stoics, fitted by their narrowness, their stern simplicity and devotion to duty for the almost Semitic earnestness of the new doctrine. In Greece its insensibility to art and the cultivation of life was a fatal defect; not so with the shrewd men of the world, desirous of qualifying as advocates or jurists.

The principal belief of the Stoics was that man's supreme duty was devotion to virtue. Whatever vicissitudes life might bring, man must follow his conscience and by doing so he would be fulfilling the will of God. Everyone had a purpose in the world, the ruler to rule, the artist to create, the farmer to raise the crops for his fellow men, and the lawgiver to dispense justice. Some 300 years before the birth of Paul, the Stoic philosopher Cleanthes in his magnificent hymn to Zeus, the creator of all things, had given expression to religious sentiments which could hardly have been taken amiss by even the most orthodox Jew:

> Most glorious of immortals, O Zeus of many names, almighty and everlasting, sovereign of nature, directing all in accordance with law, thee it is fitting that all mortals should address . . . Thee all this universe, as it rolls circling round the earth, obeys wheresoever thou dost guide, and gladly owns thy sway. Such a minister thou holdest in thy invincible hands – the two-edged, fiery, everliving thunderbolt, under whose stroke all nature shudders. No work upon earth is wrought apart from thee, lord, nor through the divine ethereal sphere, nor upon the sea; save only whatsoever deeds wicked men do in their own foolishness. Nay, thou knowest how to make even the rough smooth, and to bring order out of disorder; and unfriendly things are friendly in thy sight. For so hast thou fitted all things together, the good with the evil, that there might be one eternal law over all . . . Deliver men from fell ignorance. Banish it, father, from their soul, and grant them to obtain wisdom, whereon relying thou rulest all things with justice.

The most powerful intellect in Rome at this time, and a man whose influence through his writings had spread far and wide, was Seneca. His was a stoicism that had refined earlier teachings until it embraced such concepts as those propounded in his treatise *On Providence*, where he says that the wise man can never really meet with misfortune. All apparent misfortune is sent by God to train man how to live and how to disregard external conditions. The body is a mere husk, the prison of the soul, and it is not until the death of the body that the soul can begin its real life. Seneca committed suicide at the Emperor's orders in the reign of Nero. As the latter's tutor, when Nero was a young man, Seneca had done everything he could to check the future Emperor's vicious inclinations. He failed in this, as probably any man would have done. It was in the reign of Nero that Paul too would one day meet his end. Some of the ideas contained in the Stoic doctrine seem to have permeated Paul, and he was later to use them for his own purpose.

Quite apart from the Stoics, but a link between them and the great Socrates, were the Cynics – whom Paul must certainly have seen in the market-place of Tarsus. For whereas the Stoics carried out their philosophy in their normal daily life, or endeavoured to do so, the Cynics made a parade of their rejection of contemporary society. Nowadays they would be called 'drop-outs', and their appearance was certainly such as would be easily recognizable in any modern 'commune'. To emphasize their contempt for society and the world in general they went long-haired and bearded. Boasting of the lice in their locks, with foul uncut fingernails and tattered cloaks, leaning upon rough staves, they scorned all comfort and called upon men to repent and leave the artificiality of evolved convention.

The originator of their philosophy, Antisthenes, had been a pupil of Socrates and had carried his master's saying, 'Virtue is knowledge', to a logical if extreme conclusion, that nothing matters except the harmony of morality with reason. Everything else must be despised. The pleasures of life are harmful since they interfere with the operation of the will. Power and wealth corrupt, since they substitute in the soul the artificial for the natural. Back to nature, then, and wander homeless, sleeping on the ground and begging for scraps of bread from the very people whom you despise. The good man needs nothing. 'Let men gain wisdom – or buy a rope,' Diogenes had remarked. Poverty and disrepute are if anything an advantage, since they force a man out of society and turn him in upon himself, and it is only in himself that he can best learn to do without external things and achieve purity of intellect. The Stoic philosopher Epictetus, who also lived in the reign of Nero, referred to them admiringly as 'the athletes of righteousness'. They were in many respects akin to the Stoics. The poet Juvenal remarked of them: 'A Cynic only differs from a Stoic by his cloak.' The tattered and bedraggled cloak of the Cynic was, like the garb of the modern 'drop-out', his badge of office, the evidence of his superiority to the materialistic consumer world by which he was surrounded.

But – and again like some of his successors – the Cynic was prone to one great error. By placing so much emphasis on the animal side of life, 'the return to nature pure and simple', he inevitably lost so many of the advantages – if not possibly the virtues – of the civilization that he despised. If virtue is knowledge, the question must inevitably be asked, 'Knowledge of what?' To this, the answer, for many of the simpler followers of Cynicism, was a return to a more than Rousseauesque 'Noble savage'. Civilization must go, animals were happy (if not dominated by man and killed for man's convenience). Theirs was much the same dream as that of the nineteenth-century anarchists, believing in their simplicity that man was essentially good at heart and, if left on his own, had no need for social laws.

Paul, on his way to and from school, must often have seen and heard them. As a strict Jew (and as a Roman citizen acknowledging the rule of law, quite apart from the Law of Jehovah), he cannot have accepted their doctrines. At the same time, something in their abnegation, their contempt for comfortable living, may have appealed to his desert heart. They were wanderers – as he was to become. They had no permanent homes. They said that Truth was above all and that it did not matter where the next meal came from. They were *free* because they had rejected the world.

[4]

Emperor-worship

The worship of the ruling monarch and his consort was as old as the Pharaohs. Other gods the ancient Egyptians had in abundance, but the ruler of the Two Kingdoms of the Nile was always accepted as a divine being. To a modern, accustomed to a distinct separation between the divine and the mortal, this seems strange, but it is not so curious a conception. One may pray to the gods and goddesses, whether they be Isis Queen of Heaven or Osiris her consort, or Horus her son, but the results of such prayers are not immediately obvious. These remote gods may confer comfort, or appear to answer some bequest, but usually the result of such prayers is intangible. The Pharaoh on the other hand is himself visible, and the evidence of his rule is there for all to see. If times are good, the country peaceful, and law and order prevail, all this may be ascribed to him. On the other hand if there is famine or drought, or the Nile fails to flood, it is only the Pharaoh who can order the royal granaries to be opened and the people issued with food. He is conspicuous in his life and acts, and his power is immediately evident. He can condemn to death, and he can also grant pardon. Over all his subjects he has complete sway. When most of those subjects are illiterate peasants it is not difficult to see how the Pharaoh, remote in his splendour, surrounded by priests and advisers, magnified by the army over which he has control, and enhanced by the works of art which his architects and artists create to surround him, acquired a completely godlike quality.

The Romans of the old republic, rejoicing in the fact that there were no more kings of Rome, could never have accepted the deification of any living man. All this had begun to change even before Augustus. Julius Caesar had been deified after his death, and from now on emperor-worship was to become an accredited part of the Roman system. It was natural enough perhaps, but it did not really fit the old Roman pattern. In a sense it had largely been an importation from Egypt and from Caesar's entanglement with Cleopatra. It was in Egypt, or more particularly in Hellenistic Alexandria, that Caesar had observed the aura of divinity that enshrouded Egypt's queen. The Macedonian Greek rulers of Egypt had followed the pattern set by the Pharaohs. In order to show the native Egyptians that they too were as much gods and goddesses as the ancient rulers had claimed to be, they had even adopted the custom of royal incest – since a god clearly cannot mate with a mere mortal. Caesar with his political astuteness had observed how convenient it was for a ruler to be considered by his people as something more than mortal. Since he himself claimed through the Julian line to be descended from Venus it was natural enough for him to see himself as potentially a god. After all, Alexander the Great had been acclaimed as such, and were not Caesar's achievements on a par with his?

After Caesar's death Antony had absorbed the same mystique. He for his part claimed to be descended from Hercules – something to which he attributed his physical strength and his great prowess with women. But, as has been seen, he went even further than that. When he was joint ruler of the Roman empire along with Octavian he had not only inherited the eastern part of the empire but he also, as it were, inherited Cleopatra.

Even before he met the queen at Paul's city of Tarsus he had begun to imbue himself with more than mortal characteristics, claiming to be the new Dionysus, a god with whom he had a particular affinity because of his more than average love of wine. But his assumption of this title was well justified on political grounds. The peoples of the East, and not only the Egyptians, were accustomed to identifying their rulers with gods, and Antony, to regularize his position with them, was wise to claim such an identity for himself. After all, Cleopatra's father Ptolemy XII had adopted the title of the New Dionysus. In view of Antony's relationship with the queen who was to bear him three children, it was intelligent enough to claim a similar divine status. The Egyptians certainly expected it of him if he was to be the father of their queen's children. The tradition then had been established whereby a Roman could, like an oriental potentate, claim divine honours for himself.

The cult of emperor-worship, which was to become a standard feature of Roman imperialism from the time of Augustus onwards, served the useful political purpose of unifying the innumerable peoples who had now come under the sway of Rome. Although Augustus himself was always determined to maintain the apparent trappings of republicanism, referring to the 'Restoration of the Republic' – and many Romans, content in the peace that he had brought them, were prepared to believe him – to the peoples of the east the ruling emperor was generally considered to be a god. If they rarely, if ever, saw him, they had proof enough of his power. The one nation which refused to acknowledge the divinity of the emperor was of course the Jews. To them it was anathema that any man should outstep his station in the world to the extent of claiming to be other than mortal, and subject to the laws of the one and only God.

It was, despite the imposed peace that had followed upon the success of Augustus, a period of intense emotional distress. All around the Mediterranean basin men sought for a sign, for a saviour, for some reason and justification for their lives. Astrologers flourished, and people would hardly embark upon any enterprise of consequence without consulting their favourite soothsayer. To quote Peter Green's translation of Juvenal:

Rich ladies send out to hire their own tame Phrygian
Prophet, they skim off the cream of the star-gazers, or
Pick one of those wise old parties who neutralize thunderbolts:
The Circus and the Embankment preside over more
Plebeian destinies. Here, by the dolphin columns
And the public stands, old whores in their off-shoulder
Dresses and thin gold neck-chains come for advice –
Should they ditch the tavern-keeper? marry the rag-and-bone man?

Fate and the stars occupied people's minds. Pliny the elder, writing in the first century, commented that all over the world, in every place and at every hour, 'Fortune alone is invoked and her name is spoken'. As it seemed that the whole world was ruled by Chance or Fortune, she was the goddess to whom most people turned. Every city was deemed to have her own Tyche or Fortune, and in private houses there was more often than not a statuette of the goddess. On some coins of this period there is to be found 'The Fortune of Augustus', a symbol not only of his emperorship but of the special relationship he had with the blind goddess who ruled the world.

And what of this man who ruled the *visible* world and who was in due course to be proclaimed divine? He was a remarkably fine politician and statesman, and a man who worked incessantly for the good of Rome. Even the gossip Suetonius is compelled to write his life in terms that are tinged with admiration. Unlike Caesar or Antony, or many of the emperors who were to succeed him, Suetonius is unable to lay the charge of unnatural vice at his door – nor of the violence and sadism that were to characterize so many of the subsequent emperors. He was in short, despite his sexual promiscuity, something of a puritan at heart. Frugal in his eating habits, he 'preferred the food of the working classes, especially coarse bread, whitebait, fresh cheese, and green figs. . . .' He wrote in a letter to his successor Tiberius: 'Not even a Jew is as meticulous as fasting on the Sabbath as I was today. I did not touch a thing until after dusk, and that was when I was at the baths, before my oil rub, when I had two mouthfuls of bread.' (Augustus made one mistake here, for the Jews did not fast on the Sabbath; he was probably confusing it with the annual Day of Atonement.)

His quiet and efficient management of the vast empire, an empire which for the first time united the Mediterranean world, made his ultimate deification inevitable. The stability of the trade routes had enabled him to see that his policy of cheap bread could satisfy the citizens of Rome. There was another way in which he bought their approbation – circuses. In this respect this apparently mild-mannered man was as blood-thirsty as any of his citizens. He recorded with pride how 'in my own name I have three times given a show of gladiators, and five times in the names of my sons or grandsons. In these displays about 10,000 men were engaged.' He goes on to enumerate other displays which he gave the people, recording also how 'on twenty-six occasions in the circus, in the Forum, and in the amphitheatre I gave for the people hunts of wild African beasts – during the course of which some 3,500 beasts were killed. Also I gave the people the spectacle of a naval battle beyond the Tiber.'

The Roman empire itself was built on a desert of bones – the bones of all the other empires and states it had destroyed, and the hundreds of thousands of men who had been killed because they had fought for their liberty. But even in peace it was considered necessary to provide the most hideous spectacles of bloodshed to entertain not only the masses, but every stratum of the population, including the emperor himself. Augustus, far from condemning these displays, actively encouraged them. They were a symbol of a world of infinite cruelty in which, in the final analysis, there was no hope for any man. All this was to be challenged in due course by a doctrine that was practically unthinkable to Augustus or any other Roman of that time – that every individual is a unique being, valuable in the eyes of the creator of the universe, and possessing a soul. It would be centuries yet before the horrors of the games would be abolished throughout the empire. In the meantime arenas blossomed in all the big cities of the countries dominated by Rome.

At the core of so much of this indifference to human life lay the fact that the whole of this world operated upon the basis of slavery. Michael Grant in *The World of Rome* makes the following comment: 'Although slavery was endemic in the ancient world, it is difficult to think of any ancient people, except possibly the Assyrians, who can have exceeded many slave-owning Romans in the scale of their callous brutality. . . .' It was upon this human reservoir that the aqueducts of the empire were fed. 'Nasty, brutish and short' were the lives of most slaves; perhaps the only exception being those of talented and cultured Greeks who were employed as private secretaries, amanuenses or tutors. But for the slaves who toiled on the land or, worst fate of all, in the mines from which Rome derived much of her wealth, the life expectation can have been little more than the early twenties. Everywhere throughout this empire, which curiously enough has elicited the admiration of so many Christian historians, every kind of brutality and perversity prevailed. It was against all the forces of this iron-masked world of infinite violence that the Jewish boy now growing up in Tarsus was to pit himself.

[5]

A Student in Jerusalem

The boy was intelligent. The family was strict. It was clear from the progress that Paul had made in his studies that he was more than a tent-maker. The highest ambition he could aspire to was to become a rabbi, and in his knowledge of the Law he had already shown himself to be worthy of higher training than could be provided locally. His father, in any case, may well have felt that so clever and sensitive a youth should for both reasons be removed from the potentially corrupting society of Tarsus.

From his subsequent history it would seem more than likely that Paul had already begun to display an unusual interest in the non-Jewish communities, in those Gentiles who, his father would certainly have believed, were all destined for hell. Paul must leave Tarsus, then. The finest thing that a caring and careful father could do was to send him to Jerusalem. There, in the holy city, his only son would learn right thinking and right ways every day of his life. He would be surrounded by the finest Jewish teachers in the world, and he would have abundant opportunity to expand his intellect and his soul. Paul's father, though he is a man about whom little or nothing is known – not even his name – was undoubtedly a good parent. There was only one other child of the marriage, a daughter. So he was sending away his only son for a higher education that, though it might mean he would attain great distinction, meant also that there would be nobody to inherit the family business. It was in many ways an act of considerable self-sacrifice, and the father should be remembered for it.

Paul would have been about fifteen years old when he first took ship on the sea that he was later to grow to know so well. No doubt his father sent him to Jerusalem under the protection of some friend, perhaps a rabbi returning to the city. All his life the boy would have heard about Jerusalem and he would have known well that it, like Judaea itself, now fell within the aegis of Rome. In A.D. 6 Augustus had exiled Archelous, the corrupt and vicious son of Herod the Great, and had put all Judaea, Samaria and Idumaea under the rule of a Roman procurator, who in his turn was subject to the governor of the province of Syria. A Roman garrison was based in the Herodian fortress of Antonia which overlooked the great temple platform – a permanent affront to the orthodox. And Jerusalem itself was no longer considered the capital – a further affront – the country being ruled from the great coastal city of Caesarea. This was named in honour of Augustus Caesar by Herod the Great, who had also enlarged the port and built a splendid palace, now the residence of the Roman governor. It was, whatever the Jews might feel, political tact as well as strategic wisdom to have made Caesarea the capital. It did not make the Roman presence too heavily felt in Jerusalem, where the population was particularly sensitive.

The Romans during this period were careful not to upset the religious susceptibilities of the Jews. Many a procurator, as well as the governor, must have wished that he had a different appointment – to some other part of the world where people took religion as it came, and where gods and goddesses mingled in cosmopolitan confusion. Although the procurator could give the death sentence for political offences, and was responsible for the collection of taxes, the city was in effect ruled by the Jews themselves. The High Priest, former high priests, members of priestly families and the Sanhedrin (a council composed of seventy-one elders) administered justice and, among other things, collected the Temple tax. The only thing that the Sanhedrin, the highest court of Israel, could not do was to have anyone put to death. For this they needed the procurator's consent.

It was into this web of complexity – military, political, religious and civil – that the young Tarsian was now headed. The ship aboard which he and his companions were embarked would have coasted down the province of Syria, passing such ancient and famous cities as Tyre and Sidon, until finally it docked at Caesarea in the shelter of the great harbour arms. Familiar though he was with the world of Rome from his boyhood years in Tarsus, Paul would first have realized in Caesarea the omnipresence throughout the Mediterranean of the Roman army, navy, and administrative system. All races and all religions might be tolerated, and indeed accepted, throughout the empire. But in the final analysis it was the hard right hand of Rome, the legionary's sword, that held together this extraordinary compendium of the human race, which stretched from the plains of Asia Minor, through all the islands and lands of the Middle Sea, to distant Spain and Gaul and even as far afield as rainy, fog-enshrouded Britain.

It would seem from all the evidence of this power that a small people like the Jews, even though they considered themselves the chosen people of the only God, had little chance of changing the pattern of the world. The great galleys bridling against their hawsers in Caesarea, the merchantmen larger than any Paul is likely to have seen in Tarsus, the sound of trumpets as soldiers disembarked, the bales of cargo rising and falling, all these were visible signs of *Imperium*. Nothing, it would seem, could possibly challenge this strength and this security.

Thirty-four miles away, the city of Jerusalem beckoned the Jews aboard the freshly arrived coaster. It represented far more to them than all the power of Rome, than all this evidence of that power. It is certain that the youth must have felt this, however much he may have been dismayed by these outward and visible trappings of worldly dominance. Jersalem was more than just another city. It was a spiritual entity – something quite distinct from far larger cities such as Rome or Alexandria. One day he would see Rome, that steaming cauldron from which the world was ruled, but in the meantime he was bound for the holy places of his fathers and for the Temple where he would study. There he would try to learn the true and only right ways for a man to live.

'Central, but aloof, defensible but not commanding,' writes G. A. Smith in *Jerusalem*,

> left alone by the main currents of the world's history, Jerusalem had been but a small highland township, her character compounded of the rock, the olive and the desert. Sion, the Rock-fort, Olivet and Gethsemane, the Oilpress, the Tower of the Flock and the wilderness of the Shepherds, would still have been names typical of her life, and the things they illustrate have remained the material substance of her history to the present day. But she became the bride of kings and the mother of prophets.

The desert came almost up to the city's walls. Jerusalem was lodged between the sea and the desert. With a scanty water supply and little timber the city's main export was religion.

Augustus had claimed that he had 'found Rome brick and left it marble', and Herod the Great had endeavoured to do as much for Jerusalem. He and Solomon, architecturally speaking at any rate, were the city's greatest benefactors. Herod had had the Temple completely rebuilt and had doubled the area of the enclosure. It was now one of the most – if not the most – splendid buildings in the world. No pagan might enter it, and it was fenced off from any such contamination by the 'middle wall of partition', where notices written in both Greek and Latin forbade any Gentile to go any further on pain of death. It was this 'middle wall', although it was one in the mind, that Paul would one day endeavour to breach.

Herod had also restored the fortifications of the city, making it one of the most strongly defended places in the world. He had added to the existing walls and towers the great fort of Antonia, called after his friend Mark Anthony. Founded on a rock and about ninety feet high, the sides of the fort were sheathed with smooth stone so that they offered no foot- or hand-hold for any attacker. At three of its corners were towers of equal size, each about ninety feet high, while on the fourth corner rose the king tower, 100 feet of it, from which the whole Temple area was commanded. Whether so intended or not, what this said in effect was: 'Your God, as you maintain, may be the greatest of all, but, see, the power of Rome looks down even upon *him*!' Paul one day, as a captive, was to acquire an unpleasant acquaintance with the interior of the fort and its prison facilities.

Other improvements that Herod had made to the city were to give it, in the Greco-Roman manner, a theatre and a gymnasium. There was, however, no arena: this would not have been tolerated. His crowning adornment of the city was the magnificent palace which he had built, soaring above the western hill, shining in the sunlight, plashing with fountains even in the searing heat of the Jerusalem summer. The new visitor cannot have failed to notice all these things with a sense of awe. Tarsus was now seen as provincial – as indeed it was – and even Tarsus with its cosmopolitan population could show nothing to the mixture of races that moved here through the narrow streets: men from every nation under the sun. A young Jew viewing it all for the first time must certainly have felt an immense, and almost overweaning, pride at the sight of his city, and at the fact that all the nations of the earth came here, some on business, some to pray, and others just to admire. And then, as a party of soldiers led by a centurion passed him by, plumes swaying, armour gleaming, the Roman sword that had mastered the world at their sides, he would remember that Jerusalem was in bondage.

But there was one place which he might enter – to which even these all-powerful, all-conquering Romans were forbidden. He could pass beyond the barrier, leaving behind the world of Gentiles, and enter the place where God himself dwelt. He could become absorbed into the history of his own race and sense the presence of all the Prophets and hear the heartbeat of the God who ruled the universe. The Inner Sanctuary was enclosed by a wall over forty feet high, nine portals giving access to it, and revealing within – like the sudden dazzle on opening a dark box and finding myriad gems – the splendours of the Temple. White marble was everywhere, gold adornments, hangings of Tyrian scarlet, the shiver of incense on the air, and over all an incessant rumour – cries of money-changers, the bellowing of cattle waiting to be sold for sacrifice, and the voices of men haggling over prices. It was this latter aspect of the Temple that some fourteen or fifteen years later was to drive a young Nazarene into a frenzy of righteous indignation. God himself might dwell within the deep and scented silence of the Holy of Holies, but the area beyond resembled a cross between a stock market, a businessmen's convention, a currency exchange and a butcher's shop. For Jahweh still demanded, like any pagan god, the incessant tribute of roast flesh.

Jahweh was still very much a tribal god. Although the Law and the Prophets enjoined a standard and code of behaviour immeasurably in advance of anything elsewhere in the known world, the ceremonies with which He was honoured would not have seemed out of place in the temple of Capitoline Jupiter. In front of the veil of the Temple (which hid the Holy of Holies) stood an altar of gold, on which incense was sprinkled at the beginning of a service. As it wafted up in a dark cloud it was believed to carry away with it part of the sins of the people. Attendants, having lit the candles on the seven-branched candelabra – representing the seven planets – made sure that the fire was burning strongly and clean before withdrawing. The priest who had been chosen by lot to make the sacrifice for the day mounted the steps of the altar and placed upon the fire the chosen parts of the animal that was being offered up. Blood and wine were now thrown upon the meat and, as the offering went up in a blaze, a crackle and a stream of smoke, the priest turned to the worshippers and extended the blessing: 'The Lord bless thee and keep thee. The Lord make his face to shine upon thee and be gracious unto thee. The Lord lift up his countenance upon thee, and give thee peace.' In response, all those assembled would reply: 'Blessed be the Lord God, God of Israel, from everlasting to everlasting.' The choir now sang the psalm appointed for the day, after which the assembly rose to their feet. They were conscious that they had fulfilled their obligations, and could busy themselves once more with the ordinary affairs of the world.

Quite apart from such ceremonial offerings, individuals were allowed, indeed encouraged, to bring their own offerings to expiate some sin or guilt. The portion of those offerings not set aside for the Lord were reserved for the priests, only they being allowed to eat the flesh of the animals dedicated to expiate sin. They had other prerogatives too, including that of dealing as bankers in the vaults that lay below the Court of Women. Many of them owned large estates, and both they and their families were allowed various specific 'cuts' from the votive offerings. If their lives were circumscribed by ritual they were nevertheless men of substance and power. As servants of the Lord they enjoyed a standard of living far above that of most Jews. If the priests of innumerable divinities throughout the pagan world benefited by a similar comfortable existence – through preying upon the ignorance and superstition of their worshippers – the priests of Jahweh were no less comfortable. They fed upon the sins of the people.

[6]

A Jewish World

The young man's teacher, as he was proudly to recall in later years, was a man who enjoyed the highest reputation as an exponent of the Law. His name was Gamaliel, and he held a leading position in the Sanhedrin. At this time Pharisaism basically followed two styles of thought: the austere and strictly orthodox tradition of Shammai and the more liberal approach of Hillel. These two great Jewish rabbis had been contemporaries during the time of Herod, and Gamaliel was Hillel's grandson. In the long run the teaching of Hillel was to triumph. At the small town of Jabne, to which the rabbis withdrew after the destruction of Jerusalem and the Temple in A.D. 70, the verdict was given in favour of the school of Hillel.

If a man is lucky enough to have a good teacher in his youth it is likely that the precepts enjoined during these formative years will remain deeply embedded in his character for the rest of his life. It is interesting to see what kind of instruction Paul may have received from his master. Of the many sayings ascribed to the great Hillel (which will have been passed on by Gamaliel), a number of them bear a remarkable resemblance to the teaching of Christ. Typical are the following: 'judge not thy neighbour until thou art in his place'; 'he who has acquired the words of doctrine has acquired the life of the world to come'; 'my abasement is my exaltation'; 'he who wishes to make a name for himself loses his name; he who does not increase [his knowledge] decreases it; he who does not learn is worthy of death; he who works for the sake of a crown is lost'; 'what is unpleasant to thyself that do not to thy neighbour; this is the whole Law, all else is but its exposition.' After his death Hillel was lamented as 'the humble, the pious, the disciple of Ezra'.

According to tradition, most probably inaccurate, Gamaliel succeeded his father as Nasi, or President of the Sanhedrin. In any case he was certainly one of the most influential men of his day, as well as one of the finest intellects. There were about 1,000 students in the House of Interpretation, or rabbinical college, during the period that Paul was studying. It is evidence of Gamaliel's liberalism that, apart from the Law and the prophets, Greek literature (presumably carefully selected) was also studied. Gamaliel was clearly a remarkable man – he was the first to whom the title Rabban (Master) was given. On one occasion, as recorded in Acts of the Apostles, he saved Peter and other apostles from being put to death. He enjoined the members of the Sanhedrin not to take any action against these followers of Jesus, adding: 'Leave them alone. If their belief and their work is a man-made thing, it will disappear. But if it comes from God you cannot possibly overcome them. You could even find yourselves fighting against God!' His reputation indeed was so great that in later years it was said: 'When Rabban Gamaliel the Elder died, regard for the Torah ceased, and purity and piety died.' An exaggerated compliment perhaps, but one which indicates the quality of the man who was to be Paul's instructor.

To understand the type of thinking which Paul and his fellow students were absorbing during these years of their adolescence and young manhood it is essential to look at the backbone around which the Torah was framed. (It still remains at the core of much Western thinking, even if that thinking is now secularized.) Torah has been defined as: 'The teaching or instruction, and judicial decisions, given by the ancient Hebrew priest as a revelation of the divine will; the Mosaic or Jewish law; hence, a name for the books of the law, the Pentateuch.' Within Torah, according to Jewish belief, was embodied the revealed will of God. The Pharisees maintained that it covered the whole of human life, national as well as personal. No situation existed which could not be met by an accurate interpretation of Torah. This inevitably resulted in intense, and indeed eternal, debates on the interpretation of the Law. A large part of the students' time was spent in hair-splitting definitions, and arguments every whit as complex, and even bizarre, as those that centuries later were to trouble the scholars and divines of Byzantium.

It followed that a religious philosophy so all-embracing inevitably led to a kind of mental straitjacketing. The details of the Law were interpreted to such a minute degree that it was almost impossible even for the strictest teacher or student to comply with all its requirements. It was even said that if a single Jew could live a completely righteous life, keeping within the Law for one whole day, then the rainbow – the sign of God's covenant with man – would never more be seen, and the Messiah himself would at once appear. Although this was intended as a joke it contained more than a hint of truth. The fact was that it was practically impossible to fulfil the requirements of the Law in all their niceties. Furthermore, even in Jerusalem, the Jews, whether they liked it or not, were still living in a pagan world, and a world which revelled in all fleshly delights and pleasures.

It was for this reason that certain communities of Jews withdrew themselves altogether from contact with the world, believing that its contagion was such that a man could live according to God's Law only in a hermetically sealed community, disdaining contact even with other Jews. Among these were the Essenes who set up their cell at Qumran. They are the best known group today, since the discovery of the Dead Sea Scrolls has revealed a great deal about the Rules within which the community lived. No inquiring student, such as Paul undoubtedly was, can have been unaware of the existence of these groups, even if their doctrines were kept secret. Apart from the evidence of their beliefs contained in the Scrolls, the little that we know about them comes from the Jewish historian Josephus, the first century philosopher Philo, and Pliny the Elder. The most curious thing about them, and a state extremely unusual in Judaism, was their practice of celibacy. Although a deliberate renunciation of sex was not unknown in some Eastern mystery religions, some of the followers of Cybele and Attis even going so far as emasculate themselves, to the Jew marriage and the procreation of children were enjoined under the Law. An unmarried rabbi, for instance, was practically unthinkable.

The unmarried state insisted upon for its priests centuries later by the Roman Catholic Church would have seemed quite contrary to the injunction of God to 'increase and multiply'. In any case, Judaism was wise for, by endowing marriage and the raising of children with its blessings, it ensured that not only the generality but also the best brains in the community were perpetuated. The Essenes, however, regarded celibacy as the preferable state. Even though the tombs at Qumran have revealed some female and infant skeletons, these are only a few compared with those of many adult males.

Josephus wrote of the Essenes that 'they have renounced pleasure, identifying it with vice, and school themselves in temperance and self-control. They disdain marriage, but they adopt other men's children, while they are still young and pliable, accepting them as their kin and forming them in accordance with their principles.' He goes on to say: 'They do not condemn wedlock in principle . . . but they wish to protect themselves against the wantonness of women.' Philo confirms that: 'No Essene takes a wife, because a woman is a selfish and very jealous creature. . . . He who is bound fast in the love of a wife, or under natural causes, makes his children his first care, and cannot be like the others [of us]. Without knowing it he has become a different man and he is no longer free but a slave.' He also comments that the Essenes have renounced riches, eat only the simplest food, and wear their clothes and shoes to pieces before they will think about replacing them.

Trace-elements of Essenism are undoubtedly detectable in early Christianity. Indeed, Jesus's injunction to his followers to be without 'wife or brothers or parents or children' would be anathema to a good Jew, for whom the family and family ties and obligations were all-important within the framework of the Law. The fact that neither Jesus nor, at a later date, Paul, ever seem to have married is surprising. In the eyes of a strict and devout Jew there was no virtue whatsoever in their celibacy: they were in fact acting contrarily to the will of God.

There are only two suppositions that one can make as to celibacy being preferable to the married state by the Master and his ardent follower-to-be. The first is, and it is not improbable, that at some time in their lives both had become acquainted with the doctrines of Essenism, or even attached for some period to an Essene cell. The other is that both believed so firmly in the imminent end of the world that to contemplate a settled state such as marriage seemed absurd. Even if Jesus, or Paul, or both, were at some time involved with Essene thought it is clear why both came to reject its basic principle of seclusion from the world. It was Jesus's knowledge that it was in the world, 'among tax-gatherers and sinners', that his mission lay which distinguished him completely from the self-righteousness of the narrow and, in the final analysis, arid tenets of Essenism. Both the Master and Paul rejected such rigid exclusiveness. Jesus by the pattern of his life quite often, and consciously, broke tenets of Judaic Law. Paul was to go even further. He was one day to say that even the rite of circumcision (all-important to the Jew) was not necessary for Gentile converts. He was to live among the heathen and maintain that it was not only the Jews who were God's chosen people, but that all could become part of the elect by an act of belief and grace. It is possible that the seeds of this rebellion were sown in his heart by the intellectual wool-winding sophistry which he daily encountered in the House of Interpretation.

The other influence upon the thinking of this eager young student, which must never be discounted, was the belief in the advent of a Messiah. He would free the chosen people from their Roman bondage and he would redress the wrongs which they manifestly suffered – and which they had not the physical strength to combat. Dr Parkes has summarized the situation at the time, the constant hope that the Lord would redress the balance:

> For many centuries there had been a Jewish belief in an ultimate 'Day of the Lord' in which human injustices would be righted and God would himself rule and deliver his people; and in a number of these expectations all nations were ultimately thought of as his subjects . . . the powerlessness of little Judaea confronted by great world empires led some to expect a day of divine vengeance rather than of divine promise. A Messiah, who was originally to rule all the earth in peace and righteousness, became a celestial figure armed with the thunderbolts of Jove. The literature embodying these ideas was all pseudonymous: the ideas themselves were 'revealed' in 'visions' so that it came to be known as *pseudepigrapha* or *apocalyptic*. As it all dwelt with a fancied end of the world, it received the general title of *eschatology*. Its menace lay in the ease with which it became the inspiration for political extremism and terrorism. For, since God was expected to level up the disparity in power between Jew and Roman, armed struggle against the latter seemed to become possible and desirable. In the half-century which preceded the open war apocalyptic expectations of the Messiah produced a continuous ferment of terrorism, disorder and assassination.

Judaea, in fact, showed all the traits – so familiar in our century – of a country occupied by a foreign invader and determined to assert its own freedom. The issue was even further complicated by the fact that the nation concerned saw itself as the chosen people of the Maker of all worlds. The desire was not only the ordinary human one for liberty and freedom from oppression. It was complicated by the conviction that, if the human animal was different in kind (not quality) from all other animals, the Jew was yet again different in *kind* from his fellow humans. Such distinctions of thought can only lead to tragedy.

[7]

A Roman World

There was another world. The minute and relatively unimportant enclave of Jews living in the small province of Judaea, who have claimed so large an amount of the world's interest, figured as only a very small part of an immense jigsaw puzzle. Judaea was a disaffected oyster, and the irritant at the base of the pearl was only a section within a city which in itself was only one of many cities within a world empire. In due course, when the Romans had been irritated enough, they were with one blow of the hand to crush Jerusalem, enslave the Jews, disperse them throughout the empire, and compel a capitulation that would last up to the twentieth century.

A year or so before Paul went up to Jerusalem the Emperor Augustus had died. He was succeeded by Tiberius, who was the son of Livia, Augustus's wife, but whose father had been one of Julius Caesar's officers. Augustus himself had no sons and Livia, for whom he had entertained an unbridled passion, had been ceded to him by the future Emperor's father when she was already pregnant with Tiberius's younger brother, Drusus. Tiberius was born in 42 B.C. and was fifty-six when he became Emperor. His full name was Tiberius Claudius Nero Caesar. One of the reasons perhaps why he has suffered from so much abuse in subsequent centuries is the fact that, while he was Emperor, far away in Judaea, an obscure Jew, who had proclaimed himself the Messiah, had been crucified in the company of two even more obscure criminals. Crucifixions, like hangings in later centuries, were no more than a routine part of the administration of an empire.

Tiberius was an unusual character, an excellent soldier and an able administrator. The portrait that Tacitus gives us of him is certainly a terrible one, and one must suspect the historian of some bias. To judge by the conduct of the empire during his reign – and before his retirement – Tiberius cannot be considered incompetent. From 22 to 6 B.C. and again from A.D. 4 to 10 he had spent almost all his time as a soldier, first in the Spanish peninsula, then in Armenia and then in Gaul. Unlike Augustus, nearly all of whose successful military and naval campaigns had been conducted for him by his incomparable right-hand man Agrippa, Tiberius had an intimate knowledge from his military experience of the frontiers of the empire. In company with his brother Drusus he had subdued the mountain tribes between the sources of the Rhine and the Danube, thus ensuring the safety of communications between Italy and Gaul, and had subsequently been victorious over the Pannonians (who occupied a territory lying between the Danube and the Alps). On the death of his brother Drusus in 9 B.C. Tiberius was clearly seen as the first soldier of Rome – a worthy successor to Julius Caesar.

But there was far more to the future Emperor than his considerable abilities in the military sphere. He appears to have been a man capable of intense love and affection. He had married Vipsania Agrippina, daughter of Marcus Agrippa, who bore him a son, Drusus. The marriage was not only successful but it is clear that, certainly on Tiberius's side, it was a true love-match. The great grief of his life was that Augustus, for reasons of state, compelled him to divorce his wife and marry Augustus's daughter, Julia. Tiberius was well aware of Julia's nature; she was a completely unprincipled adulteress. The misery of this marriage could not be compensated for by the honours that were showered upon him – triumphs in 9 and 7 B.C., the successive offices of quaestor, praetor and Consul, a further consulship, and tribunicial power for a five-year period. Despite all this proof of the Emperor's and the people's regard for him and his abilities, Tiberius felt himself degraded by his wife. 'He dared not,' as Suetonius puts it, 'charge her with adultery or divorce her on any other grounds.'

The only solution, as Tiberius saw it, was to withdraw from public life – leaving the field open for Augustus's grandchildren Gaius and Lucius. Such, at any rate, was the reason that he gave for his retirement from Rome, although it must be suspected that personal reasons largely motivated his act. He went to the beautiful island of Rhodes,

> of which he cherished pleasant memories since he had touched there during his return voyage from Armenia many years before. He contented himself with a modest town house and a villa in the nearby countryside, also of modest scale. While in Rhodes he behaved most unassumingly and, after dismissing his lictors and runners, he would often stroll around the gymnasium where he greeted and talked with humble Greeks almost as if they were his social equals.

There can be little doubt that this was one of the happiest periods in a life that was not destined to see much happiness. In due course even Augustus was compelled to recognize the real nature of his daughter, whose immorality and adulterous behaviour had scandalized even a Rome that could take a great deal of scandal. Julia was banished while Tiberius was still in Rhodes. Not long afterwards her daughter, also called Julia, was banished for similar behaviour. Augustus was unfortunate in his children. It was more than ironical that in 18 B.C. he had passed a law intended to clean up the morals of the city, under which he could in fact have had both his daughter and granddaughter put to death. Banished at the same time as Julia's daughter and her lover was the writer Ovid, whose poem *The Art of Love* had long offended many of the more strait-laced in the capital. It gave advice on the art of seduction in terms that left little to the imagination. Ovid died in the remote and unattractive small town of Tomi near the mouth of the Danube in A.D. 18, at a time when the future antagonist of all that he stood for was studying at the House of Instruction in Jerusalem.

During the early years of his reign Tiberius seems to have conducted himself with considerable modesty and circumspection. He was foremost in insisting on all respect being paid to the now deified Augustus and in encouraging the cult of emperor-worship throughout all the countries that came within the sway of Rome. At the same time, the misery of his earlier years, the habit he had acquired of solitary introspection, coupled with a natural taciturnity, did not make him attractive to the Roman people. His wife

Julia, who had been recalled from exile by Augustus (who nevertheless refused to receive her publicly), was again confined and is said to have died shortly afterwards of starvation and ill-treatment. It is quite possible. Tiberius had a proud and sensitive nature, and she had tortured him by her behaviour and infidelities. Tiberius like Augustus seems to have had a strain of the puritan in his nature – something which seems extraordinary if we are to believe Suetonius's account of his later life in Capri. One of the reasons for his unpopularity was the many stringent laws he enforced against extravagance, adultery (often punished by the death penalty) and even such apparently trivial acts as kissing in public. He also had a number of temples which had become notorious as places of assignation razed to the ground; an action hardly likely to endear him to genuine worshippers, let alone to the lovers and prostitutes who had made use of them.

A heavy drinker all his life, it is possible that he suffered in later years not only a moral but a physical breakdown. Certainly he hated the world of Rome and, when the opportunity presented itself, he left it in the hands of a brutal subordinate, Sejanus, and retired to Capri. Prior to this he had offended other sections of the community by a deliberate attack on all the foreign gods who had invaded the city in the wake of Rome's Eastern acquisitions. The Egyptian cults were the especial object of his dislike, as were the Jewish. Vast numbers of Jews were exiled for refusing to conform to the Emperor's laws (to burn their vestments and religious objects), while many others were conscripted into the army and deliberately sent to the unhealthy malarial parts of Sardinia, where 'if they fell victims to the climate they would be little loss'. Tiberius was not alone in believing that these followers of Eastern religions constituted a threat to Rome and the sovereignty of the emperor. The old Roman gods had been good enough for their fathers – and the only other addition necessary to them was the cult of the ruler.

It is difficult to know what to make of Suetonius's description of his private character and of his sexual excesses upon his retirement to Capri. If he wished for orgies, what was wrong with Rome? A number of his successors, including Nero, found that the capital contained all the ingredients necessary for every form of sensual or sexual pleasure. Everything, and everybody, was subject to the whim of the emperor. It was because, says Suetonius, his practices were so revolting that he needed the seclusion of an island where he could behave as he pleased, and yet remain unobserved by the people at large.

> In his retirement to Capri he made himself a private brothel, where all sorts of sexual extravagances were practised for his secret pleasure. Troops of young men and girls, whom he had collected from all parts of the Empire because they were skilled in unnatural practices – known as Spintrians – used to perform in front of him in groups of three to excite his jaded palate. A number of small rooms were decorated with vilely obscene pictures and statuary, also erotic books from Elephantis in Egypt. . . . He also devised special 'sporting grounds' in the woods and glades of Capri, and had little boys and girls dressed as Pans and nymphs stationed in nooks and grottoes. The island was now openly called 'Caprinium' (Goat Island) because of his goatish behaviour.

Suetonius continues: 'Some aspects of his criminal obscenity can hardly be discussed or even believed. He had little boys trained to chase him when he went swimming and get between his legs to nibble him. He called them his "little fish".'

Suetonius's recital of Tiberius's perverted habits, his sadism, and his preoccupation with oral sex is quite explicit. After all these centuries it is difficult to know what to believe, but certainly Suetonius himself lived thirty years under the Caesars. He had a great deal of his information about Tiberius and his immediate successors from contemporaries and eyewitnesses. He also had access to the imperial and senatorial archives. In general he shows himself to be a man who checked his facts and did not write with the bias of, say, Tacitus.

It is difficult to reject all the charges made against Tiberius. Even if some of them were dismissed there would still remain a host of others, particularly about his maniac cruelty and sadistic love of violence. Suetonius records that

> in Capri they still show the place at the top of the cliffs where Tiberius used to watch his victims being hurled into the sea after protracted and ingenious tortures. A body of marines, stationed

down below, beat the bodies with oars and boat-hooks to make sure they were completely dead. Another torture which Tiberius had himself devised was to get men to drink vast quantities of wine and then suddenly to have a string knotted round their privates. This not only cut the flesh but stopped them urinating.

This was the man who sat at the apex of power. This was the god-emperor before whose statues incense was daily burned and catacombs of animals were sacrificed. Even if 50 per cent of the stories told against him were to be proved untrue, the portrait that would emerge would be of a monster. If Acton's dictum is correct, then one sees in Tiberius the absolute corruption of absolute power.

Against his legions, against the wealth and might of Rome, against the imperial navy, the host of cargo-carriers moving on their trade-routes throughout the known world, against the generals, the siege-engines, the secret police, the governors and administrators, it must necessarily have seemed that no subject nation – let alone an individual – could make any impact.

[8]

Misunderstandings

Against the wealth, power, dominance and unbridled licence of first-century Rome few people could oppose anything. Numb acceptance seemed the order of the day. The occupied territories of Hitler's Europe in the twentieth century offered more chances for opposition, for beyond that pseudo-empire there lay free countries with warlike capabilities and scientific and intellectual attainments. Beyond the world of Rome lay nothing but savages, barbarians, or crushed nations – like the Gauls, over whom Julius Caesar had triumphed by blood-bath after blood-bath. Greece had helped – was helping – to civilize Rome and impose upon her rude conqueror her incomparable culture – to which the Roman paid lip-service, but which he despised for being subject. Egypt, which her last queen, Cleopatra, had done her best to preserve as independent by the use of her body and her wits, now lay equally supine – cheated into the belief by subservient priests, Alexandrian Greeks and Roman officials that the Caesar of the day was a divine monarch, just as the Pharoahs had been. Out of all this immense wealth of territory only a small and relatively unimportant Judaea maintained opposition to the rule of the Caesars.

It was an astonishing situation and, even if not yet apparent to men like Tiberius and his administrators, it was to end centuries later with the subservience of Rome to an alien religion – to the completely extraordinary conception that a man who had died as a criminal on a cross was more powerful than any Caesar. It was as if in the modern world of great states like America, Russia or China the whole system would one day be overturned by an obscure man who had been executed on a capital charge. By declaring himself the Messiah, he had declared himself an enemy of the State. His follower, the young man Paul, would in due course create a revolution that would make all subsequent ones look relatively minor affairs. The influence throughout the whole world, creating 'a kingdom not of this world', would one day spread beyond any knowledge or memory of the Roman Caesars.

Paul in his young manhood was certainly a highly puritanical Pharisee – something that was not so surprising in view of the dissolute world against which he was destined to react. He was also, as his writings were later to show, one of the greatest poets the world has ever known. But this was in the future. In the meantime he had to learn, and in learning he had to suffer the intensive discipline that the Jewish system of education imposed upon its students. It was this 'Holier than Thou' attitude inculcated upon the Jew which so incensed the Romans, and indeed the Greeks. The latter felt that, as the most intelligent and cultured people in the Mediterranean, they had no need of instruction from this Semitic people in the Levant, whom their own Alexander the Great had once taken within the shield of a Greek world empire. The rite of circumcision was regarded by them with a peculiar mixture of amusement and contempt. To partly unman oneself, as they viewed the act, seemed the mark of a people destined by nature to be inferior. Why not go the whole way and join the eunuch priests of Attis?

Circumcision was in fact far from being an exclusively Jewish practice. Cutting off the foreskin was a rite widely diffused throughout ancient nations, as indeed it still is among many modern ones quite apart from Jews. At least 3,000 years B.C. it was familiar to Egyptians. Indeed, it is possible that the Jews acquired the rite during their days in Egypt. The Egyptian custom was to circumcise boys at the age of puberty or just before, and, as Fr Roland de Vaux writes in *Ancient Israel*: 'Originally, and as a general rule, circumcision seems to have been an initiation rite before marriage. Consequently, it also initiated a man into the common life of the clan. This is certainly true of many African tribes which practise it today, and was very probably true of ancient Egypt. . . .'

The ceremony is clearly portrayed in a temple at Karnak, and the evidence of most of the male mummies which have been examined shows that the great majority had been circumcized. Since this rite was later to play so great a part in Paul's struggle with legalistic Judaism it is important to see whether it had any other meaning than ritual. It is doubtful whether, considering the primitive nature of the peoples among whom it was and still is found, that sanitary reasons had anything to do with it. It seems to have served more as a 'tattoo' designed to mark the circumcized one as a member of the tribe, and qualified therefore to take part in its religious rites. In Ezekiel, for instance, one finds that a man who dies uncircumcized will not be permitted to join in communion with his dead forefathers, who bear the mark of their initiation. At the same time, along with the Egyptians, it is noteworthy that many of the tribes by whom Israel was surrounded also practised circumcision, among them the Edomites, the Moabites and the Ammonites. According to Herodotus all the Phoenicians and Syrians of Palestine were circumcized. Pre-Islamic poets reveal that ancient Arabs were also circumcized. It is noticeable that the only people with whom the Israelites came into direct contact who are expressly described as 'uncircumcized' were the Philistines. The epithet, directed at them sneeringly, is quite enough to identify them without any other reference to their name. The Canaanites, for instance, are never so described, so one must presume that they too followed the same ritual as the Hebrews. Professor S. M. Zarb has pointed out the interesting fact that, while the word 'circumcision' derives from the Latin for the surgical operation,

> in the Semitic languages it gives the real meaning of the rite. It is from the root *hatan* [from which] derive the word bridegroom, son-in-law, father-in-law and even the wedding ring which according to some writers, the foreskin being in the form of a ring was worn on one of the fingers and later on it was replaced by a metal ring.

It would seem that the reason the rite came to assume such importance in Jewish eyes was that after the exile the nations under whose sway Israel lived – the Babylonians and the Persians – did not practise it. It was during this period that the religious significance was attached to it. It was the visible sign of the covenant between God and his chosen people, setting them apart from their oppressors. Later on when they were subject to the Greeks, and then to the Romans, both of whom regarded the act with derision, the Jews clung to it even more fervently as being the sign that set them apart from their oppressors. The controversy that would later ensue between Paul and the orthodox must be seen in the light of Jewish history. He was to assert that the 'true circumcision' occurred in the heart, and that Gentiles, who did not bear this Jewish caste mark, might equally be accepted within the New Covenant.

There were other aspects of the Jewish nation and its religious beliefs which irritated most pagans. It was bad enough that the Jews so clearly despised the Gentiles, finding it difficult even to accept those who had become converts to Judaism. What seemed so absurd were their complicated dietary laws, for instance their shunning of one of the best meat dishes available in a world where meat was a luxury. What was wrong with the 'other thing', as the Jews euphemistically referred to the pig? And then again, the refusal to honour the statues of the emperor, which meant in effect not acknowledging the sovereignty of Rome, seemed to other nations not only a discourtesy but a stupidity. After all, the Jews were ruled by Rome just as much as they themselves were. A proud, haughty and stubborn people, they seemed with their strange laws and grave demeanour even to dislike life itself. Life was short, and in its brief span a man might surely enjoy a little of the honey on the branch that was certain to snap and hurl him in the darkness.

The Jews appeared to think differently. They bound themselves in by a code of behaviour that made normal human life seem scarcely possible. For instance, it was said that within their laws, deriving from some ancient leader called Moses, there were over 600 specific commands and prohibitions to each of which a Jew must subscribe. Even more extraordinary, on their holy day, the Sabbath as they called it, there were exactly 1,521 things which the stricter of their members, like the Pharisees, were forbidden to do. How could a man live like that? It was clear, though, that within their homes they did not deny themselves their wives. Why, they bred like rabbits, and there were thousands of them all over the empire! But yet in some way they seemed to deny the pleasures of sex, looking with horrified scorn on the processions of the Great Goddess, and on the fertility rites which were designed to ensure the continuance of man and beast, and the return of the spring with its flowers and its promise of future crops.

If the Jews despised the Gentiles, the latter were not slow to return the compliment. We know from Josephus, Tacitus, Cicero and others just how the Roman regarded the Jew, and he was every whit as uncomplimentary about them as Paul was later to be about the Cretans. Here are some of the epithets applied to them: 'Haters of mankind, so ill-natured as not to direct a stranger to a fountain; superstitious worshippers of a pig-God [the belief being that this was why they were not allowed eat pork]; dirty, smelly lepers.' In Petronius's novel *The Satyricon*, written in the reign of Nero, the rich vulgarian Trimalchio says mockingly of one of his slaves: 'He's only got two faults. He snores and he's circumcized.' No, the Jew was not popular within the empire – 'a nation of wandering glass- and sulphur-peddlers' and, what was worse, 'unruly and treacherous to all government'.

If these were the general opinions it was hardly surprising that Tiberius expelled them from Rome and that Nero, looking for a scapegoat after the great fire, picked on the most intransigent of all Jewish sects – and one disliked and despised by most Jews themselves – the Christians.

There is no evidence of how long Paul remained under instruction in Jerusalem. It would have been normal for him, if he went to the House of Interpretation at fifteen, to have stayed on for at least a further five years if he wanted to aspire to the title of rabbi. It is somewhat doubtful if he ever did, as it were, 'take his degree', or we would probably have had some reference to it. It is interesting to speculate whether he was in fact a failed student. This might account for his first fury against the Christians (proclaiming their absurd 'Messiah' while he, Paul the failure, knew enough of the Law to discredit them). Secondly, it might to some extent account for his later conflicts with orthodox Judaism, under whose restricting shadow he may have felt that he had wasted many years. But such speculations are in the main as fruitless as most modern attempts at psycho-biography. One cannot be dogmatic about a man who has been dead nearly 2,000 years. One can guess, but must admit that it is no more than guesswork.

While Paul was still either studying in Jerusalem or had reverted to his father's trade of tent-making, in the same year that Tiberius retired to Capri, a new procurator of Judaea had been appointed. Pontius Pilate took up his charge in A.D. 26 and was to remain procurator for ten years. This in itself was something of an achievement for, as has been seen, Judaea was a notoriously tricky country to rule. Pilate seems to have maintained the Roman Peace with some success during his period of office. Of equestrian rank, he was the fifth Roman procurator of Judaea and Samaria and, despite some administrative incidents to his discredit, seems to have been no worse, perhaps even better, than some of his predecessors and successors. One of his gravest errors was to use some of the Temple funds for building an aqueduct into the city; an act which he no doubt saw as being to the citizens' benefit, but which infuriated the Jews and led to a riot. The fact was that he had little understanding of their temperament – what Roman ever had? – and he no doubt found them a singularly infuriating people to deal with.

On his arrival in the city he had made his first politico-religious error by marching in with his men at night, carrying the standards of the legion (which bore the head of Caesar) and having them planted near the Temple. This was his first experience of a Jewish riot, and no doubt it did not predispose them in his favour. Luke records that at a later date he had some Galilean pilgrims massacred while they were in the act of sacrificing; but again one must suspect that it was not as simple as that, and that there was probably some semblance of riot or other disturbance to provoke so harsh a response.

Pilate's part in the death of Joshua, the Christ, the King of the Jews, has long been debated. The early Church tended to exonerate him, putting the blame on the Jews themselves. Certainly, to judge from the third and fourth Gospels, it seems that Pilate did what he could to save a man in whom he could find no fault against the law, and only reluctantly yielded up his victim. He was finally recalled in A.D. 36 to answer charges brought against him of mismanagement of Jewish affairs. Many stories, most of uncertain or indeed apocryphal nature, were later told about his end; one being that he committed suicide; another that he was banished to Vienne on the Rhône. His wife, Claudia Procula, was to be canonized by the Eastern Church for her action in warning him not to put this Messiah to death. The Abyssinian Church, taking its line from the thinking of the early Fathers, has even canonized Pilate for his attempts to save the Founder's life. Not a completely unattractive figure, he must be seen in the light of his times: a Roman occupying the most uncomfortable seat in the whole of the empire. In the year in which he was recalled to Rome, Paul, who had been away from the city for several years in Arabia and Damascus, was to return to Jerusalem – only to have to leave again in a hurry because of a Jewish plot against him. There was little peace to be found in Jerusalem by either the Roman or the Jew. But by that time Paul would have become a convert to the Messiah who had been crucified during the rule of the departing governor.

[9]

Compulsions and Revulsions

It is very unlikely that Paul was in Jerusalem at the time of the crucifixion. It is scarcely believable that this man – who was so honest about his part in the persecution of the early members of the Christian sect – would not have said openly that he had been present in Jerusalem, or even that he had seen his future Master had he done so. The references in his letters to the Corinthians never suggest that he had been an eyewitness to the crucifixion itself, or to any of the events leading up to it. It is inconceivable that, if he had, he would have omitted saying so. His authority for proclaiming 'the good news' seems to be based entirely upon his experience on the road to Damascus. One might almost say that Paul's vision, whatever view one takes of it, was necessary to him – just because he had never seen Jesus in the flesh.

At the time of the crucifixion (A.D. 29–30?) Paul, as probably as not, was back in his native Tarsus. Whether he had in fact qualified as a rabbi is not really material. Even if he had, a rabbi was expected to keep himself by some respectable craft or trade, and Paul had only the one that he had learned from his father. There was no conception in the practical sphere of Judaism that, because a man was learned in the Law, he should be absolved from earning his own bread. Paul later lays great stress on this. The case of the priests in the Temple at Jerusalem was slightly different, but the rabbi in any ordinary synagogue was expected to support himself and his own family.

If Paul was not married by the time he returned to Jerusalem aged about thirty he was an exception to nearly all other Jews. Indeed, if he was ambitious, he could not qualify to be a member of the Sanhedrin unless he was a family man. If he did marry during these years one can only suppose that his wife died young, possibly in childbirth, something that would explain Paul's tenderness towards Timothy as the son he never had, or possibly had lost. Paul was not a woman-hater as has been maintained by some of his later critics who mistake his thinking on the proper and decorous way in which he maintained that woman should behave for misogyny. There is little or nothing in Paul's instructions for women that would not have been given by a rabbi to an orthodox family. Furthermore, Paul's Gentile converts had been brought up as pagans amid the myriad gods and goddesses of a world that seemed, even to a lax Jew, to be heading for destruction. It was therefore necessary to instruct them carefully about the Jewish mode of life as compared with the pagan way. If Paul was later to bend the Law regarding the matter of circumcision, in all other matters he was inflexible. Some of the comments hostile to Paul that have been expressed centuries later derive from the inability of their authors to grasp what kind of society prevailed in the first century A.D. The lives of Tiberius, Caligula and Nero were not unique. They were paralleled by many other rich and powerful men.

During these lost years, whether Paul was preaching in some obscure synagogue in Syria or Cilicia, or at home in his native Tarsus, it is unlikely that he did not hear of the death of one Joshua (anglicized Greek: Jesus), who had claimed to be the Messiah and who had died an ignominious death on a cross. Messiahs were an almost constant event in the Jewish world. Günther Bornkamm comments: 'As late as the thirties of the second century, in the time of the emperor Hadrian, the most highly esteemed contemporary teacher of the Law, R. Akiba, proclaimed the leader of the final Jewish revolt against the Romans, Bar Cocheba, as the Messiah.'

The news that yet another claimant to the title had met his end would scarcely have surprised Paul, although the end itself would almost certainly have proved to him that this one had been the most pathetic and deluded. The pain and shame that that inscription, 'King of the Jews', nailed to the cross, must have brought to any member of the nation is difficult to conceive in modern terms. It was as if, for example, Britain had been occupied by Germany during the years of Hitler, the royal family fled or dead, and that sporadic rebellions broke out against the administering authority led by claimants to the throne. What greater shame or insult could one inflict upon the occupied country than by hanging the leader of an unsuccessful revolt and announcing to the press and over the radio, 'The King of England was hung today in the company of his fellows, two other common criminals.' But it was even worse than that. The expected Messiah was to be far more than royal, far more than an ordinary man. He was the Righteous One, the chosen of God, the Ancient of Days. His coming would foreshadow the end of the world and the judgement of all peoples and nations. That mocking inscription meant more than: 'Here is your King – See what we think of him!' It meant also: 'Here is your God – See what we think of Him!'

Some of Paul's hatred of the early Christians may well have stemmed from the fact that they had shamed not only the Jewish nation by their advocacy of a common man who had died as a criminal; they had shamed also Jahweh. They had allowed the Romans to make it appear that even the Lord of Lords could not triumph over Roman might, but was a despicable and dead figure. After all, no one could nail up Jupiter. He was in the clouds, far above the bondage of ordinary mortal flesh. So this was the Jewish God and Saviour, a corpse carted off like a hunk of meat – just as so many others were, every day, all over the empire. It was a triumph of propaganda, likely to break any Jewish heart with mortification.

Then no doubt the rumours began to come through – tales that this man's followers claimed to have seen him after his death, that he was not dead at all but triumphed over the tomb. Unbelievable! And yet, if his claim to be the Messiah was to mean anything it was essential that the story be true. The Jews, almost alone among ancient peoples, believed in the actual physical resurrection of the human body. A number of Eastern mystery religions promised their followers a life beyond the grave, but it was a life conceived in far different terms from this. The 'body' of this death would itself be shed away, the spirit would triumph and enjoy – according to whichever doctrine the follower believed in – the joys and benefits of a completely different world. The philosophers might see the spirit as a fiery spark united in the great creative sun, or the primal fire that made all things – somewhat similar to the Buddhist conception that 'the dewdrop slips into the shining sea'. Those Greeks who still envisaged life in Homeric terms knew that, yes, in some dim world among the asphodels they would meet again, but only as shadowy ghosts, lamenting the days when they had lived with the sea, the mountains, the wild flowers, wine and sexual pleasure, in the sunlit world above.

Traces of the idea of the literal resurrection of the dead body, which was to become a peculiarly Christian part of doctrine, are to be found in the Persian religion of Zoroaster and also in later Judaism. It was something that was always denied by the great rival group to the Pharisees, the Saducees. There is no mention of it in the earlier Hebrew scriptures, although some claim to have found references to it in Isaiah and particularly in Ezekiel, in the chapter about the revival of the dry bones in the valley of vision. In the last chapter of Daniel there is a clear statement that 'many that sleep in the dust of the earth shall awake, some to everlasting life, and some to shame and everlasting contempt'.

By the first century it had become accepted doctrine among the Pharisees, and probably among a large part of the Jewish people, so that one may conclude that Paul believed in it – although on exactly what terms has provoked argument that still rolls down the ages. To the sophisticated Greeks, of course – philosophers such as those whom Paul would one day meet in Athens – the idea was derisory. It was a joke. It was part of some foolishness of fanatics like this one coming out of the East, unlettered in the true nature of life and of the universe. How could you fix all those old bones, with which Greece alone was littered, together again? And if you did, to what purpose? Why, there would not even be standing room!

On this whole subject there must have been an immense range of conjecture among the Jews themselves about the age at which the mortal life of the body would be so restored, and whether children would always be children, and grandfathers always grandfathers. Byzantine speculation such as the famous query as to how many angels could stand on the head of a pin were as nothing compared to the intellectual cats'-cradles evolved by many of the Jews. The Alexandrian school, with typical subtlety, had refined upon earlier simplicities, maintaining that the body that rose at the Last Judgement would be, as it were, something quite new and different. Paul seems to echo something of this in his first letter to the Corinthians where he says: 'When buried it is a physical body; when raised it will be a spiritual body. There is, of course, a physical body, so there must be a spiritual body.' It is little wonder that assumptions like this made the philosophers and intellectuals of Athens laugh, decry him, and finally abandon him to his absurd opinions – which were clearly not worth debating.

But that was in the future. Now he must surely have heard, wherever he was, that these followers of the crucified Joshua were everywhere proclaiming that they had indeed seen the man, and that he had spoken to them. Perhaps he had been cut down before death? Such cases were not all that uncommon. Sometimes, if a Roman governor or conqueror wished to show mercy, he would leave the victims long enough on the cross for what he considered sufficient punishment, and would then have them cut down to go free. He knew well enough that after that agony, even if they ever recovered fully, they would never trouble Rome again. The pain of crucifixion was intense, but it was usually a slow death, the condemned man often lingering on for several days. Julius Caesar, on one occasion when he had condemned to death some pirates who had previously captured him, considered himself merciful in ordering their throats to be cut. Paul can hardly have escaped hearing about, or even seeing crucifixions, in his thirty years. They had in any case been known in the East long before the Romans came. Phoenicians and Carthaginians had used this method of punishment as well as for sacrifice to the supreme lord, Baal. In just such a way the Carthaginian general Malcus, to obtain some special favour, had invested his son Cartalo in royal robes, set a crown on his head, and sacrificed him to Baal.

The simplest, and it would seem original, form of the cross (the Roman *crux*) was merely an upright stake to which the condemned were either fastened and left to die, or impaled upon it. More generally a cross-piece (*patibulium*) was added, to which the arms of the man were tied, or his hands nailed, or both. There were three variants upon this, the one in which the cross-piece was fastened at right angles below the summit of the stake (*crux immissa*), the second where the cross-piece was fastened at right angles across the top of the stake (*crux commissa*), and the third where it was formed by two beams crossing one another obliquely (*crux decussata*). It was customary for the Roman officer in charge of such an execution to have the victim's name and crimes proclaimed, or to have fixed to the cross a tablet (*album*) on which they were inscribed.

Paul must have known all this, must have heard too about that disgraceful, degrading inscription which said that this man's crime was to have been the King of the Jews. Insult, upon insult! And now his degraded followers were proclaiming that he really had been the Messiah, and that he had risen from the dead. Peasant followers, too, he heard; scum out of Galilee, the riff-raff of the nation, primitive, superstitious and uneducated. No true Pharisee, no Jew of spirit, could possibly have condoned such people who, by giving their backing to this madman, had put the whole Jewish nation to shame.

[10]

Fire – and Stones

Unlike so many other Messianic movements in the past – which had swiftly been forgotten after the failure of their attempts to free Israel from Rome – the new one continued to spread. What had reinforced it was not only the certainty of some of the Galilean's followers that the dead man's sealed tomb had been found mysteriously empty, but that they had even seen him after death. It was easy enough for Jews and pagans alike to say that the mystery of the tomb was easily solved. Some of his people believing, in their simplicity, in the literal meaning of his words about being resurrected, must have stolen the body overnight. It was more difficult to combat the second of their stories. They were so entirely convinced they had seen him that, instead of slinking back in fear to the hamlets from which they had come, they were openly proclaiming in Jerusalem that he had risen from the dead.

Both the Jews and the Romans would have been glad to see them disperse, and be heard of no more. The Sadducees and the Temple administrators (who had to reach some kind of *modus vivendi* with the Roman authorities) were anxious for no more trouble. The Sadducees have been harshly treated by some later commentators, but they were far from being 'Quislings', in any sense of wanting to betray their religion or their country. They were conservatives – in many ways more so than the Pharisees – but the centre of their interest revolved around the Temple itself. So long as the Roman rulers left everything to do with this heart of Judaism undisturbed, they were prepared to accept the physical dominion of Rome. Their fear was that there was always the danger that some popular mass movement could cause a change in this benevolent policy. This put the Temple in danger. As the events of A.D. 70 were to show, the Sadducees were right in trying to seek a working *rapprochement* with Rome.

But the new religious movement continued to spread like a bush fire, aided above all by the extraordinary events which occurred about two months before the Passover feast. At the Feast of Weeks, which marked the end of the corn harvest, a gathering of the dead man's disciples were convinced that fire had fallen from heaven, and had imbued them with the gift of tongues. *Glossolalia*, to give it its technical name, the gift of speaking in languages which – theoretically at least – were unknown to the speaker, was not a unique phenomenon in the East. During the rites of Bacchus, inspired not only by wine but by hysteria, the followers of the god would give vent to cries and indecipherable sounds, which were considered as evidence of their possession by the spirit of the god. Similarly, during the rites of Attis and the great Syrian goddess, the ecstatic behaviour of the priests and acolytes, lashing themselves into a frenzy, and wounding themselves with knives, inspired words and incoherent non-words poured from their lips and often triggered off a similar reaction among the watching crowds.

The difference on this occasion was that the leader of these people, a man called Peter, had interpreted the words of inspiration. He had told the crowds assembled round the house where all the confusion was going on that they must all repent, accept his Master as the Saviour–Messiah, and be baptized. Again, far from dying away, as such wild moments of enthusiasm usually did after a Bacchic orgy or the passage of Mother Cybele through the streets, the movement spread. Thousands rushed to be baptized, and to accept Jesus as the Messiah. There was consternation in the Temple, where the hard core of these revolutionaries were stirring up trouble (by calling on everyone to repent). But even worse, the new converts, most of whom no doubt were somewhat unsure of what they were preaching, were buttonholing everyone they came across. This was what the Jewish authorities had been afraid of: trouble in the city, leading to trouble in the Temple, leading logically to Roman intervention. It was hardly surprising that the Sanhedrin held an emergency meeting, summoned before them Peter and John, another of the leaders, and had them swiftly imprisoned. It was a religious matter and, since there was no question of execution, the Sanhedrin was acting entirely within its rights.

Called upon to explain himself to the Council, Peter had the effrontery to insist that a lame beggar, whom he was alleged to have healed, had been cured through the efficacy of 'Jesus Christ, the Nazarine, whom you crucified and whom God raised from the dead. . . .' The fury of the elders of the Temple is easy to comprehend. They were men schooled in the Law, the finest intellects of Judaism; and here they were being insulted and instructed by an untutored country bumpkin, as well as uncomfortably reminded that it was they and not the Romans who had insisted upon Joshua's death.

They ordered the prisoners to be taken away while they had a consultation as to what they should do about the whole affair. The only sensible solution seemed to be to get these people to hold their peace, and never more to mention 'this name' – for the Council members refused to let it pass their lips – and to stop stirring up the people. The Sanhedrin could hardly take any further action, for the rabble were swarming outside, and even in, the Temple itself. Silence, if it could be obtained, seemed the only answer. With astounding insolence the two men said that they intended to obey God and not men. They would continue to tell all who would listen to them what they had seen and heard about the life and the life after death of their Master. The movement continued to spread. The followers of the Nazarene now formed themselves into a kind of communist community, in which all shared alike. This was a practice, it must be said, that had long been established among the Essenes.

Two of the members of the new sect, so the rumour went, a man named Ananias and his wife, Sapphira, who had attempted to keep back some property from the general fund, had immediately been struck dead for their sin. The East was always full of rumours, but never so much as in these perfervid days when a wave of religious mania was storming through the always tempestuous heart of this city. Another thing which must really have disturbed the orthodox was that these followers of the Nazarene, after the conclusion of their evening meal, celebrated a supper in memory of their Master, and of the last Passover meal which he had taken with his intimate disciples before going to his death. There was nothing so extraordinary in the supper itself. It was well known that the Essenes also, according to their Rule, ordained a similar solemn Meal: 'When the table has been prepared for eating, and the new wine for drinking, the Priest shall be the first to stretch out his hand to bless the first-fruits of the bread and the new wine.'

This ritual meal was not considered harmful in itself. But there was an ugly rumour circulating that, unlike the Essenes' supper, which derived from that of Pentecost, and which was little more than a consecration of the members in their vows, this crucified troublemaker was being openly identified in this new community with the Messiah, that is to say, with Jahweh himself. It was little wonder that members of the Sanhedrin, and indeed all good Jews, should view this new sect not only with suspicion, but with detestation. They were identifying a justly condemned criminal with God. They must, of course, be crushed, and the rotten root must be extirpated from Israel. In due course the opportunity would surely occur for all right-thinking Jews to make an example of them.

But, before that happened, both Peter and John had once more been brought before the disciplinary court. Despite the ruling of the Sanhedrin that they were not to mention 'this name' again, they had carried on preaching within the precincts of the Temple.

Anathema! Imprisoned for a second time they managed to escape, either by bribing their jailers, or by converting them to this slave-doctrine (suitable as much for jailers perhaps as for illiterate peasants). They had not attempted to flee for safety, but had calmly gone back to preaching in the Temple. The understandable anger of many members of the Sanhedrin, when these escaped prisoners were again brought before them, was that they had now certainly deserved the death sentence, for having defied the earlier ruling of the court. (The sentence, of course, would have been subject to confirmation by the Roman governor, but he was surely as little inclined to have the city disturbed by rioting as were the Jews themselves.) It was only the cautious and sagacious words of Paul's tutor Gamaliel that prevented the elders from asking for the men to be put to death. As he wisely pointed out, if what these men said had no divine justification then they would certainly fail to achieve anything. On the other hand, if what they said was sanctioned and indeed inspired by God, the Sanhedrin by fighting against it would be 'fighting against God himself'.

Pilate must have looked on the whole matter with indifference – but with a concerned indifference. He wanted no disturbance in the kingdom. The interest of Rome was to see that the taxes were paid, and that the countries within the empire thrived, and lived quietly (no need to expend Roman lives in ensuring their subjection). The Council finally concurred with Gamaliel's views and, after having had the two dissidents soundly thrashed, they let them go. To have asked for the death penalty from the Governor would, they now realized, have only created a further mystique around this cult of the Crucified Man. Better by far to let them slink away, conscious of the pain of their bruised and bloody shoulders. Let the whole movement disappear like water poured from a jar into the desert sands!

The first act of outright violence – of violence that did not sit within the framework of Roman law as it related to the city – occurred about three years after the death on the cross which had inspired this further crackling of twigs beneath the eternally boiling cauldron of Judaea. It is at this moment that Paul once more appears upon the scene. He had been away from Jerusalem; he was back again, and he would soon afterwards disappear once more, until his return in the year that Pilate left for Rome. It is more than probable that Paul, like many others, was only a tool in the hands of the Sanhedrin. They could not themselves take any violent action against these detestable followers of the Galilean, for fear of giving the Romans an excuse for involving themselves in the affairs of the Temple. But that was no reason why they should not secretly encourage the more hot-headed of the young Jews to take matters into their own hands, and to engage in open action against this troublesome and dissident sect. After all, the Romans and the Governor himself would be delighted to see the air of Jerusalem and the whole country purged of this sulphurous atmosphere. The interests of orthodox Judaism and the Roman *Imperium* coincided. How often, centuries later, in the histories of other imperialisms, would the governing powers stand back and close their eyes, while certain citizens of their colonies undertook acts which suited them, but were certainly not within their official jurisdiction?

The issue was raised by the actions of a young man (a word which meant anything between manhood and forty) called Stephen. He had been appointed one of seven deacons, or servants, of the new church, whose duty it was to supervise charities and to adjudicate in any disputes between church members. Although not one of the apostles, Stephen was noted for his remarkable eloquence and oratorical ability. He was accordingly dispatched to spread the word of the Messiah throughout the Jewish nation. He was eminently successful, a fact which naturally put him on the Sanhedrin's black-list. Ignorant and unconvincing speakers might be tolerated, but a man who could quote chapter and verse from the scriptures to prove to orthodox Jews that this Jesus was indeed the Messiah must be eliminated.

It was the year 33, the fourth Passover since the death of Christ. Jerusalem as usual was bustling with preparations for the feast, the air trembling with the bleating of lambs, the women everywhere busy cooking, making the bread and pounding herbs, and the city full of Jews returned from all over the empire for the great day. Stephen, who was naturally making use of the anniversary of his Master's suffering to win converts, was arrested by the Temple police on orders from the Sanhedrin. Taken before the Council he was charged with having spoken against Moses and against God. False witnesses were produced. They said they had heard Stephen say how Jesus would tear down the Temple, and change all the laws and customs that had been handed on from Moses.

Confronted by the full panoplied might of the Sanhedrin, Stephen's eloquence did not desert him. Indeed, he deliberately set out to antagonize the Council by pointing out that the Jews had always been treacherous to their great men – citing Joseph and Moses – and that they had destroyed his Master, Christ. Yes, and he would not bother to deny the charge that Christ would destroy the Temple. The Temple in itself was nothing. Had not Isaiah declared that heaven was the throne, and the earth God's footstool? God did not live in houses built by men. If he was in search of death, Stephen could not have been more successful. Every word he spoke was calculated to inflame the prejudices of his hearers. Among them, sitting most probably with the students, was Paul.

The climax of Stephen's speech – the words that sealed his fate – came when he looked up with 'a face like an angel', and said: 'I see heaven opened – and the Son of Man standing at the right hand of God!' This blasphemy was more than anyone present could bear. 'They covered their ears with their hands. Then they all rushed at him at once.'

Their fury was so great that murder was very nearly committed in the Temple itself. Wiser counsels prevailed. Stephen was dragged outside the city walls – so that his blood would not fall within Jerusalem. He was stoned to death. A cruel and ancient punishment for all grave sins against the Law, stoning implied that no single individual was guilty of the condemned person's death, but that all who agreed with the charges against him or her (adultery was another sin punishable in this way) shared equally in the taking of life. Those who had witnessed against the condemned were the ones who cast the first stones.

They took off their cloaks so as to have freedom of movement. They laid them for safe-keeping at the feet of 'a young man named

Saul'. The latter had not been one of the witnesses, but he had heard the blasphemies. He had also been among the mob that had hurled Stephen out of the Temple to meet his end on this barren ground, where the dirt, refuse and dust of centuries served as a reminder of the antiquity of this city which, in theory at any rate, was but a pale mirror of the eternal Jerusalem in the sky above. Under the splintering hail of jagged limestone rocks the blasphemer stood upright for a time, compounding his blasphemy by calling on this Jesus to revive his spirit. Then, under the skin-tearing, bone-shattering hail of blows, he sank to his knees. A life was flowing away before their bloodshot eyes. His last words before the stones stopped his mouth for ever echoed those of his Master: 'Lord, do not hold this sin against them!' Blasphemy even at the moment of death! And the man at whose feet lay the pile of bleached cloaks looked down regardless at the crumpled heap of flesh. He consented to this murder.

[II]

'Flashes of light . . .'

Did Paul *essentially* approve, or did he only possibly approve – as many have done of the death of others – only to find at a later date a vast sickness in the heart? Visible, violent death leaves a stain upon the eyes and upon the memory. Paul was far from insensitive. As events were to show, however, he was a man of violence. It was only after his whole nature had changed in the most extraordinary manner – rather as if a switch had been thrown in his mind – that his dynamism was directed into another channel. He would then become the man of whom F. W. Myers was to write:

> Desperate tides of the whole world's anguish
> Poured through the channels of a single heart

But for the moment, all his energy and passion were turned against the believers in this false Messiah. Paul, and the mob that followed him, now set about a systematic persecution of the Christians. It is the very excess of his behaviour that may give one a clue to the ferment that was seething in his mind. His reaction to the idea that Jesus was the Messiah was positively pathological. It far exceeded the normal scorn and dislike felt by most Jews for this pitiable – although indeed dangerous, and intellectually poisonous – belief that the Messiah had already come, had died a criminal's death and had been translated from his tomb. 'For each man kills the thing he loves,' as Wilde was to write with infinite perspicacity. It is this element which seems so readily detectable in the actions of Paul after the stoning of Stephen. On the other hand, one charge can never be laid at his door – he was no coward.

> The coward does it with a kiss
> The brave man with a sword

And it was with a sword in his hand, at the head of a pack of assassins and *sicarii* (the dagger-men sometimes surreptitiously employed by the Temple for judicial murders), that Paul now descended upon these followers of the Crucified One. Possibly among his helpers were members of the extremist group known as Zealots.

The latter were fanatical Jews called in Aramaic *Quanna* (the Zealous), *Zelotai* in Greek, on account of their zeal for the salvation of Israel from Roman dominance. They looked for a warrior-king who would lead the Jewish nation in a war of liberation, in which the oppressor would be overthrown and Israel under the Messiah would govern the world. Not unnaturally they were regarded with mistrust and fear by the other Jewish parties, who were prepared to accept the physical dominion of Rome so long as the Temple and their religious beliefs were left untouched.

The Zealots had first sprung into prominence as a politico-military group in protest against a census that was being held by the first procurator of Judaea in A.D. 6–7. Their rebellion had been crushed, their leaders killed, and all the Zealots scattered. Nevertheless they never ceased to maintain that the only solution to Israel's problems was by force of arms. It was their influence which largely sparked off the last and fatal revolt that led to the capture of Jerusalem and the destruction of the Temple. It is easy to understand why some of these extremists might willingly join in a persecution of renegade Jews who maintained that the Messiah had already come. What, a peasant crucified in the company of thieves? Nothing could have been more calculated to infuriate them than the suggestion that the great war-lord, the descendant of David, whom they expected to lead Israel with javelin and sword to the extermination of the Romans, had been no more than a criminal weakling, yes, the first out of the three condemned men to die.

The members of the Sanhedrin, for the comprehensible political reason that they considered these Christ-followers were making even more trouble than the Zealots, and were likely to lead to Roman intervention, were happy to see them being persecuted and driven out of Jerusalem. Let them get back to Galilee and to their obscure villages where, sooner or later, the whole movement like so many others before it would break up into mini-factions and finally cease to exist. Paul was their man, this dedicated Pharisee with the burning eyes and the implacable determination to root out – not heresy, for to believe in a Messiah, however mistakenly, was not heretical – but these troublemakers who were imperilling the security of the Jews and their religion.

Some of the Christians were prepared to recant, but only a few. The majority clung obstinately to their beliefs and paid for doing so by imprisonment or scourging. The latter was a singularly agonizing public flogging, 'forty stripes save one', liable to leave the victim severely injured. But it was within the jurisdiction of the Sanhedrin to administer it. If we are to trust the author of Acts (whether Luke or some unknown writer) Paul himself said at a later date that:

> I myself thought that I ought to do everything I could against the name of Jesus of Nazareth. That is what I did in Jerusalem. I had authority from the chief priests and I put many of God's people in prison. When they were sentenced to death I also voted for it. I often had them punished in the synagogues and tried to make them deny their faith. I was so furious with them that I even went to foreign cities to persecute them.

One thing immediately stands out from these words – 'sentenced to death'. The Sanhedrin could not impose the death sentence, for this was the prerogative of the Roman procurator of Judaea. Either Paul was exaggerating, or the writer was, or Pilate as procurator had given his consent to the death penalty. Assuming that neither Paul nor the writer were laying things at Paul's charge which were in excess of what really happened, the only conclusion must be that Pontius Pilate was content to see these Christians exterminated. The latter is the most likely supposition. He had, however reluctantly, consented to the crucifixion of this 'King of the Jews'. He had hoped that that would be an end of the matter. Now he saw the whole of Jerusalem in a state of ferment, aroused by the supposed physical resurrection of this man, and his subsequent appearance to his close followers. If these old Jews in the Sanhedrin were prepared to maintain that this dissident sect deserved the death penalty, then there was no reason why the Roman who was responsible for law and order in the province should contradict them. Anything, within reason, for peace and quiet; this must have been the thought of all Romans who at one time or another were unhappily responsible for the fiery little state of Judaea.

What happened to Paul during this reign of terror? The behaviour of the people he was persecuting shook him to the roots of his own belief. They followed the same pattern that Stephen had set. They were scourged, or they died, forgiving their enemies.

The most surprising thing of all to be found in the record as found in Acts is that Paul was now given authority by the high priest in Jerusalem to carry out the purge far beyond the boundaries of Judaea. He was to undertake a journey to Damascus to find out, through the synagogues, if there were any adherents of this belief present there and to bring them back under arrest to Jerusalem. Now Damascus was one of the most important cities in the Levant – but it was in Syria. The Sanhedrin, as has often been pointed out, had no jurisdiction so far afield. The fact remained that, since all the synagogues scattered throughout the Roman empire acknowledged Jerusalem as their spiritual home, and the Sanhedrin as the supreme authority of the law, any man coming to them furnished with orders from these elders of the church would be obeyed. The only thing one must question is whether Paul could possibly have brought any of these Christians back across the frontier to Jerusalem as prisoners. If this was indeed the case, then there can be no doubt of the complicity of Pilate in the whole affair. On the other hand, Paul may have been given authority to have them brought before their local synagogues, and scourged or excommunicated from the Jewish community. This would have been a purely local, religious matter involving only the Jewish settlers in Damascus, and would not have troubled the Roman governor of Syria. In any case, Paul now set out with a group of similarly minded companions to ensure that such cells of Christians as might have got as far afield as Damascus were eliminated.

Riding on donkeys, and probably accompanied by a camel bearing their baggage, the party left the ancient walls behind them, passing the ground where Stephen had been stoned to death. They headed north. They already knew that many of the people whom they were seeking had fled to other areas of Judaea, as well as to Samaria, and that – far from keeping quiet as had been hoped – they were actively seeking converts to their maniac belief.

The rage felt by Paul against this dissident Jewish community is beyond normal comprehension. If it is paranormal, then there is justification in seeing that the events which occurred on the road through the desert to Damascus were equally so. Innumerable theories have been evolved concerning the sudden and blinding conviction entertained by this Jewish heretic-hunter that everything he had hitherto believed was false. Conversion to a belief, as history has shown time and again, is something paranormal. The mind becomes molten and – to use a simple electrical term – all 'the fuses blow'. At the same time, something must have happened to activate this state. It does not arise under the circumstances of ordinary existence. But Paul had not been living in an ordinary manner: he had been a witch-hunter, a man as driven by some terrible compulsion as those who centuries later were to gas or burn the Jewish population of Hitlerian Germany.

Dr Hugh Schonfield has come up with the interesting theory that Paul was not only an extreme Pharisee, but a mystic who had progressed so far that he had reached the point where he believed that he himself was destined to be the Messiah. His rage, therefore, was occasioned by the fact that he came across this group of Jews who asserted that the Messiah had already come. His role had been taken from him! He could not claim to be one of the apostles who had actually known and talked with this saviour, so the only thing left to him was, as it were, to invent a meeting. This was something that no one could deny, for did not the apostles maintain that they themselves had seen the Messiah after his physical death on the cross? But the type of temperament that 'converts' (that changes entirely) does not need any logical or pragmatic reason. Always it is a passionate temperament – usually without much premise, but guided almost entirely by emotion. The nineteenth-century French poet Arthur Rimbaud, who did at one time imagine that he had become God, knew this blinding flash of revelation:

Elle est retrouvée!
Quoi?—l'Éternité.
C'est la mer alliée
Avec le soleil.

One should seek for no more conviction about the experience of Paul on the road to Damascus than the simple statement: 'A light from the sky flashed about him.' However, since so many have devoted their time to attempting to come up with some explanation acceptable to reason and materialistic concepts, the alternatives to a mystical experience must be considered. There is the simple meteorological one – that the party ran into a summer thunderstorm (not at all unlikely in that part of the world) and that Paul was struck by lightning. A small group of mounted men crossing the desert generate a pillar of humid heat and, just as clusters of animals tend to get struck by lightning in a field, such a column will similarly attract an electrical discharge.

A man who has been brooding incessantly on one subject, who has met people who have personally spoken and lived with the one they call the Messiah, is more than likely – when he recovers from his physical experience – to equate it with the object of his concern. It has to be remembered that for evidence of the whole experience we have no more than the words of the author of Acts, words which it may be presumed – though not assumed – were related to him by Paul himself. What one would like, but will never get, would be the report of one of the members of the party accompanying Paul. Was the whole experience, in fact, objective or subjective? Did the others who, according to one account, 'heard the voice but could not see anyone', really have any such an experience, or was the whole event entirely in Paul's mind?

Quite apart from the simple supposition of a summer thunderstorm, there remains the theory that Paul was epileptic. Authorities today tend to dismiss this on sight, despising their nineteenth-century predecessors who were eager to find a rational explanation for Paul's vision. Epilepsy often accompanies extreme intelligence. Examples of known epileptics include Julius Caesar, Napoleon Bonaparte, Mohammed, Peter the Great, the poet and painter Edward Lear and the novelist Dostoevsky. The latter in his violence, his mysticism, his impulsiveness and his persecutory beliefs has been described by J. A. C. Brown as 'typical of the epileptic character'. It is significant that this authority does not mention Paul among those who may have been epileptics – perhaps the subject has become an awkward one. But if it is conceded that the founder of the Moslem faith was subject to epileptic attacks, why should it be impossible that the man who was to become the thirteenth apostle was an epileptic? He was, as his life story shows, violent, impulsive, subject to persecutory beliefs and a mystic. No one denies, just because he was subject to epileptic fits, that Julius Caesar was incapable of governing an empire – and writing fine Latin prose. Is the Koran to be discarded because its author was an epileptic? Many millions would disagree.

Here is a description from a medical authority on this 'chronic functional disease of the nervous system'. In the severe form or epileptic 'fit' proper (the *grand mal* of the French):

> The patient, it may be without warning, utters a strange and inarticulate cry, and falls suddenly to the ground, *as if struck by lightning* [my italics]. He usually has no time to save himself, but knocks against any object near him, and may thus receive serious injury, or he may fall into the fire, or into water. He becomes deadly

pale, his body rigid, with the back arched and the features set, and he ceases to breathe. Soon the colour changes, the face becomes livid purple, the veins of the neck swell and pulsate, the eyeballs protrude, a gurgling sound is heard in the throat, and death seems imminent. But almost immediately breathing begins again, and the whole body is thrown into a series of successive convulsive twitching or jerkings. . . . After about two or three minutes the jerkings cease, leaving the patient prostrate and comatose for a time. Then he may open his eyes, look around him with a dazed expression, and go to sleep. On awaking he is quite unconscious of what has happened; he may have a severe headache, or be morose and irritable. In rare cases, he feels much freer mentally than before the fit. . . . The fits are usually separated by intervals varying from some hours to some months; but a very grave condition supervenes (called the *status epilepticus*) when one fit succeeds another before the stage of coma has passed off. The attacks may be preceded by a distant 'warning', or *aura*, as it is called. . . . The *aurae* vary very greatly, but in each case the same *aura* usually precedes the fits. There may be peculiar sensations, such as flashes of light, perceptions of colour, strong odours, or strange tastes or sounds, or visions of various forms.

To quote from Acts:

> As he was on his way to Damascus, and nearing the city, there came suddenly a light from the sky, which flashed around him. He heard a voice saying 'Saul, Saul, why do you persecute me?'
>
> 'Who are you, Master?' he asked.
>
> 'I am Jesus, whom you persecute,' the voice replied. 'But now you must get up and go into this city where you will be told what you must do.'

The later account, which Paul is supposed to have given to King Agrippa, is that, 'I was on the high road, your Majesty, when I saw a light much brighter than the sun, shining from the sky around me and the men who were with me. I heard a voice saying to me in the Hebrew language, 'Saul, Saul! Why are you persecuting me?'

When he asked who was talking to him he was told that it was Jesus, who was appointing him to be his servant. According to the first account, the people who were with Paul could not see anything, but they heard a voice. Whose voice? Almost certainly that of Paul. Thunderstorms or not, unnatural event or not, the spectacle of an epileptic fit is an extremely frightening one – particularly if the *status epilepticus* ensues, in which a constant succession of attacks occurs extending over many hours, and 'with such rapidity that the patient appears as if he had never come out of the one fit'.

'Saul got up from the ground and opened his eyes, but he could not see anything. So taking him by the hand they led him to Damascus, and for three days he was not able to see, nor during this time did he eat or drink anything.'

[12]

Truth

Damascus was said to be the most ancient city in the world. Its date of origin was unknown, and there is still some reason to believe that it is the oldest city to be continuously inhabited by man. Lying over fifty miles from the sea, approximately equidistant between the great ports of Tyre and Sidon, its position on one of the principal high roads between upper and lower Asia naturally made it a major centre of trade. Damascus is mentioned in the Book of Genesis when Abraham, in the battle of the four kings against five, is said to have pursued the routed kings of Hobah 'on the left side of Damascus'.

For a long time Damascus was the capital of the independent kingdom of Syria, but it was then captured by the Assyrians, passing successively under the control of the Babylonians, the Persians, the Greek rulers of Syria and finally the Romans. Lying in an area of great fertility, it was well known from early times for its fruits and flowers, as well as for its manufactured goods. (The English words 'damson' and 'damask' are both derived from 'Damascus'.) Under the Roman emperors it became renowned for the quality of its weapons; the decorative inlay of Damascus sword-blades gives us the word 'damascene'. Many centuries after the blinded Paul entered its walls, the founder of another faith, the camel-driver Mohammed, was to say that he would never enter Damascus in case the beauty of the city might make him forget the real paradise that lay in heaven.

Paul's companions, no doubt thinking that he was dying, took him immediately to the house of a prominent Jewish citizen called Judas. He was very probably an elder of the synagogue, and the man whom they had been told to contact by the Sanhedrin. Judas lived in Straight Street, purposely named for its character. It was the main thoroughfare of the city, where all the import merchants and traders had their houses and shops. After depositing their stricken leader the others seem to have dispersed. Certainly there is no mention of further action being taken against any section of the Jewish community in the city. This is an indication of the immense driving power and leadership exerted by Paul; that everything should cease with his apparently imminent death.

The news of the arrival in Damascus of this persecutor of the new sect must have been immediately flashed to all Jews. No one entered cities in those days except through their guarded gates, where the identity of all travellers as well as their destination was established. Even under the great shield of Rome it was not a secure world. Every city was potentially vulnerable to riots inside it, as well as to deliberate attacks directed against its walls. The arrival of a man as notorious as Paul – and especially in his condition – can hardly have gone unnoticed. It would certainly have been recorded and passed by word of mouth throughout the large Jewish community living in Damascus. The man who had so recently been indicting and persecuting the Messiah-followers in Jerusalem had arrived.

For this reason, whatever one's belief, it is not difficult to understand how a prominent member of this new sect came to hear about Paul being in the house of Judas in Straight Street. The traditional account is that Ananias had a vision in which God told him that 'a man of Tarsus called Saul' needed his help, and where he would find him.

Sudden conversions have happened in many ages, conversions to a religious commitment or even – in a quite different sense – to a materialistic one. In the twentieth century alone there have been a number of thinking men and women in the Western world who, having embraced communism in the depression years before the Second World War, subsequently rejected it totally – the Vision that Failed – and then became dedicated Christian converts. Professor Starbuck in his work on the psychology of religion showed by statistical inquiry the number of genuine 'conversions' that occurred in adolescents. Paul was no adolescent. He was a man of mature years, but a man of highly sensitive and passionate temperament, a type of which converts are so often made.

William James in *The Varieties of Religious Experiences* quotes numerous recorded conversions which to one extent or another parallel the experience of Paul. 'The most curious record of sudden conversion with which I am acquainted,' he writes, 'is that of M. Alphonse Ratisbonne, a free-thinking French Jew, to Catholicism at Rome in 1842. In a letter to a clercial friend, written a few months later, the convert gives a palpitating account of the circumstances. . . .' James goes on to quote the letter at length, but even a small extract will give some idea of the experience. M. Ratisbonne had casually entered a church, not with any religious intentions but just as any sightseer might do.

> The church of San Andrea was poor, small, and empty; I believe that I found myself there almost alone. No work of art attracted my attention; and I passed my eyes mechanically over its interior without being arrested by any particular thought. I can only remember an entirely black dog which went trotting and turning before me as I mused. In an instant the dog had disappeared, the whole church had vanished. . . .

He goes on to describe the blinding revelation that came to him and how, when a friend came to pick him up from the floor where he had fallen in floods of tears,

> I did not know where I was; I did not know whether I was Alphonse or another. I only felt myself changed and believed myself another me; I looked for myself in myself and did not find myself. In the bottom of my soul I felt an explosion of the most ardent joy; I could not speak; I had no wish to reveal what had happened. . . . I came out as from a sepulchre, from any abyss of darkness; and I was living, perfectly living. But I wept, for at the bottom of that gulf I saw the extreme of misery from which I had been saved

> by an infinite mercy; and I shuddered at the sight of my iniquities, stupefied, melted, overwhelmed with wonder and gratitude.

William James goes on, 'I might multiply cases almost indefinitely. . . . There is too much evidence of this for any doubt about it to be possible.' Not long before his death John Wesley wrote:

> In London alone I found 652 members of our society who were exceeding clear in their experience, and whose testimony I could see no reason to doubt. And everyone of these (without a single exception) has declared that his deliverance from sin was instantaneous; that the change was wrought in a moment. Had half of these, or one third, or one in twenty, declared that it was *gradually* wrought in *them*, I should have believed this, with regard to *them*, and thought that *some* were gradually sanctified and some instantaneously. But as I have not found, in so long a space of time, a single person speaking thus, I cannot but believe that sanctification is commonly, if not always, an instantaneous work.

The photism, the blinding light that Paul experienced, has been experienced – and recorded by psychologists – in a very great number of religious conversions; so many in fact that the simple explanation that Paul was merely an epileptic will hardly hold water. One of Professor Starbuck's correspondents wrote:

> I have been through the experience which is known as conversion. My explanation of it is this: *the subject works his emotions up to breaking point* [my italics], at the same time resisting their physical manifestations, such as quickened pulse etc., and then suddenly lets them have their full sway over his body. The relief is something wonderful, and the pleasurable effects of the emotions are experienced to the highest degree.

In the case of Paul there can be no doubt whatever that his emotions had been exercised to an abnormal extent. The very rage with which he persecuted what was, after all, a comparatively harmless sect indicates the intensity of his involvement. It is difficult to accept the words of John Pollock in his biography *The Apostle*: 'Until his conversion he [Paul] had been indifferent to the words of Jesus.' Clearly he had been so impressed, so shaken to the roots of his conventional beliefs by what he had heard, that his mind was at 'breaking-point'.

One may possibly suspect in the case of many later conversions – to whatever branch of Christianity – that the person concerned had been influenced by the society in which he lived: by early schooling or religious teaching, or by the whole apparent evidence of churches, statues, literature and so on, by which he or she was surrounded. With Paul this could not be so. He had been trained and conditioned to be a good Pharisaic Jew. It would seem that he had never married, yet he was clearly a passionate and highly emotional man. He needed to canalize all this energy – and his acute intelligence – into some field or other. If the religion of his fathers, if the Law itself, had seemed to fail him, then it was inevitable that he must turn elsewhere. To say this is in no way to discount, or attempt to discredit, the paranormal or 'miraculous' nature of his conversion.

Paul now became the man who was destined to 'take my name before the Gentiles and their kings, as well as to the people of Israel'. Ananias went to the white street that flashes through the centre of Damascus. He went into the house of Judas. He laid his hands on Paul, saying that he had been instructed by the Lord he served to see that he regained his sight. In the simple words of Acts, 'something like fish-scales' seemed to fall from Paul's eyes. Many more words have been expended on this subject, optical surgeons consulted, and every attempt made to explain what is in fact no more than metaphor. Paul had been blind to the truth, and now he saw the truth clearly. There is no need for any further elaboration. Truth is like a bare bone lying on a beach.

[13]

Man and Emperor

'I let myself suffer the loss of all things. . . . Because I was apprehended by Jesus,' so Paul was later to write. The man who came to his senses in the house in Damascus was to break nearly all his ties with orthodox Judaism in support of this conviction. Yet he was also highly suspect at this moment to every member of the new sect, for the obvious reason that he had done all he could to suppress it. At the same time, the fact that he now submitted to baptism (possibly in the Abana River just outside the city) clearly convinced some of them that he was to be trusted. He went into the synagogues, confessed his former errors, and said he was convinced that the man who had been crucified by the Romans was indeed the veritable son of the creator of the universe. Paul's exceptional intelligence, which had previously been used to prove that this Messiah was false and that his followers were fools or worse, was now applied in the very opposite direction.

Such reversals are not so uncommon as has sometimes been suggested. The very temperament that needs passionate conviction is hardly one that will take the middle-of-the-road course. The 'nothing in excess' attitude which the Greeks held in reverence (even if they very often found it difficult to practise this admirable maxim) was contrary to the Hebrew temperament. Paul's mind had swung from one side of the pendulum to the other. If he himself could not be the chosen of God, he was sure that he had been appointed as another sort of Messiah – one who would take the word of truth to all those people who were not Jews. The arrogance is astounding, but so was the arrogance of his race. What other people in the whole of history had abrogated to themselves the right to be considered out of all the human beings on the earth the sole repository of truth?

Francis Bacon wrote, 'What is truth? said jesting Pilate; and would not stay for an answer.' But Bishop Andrews in a sermon in 1613 perhaps came more nearly to an explanation of Pilate's attitude. 'Pilate asked, *Quid est veritas?* And then some other matter took him in the head, and so up he rose and went his way before he had his answer. He deserved never to find what truth was.' The last sentence is unfair.

Pilate was a busy man. Paul, on the other hand, was not a Roman official with many demands on his energy and time. Undoubtedly he lived as simply as millions of peasant people do to this day. In most parts of the Roman empire bread was cheap, so too was olive oil. This sound basic diet was supplemented by whatever fruit or vegetables were in season; by fish (if one was in the right area at the right time); by salted fish in the winter, and by dried beans of various varieties whenever no fresh ones were available. 'Man does not live by bread alone' – no, but in many modern societies people have forgotten that, materially at least, he needs very little else. The expressions that recur and recur in writers about events at this time (such as 'he went into a desert') impose a strain upon modern thinking. It makes the events sound incredible – and therefore 'fairytale'.

How do you just 'go into a desert'? The answer is that people do constantly. Bread, or the ingredients to make it, salt, dates, and of course water, are all that one needs for travelling through a desert area. And Damascus stands at a central point on the great trading-routes between the Red Sea, Arabia and the whole territory of Asia and the Black Sea beyond it. It would not have been difficult for Paul to find a caravan leaving for almost anywhere in the East. His own account is that he went 'into Arabia'. Speculation has been endless – and basically fruitless – as to what part of Arabia Paul went to, or what he did there. As there is no evidence whatsoever, and probably never will be, the silence can only be taken as that of a man who has been so disturbed by a unique experience that he needed complete rest and quiet in an unfamiliar environment. Paul had had what might nowadays be called a nervous breakdown. But it was a great deal more than that.

The question still arises – and it is one that theologians tend to ignore – how did he live? Presumably he resumed his work as a tent-maker, a useful trade in a desert area and one which, rather like that of a cobbler, is absorbing and quiet. Sail-makers similarly find their occupation, while demanding great technical skill, is a restful one. Suppositions have been made that Paul immediately began preaching his new convictions, or even (a modern theory) that he became a member of an Essene community. Others have suggested that he went to the Sinaitic peninsula, where Moses was reputed to have given the Law to the people of Israel. The fact is that he disappears from history for three years.

Three years is a long time for a man in his early thirties. It is the time when most men are making, or unmaking, their lives and their careers. This was exactly what Paul was doing. His conversion to this new belief had made him a traitor to everything to which he had been brought up. It is always possible that Paul had disliked his father and that he had been searching throughout his life for a substitute. He had failed to find it in the orthodox Jahweh of Judaism. Jahweh with all His rules and requirements was perhaps too much like the father he had known in his home in Tarsus. Possibly he saw in Joshua–Jesus – the Crucified Man – the image of the rebel that was in his heart.

These followers of Jesus were all rebels too, protesting against the condition of the world. Unlike the Zealots, however, they were not saying that the Roman empire could be beaten by the sword. They had adopted a far subtler approach. They said, echoing their Messiah, that their Kingdom was not of this world. Beyond the Roman sword and javelin, and the disciplined might of their empire, there lay only one possibility: a world and a country that could only be inhabited by special people, people even more 'special' than the other Jews themselves claimed to be. Such a conviction, which Paul had now embraced, was not an easy one. Indeed it still remains one of the most difficult in the world – faced with the might of other empires and other evidences of vast wealth, power and irresponsibility. It is hardly surprising that to a man of Paul's passionate nature this total reversion in his thinking required a long period of rest and readjustment.

So he went into the desert. He experienced those blinding lights and long silences, the splendour of the sunrises and sunsets, the moon coming up enormous and orange over the horizon, and the extraordinary clarity of the night sky when the stars themselves seem as big as moons. In the desert, even if in company with others, a man is very much alone. He is conscious of the immensity of nature and of his own small stature when compared with the forces of the universe. He turns inward. Even the most unthinking begin to examine their conscience. Paul was far from being unthinking, he was one of the most formidable intellectuals of all time. If his experience on the road to Damascus had utterly changed his nature he needed those silent years not only to come to terms with his new conviction but also to formulate a workable hypothesis for his belief that Jesus was indeed the chosen of Jahweh, the Messiah promised throughout all the books of Judaism. Retreat was necessary for him for every reason. Among them was the simple one that his sudden *volte face* was hardly likely to endear him to the elders in Jerusalem, nor even to make him convincing to the Christian community there – or anywhere else.

Paul in Arabia. Tiberius on Capri. The latter was becoming even more violent and eccentric as the years went by. He was drinking as heavily as ever, and his insane cruelty and vicious sexual habits were becoming more and more pronounced. Suetonius writes that once,

> while sacrificing, he took a fancy to the assistant who carried the casket of incense. He could scarecly wait for the ceremony to end before hustling him and his brother (who was the sacred trumpeter) out of the temple and sexually assaulting both of them. Upon their protesting against this unnatural and criminal act he had the legs of them broken....

On another occasion he compelled a noblewoman to share his bed. She was so disgusted by his behaviour that she went home afterwards and committed suicide.

Medical knowledge was in its infancy in those days. It is possible that the priapism, or satyriasis, from which Tiberius seems to have suffered was due to an infection or abscess of the prostate gland. His early years seem to show him not only as a fine soldier and a good administrator, but something of a puritan. The change that came over him is most likely explicable on physiological grounds. At the same time this does not explain or condone his criminal cruelty. There was a lunatic streak in the Julian line.

Here (in the translation by Robert Graves) are some of the satirical verses that were written about this giant among men who ruled practically all of the European and near Eastern world:

> You cruel monster! I'll be damned, I will,
> If even your own mother loves you still.
>
> Saturn's golden age has passed,
> Saturn's age could never last;
> Now while Caesar holds the stage
> This must be an iron age.

He is not thirsty for neat wine
As he was thirsty then,
But warms him up a tastier cup –
The blood of murdered men.

In his earlier days, when these and other similar verses were brought to his attention, Tiberius would smile and dismiss them as the outpourings of men who had been injured by some of the reforms that he had set in motion. He would then echo the words from a tragedy by an early Roman poet: 'Oderint dum metuant.' 'Let them hate as long as they fear.'

They certainly hated, but still feared. The galleys, bearing dispatches from Rome and carrying the Emperor's replies, still passed and repassed on the indolent Bay of Naples. The Senate was crushed, the aristocracy largely destroyed, and the people supine as sheep. Even from his exile, even from his 'Goatish' island, the Emperor still had a long arm.

[14]

Preparations

Paul's conversion could hardly have been forgotten in Damascus. But the whole episode had been so brief and strange that no doubt many of the Christian sect had already dismissed it as inexplicable. Some, perhaps, may even have wondered whether the whole thing had not been an act: an attempt to infiltrate them so that he could report back to the members of the Sanhedrin the state of affairs in the synagogues of the city, and the names of the adherents to the new faith. In any case he had not been seen now for three years, and no further action had been taken against them. Presumably, then, the authorities in Jerusalem were satisfied that they were no menace to orthodox Judaism.

Suddenly the man was back. Once again he came into the synagogues and once again he preached the risen Messiah. 'He is the Son of God,' he said. To the confusion of both Christians and orthodox Jews he proclaimed with complete certainty that Jesus was and is the anointed Messiah, the one foreordained and so long awaited. Paul's skill in debate had been early established, as well as his astonishing powers of rhetoric, but what had once been used to discredit all the concepts of this offshoot branch of Judaism was now directed in its favour. 'His preaching became even more powerful. He put forward his reasons for believing that Jesus was the Messiah in so convincing a way that the Jews in Damascus could find no answers to him.'

It was hardly surprising that his return should occasion more than comment. It was even less surprising that many of the elders defeated in debate became infuriated. The Jews loved argument, loved quibbles about the niceties of the Law. They also had extremely volatile, passionate and fiery tempers – as the Romans had already found out to their cost. This turncoat and renegade, who had originally been sent by the Sanhedrin to extirpate this splinter sect and to correct any irregularities in the synagogues, had come back more violently unorthodox than anyone they had ever heard before. What, they must have wondered, had he been up to in the years since they had seen him last? Clearly he had been studying the Prophets intensely for he could quote them chapter and verse – from here, there and everywhere – that this obscure, crucified Galilean was indeed the promised of God, the Messiah who was to inaugurate the new kingdom for his chosen people. But what had this so-called 'Messiah' achieved? Israel was still in bondage. The Roman soldiers still swaggered through the streets of the Holy City. They still paid their taxes to that infernal Caesar with money that showed his head upon it. To listen to Paul was enough to make any right-thinking Jew mad with fury. Away with him! The man must go.

A plot was formed to kill him, possibly not with their own hands, for they could hardly forget the Commandment, 'Thou shalt not kill'. In any case hired assassins were always readily available. However, as Paul was clearly in their eyes an enemy to the Laws of Moses, it is not unlikely that Jewish hands were prepared to dispatch him. 'Night and day they kept an eye on the city gates in order to kill him. . . .' There was no way out for him through the gates, for these were patrolled by the soldiers of the governor. Damascus came within the aegis of Aretas, King of Arabia, who was responsible under his treaty with the Romans for law and order in the city. There can be little doubt that the governor was in collusion with the Jewish elders. His concern was to keep the city quiet and peaceful and, if this Jewish fellow was stirring up trouble, then he was as anxious as they that he should be done away with.

Paul's blinding sincerity had convinced some members of the Christian sect that he was one of them, that he had totally embraced their belief. Hearing of the plot, they hid him away in one of the old houses built into the city walls, with windows opening out on to the freedom beyond. But it was too high up for him to jump, and in any case he would have been seen by one of the guards patrolling the walls. The escape would have to be made at night, most probably a moonless one, for in that clear air the moon illuminates the whole of the city and the land with needle sharpness. They hit on the expedient of lowering him out of a window-embrasure in a basket. A basket descending, even if observed by a sentry, might not have attracted much notice. In the East to this day, the women, to avoid the fatigue of the stairs and so as not to call attention to themselves, regularly lower baskets from their balconies and high windows for pedlars or vegetable merchants in from the country to take note of, and come and call up to the rooms above to find out what is wanted. In any case, since the operation was almost certainly conducted on a dark night, there was no reason why it should be observed. Sentries are often sleepy.

But what kind of basket can contain a man? Some writers say it was 'a fish basket'. This seems highly unlikely – Damascus is not on the sea. If it was a basket at all it was probably a large one designed for fruit, and there were plenty of fruit and vegetable gardens outside the walls of Damascus. Quite possibly it was no more than a sack made of flax, a plant which was widely grown in Egypt, flax being one of that country's exports. A description of Paul given later by Titus says that he was 'of slight stature'. Since he lived hard and ate very sparingly it is doubtful whether he weighed much, if anything, more than seven stone. People were also smaller-boned in those days. Whether in a sack or a basket Paul would not have been too difficult to accommodate, and for two helpers to lower down the wall of Damascus. The rope used would almost certainly have been of papyrus or flax, both products of Egypt, and ropes of both types are mentioned by Herodotus in his *Histories*. The house may well have had a wooden arm projecting from it (for hoisting in grain among other things) and this would have been fitted with a wooden block or pulley.

Paul was at liberty, but it was hardly the way he had expected to leave the famous and ancient city of Damascus. It was his first experience of the violence that was to be directed against him time and again in his new life. He was to suffer shipwrecks, to be scourged on official orders, he was to have to endure mob violence in many cities throughout Asia Minor, and he was also to have further plots against his life formulated either by the Sanhedrin in Jerusalem or by local synagogue authorities. Paul was not a man who could just be tolerated, or tacitly ignored. The extremism of his nature was such that those with whom he came in contact either loved him or loathed him.

He had come into Damascus possibly expecting that the strength of his feelings and the intellectual arguments that he had formulated would convince all the Jewish community that he was right. He had had the arrogance to believe that those who were not Christians could be converted by the sheer force of argument. He was to learn differently: 'Though I speak with the tongues of men and of angels, and have not love, I am no more than a brazen gong or a tinkling cymbal. . . .' He had to learn that loving-kindness or the old English word 'charity' was the most essential thing, not only for making converts but equally for living life. Passion was not enough, and neither was intellect.

Three years earlier he had left Jerusalem as the chosen emissary of the Sanhedrin at the head of an armed band with instructions to rid Judaism of unorthodoxy. He had been chosen because of his high reputation in debate, his zeal for keeping the Law in purity, and his known adherence to strict Pharisaic principles. He returned a poor outcast, a refugee from Damascus, a man suspected by the

Christian sect and hated by the other Jews. His reception in Jerusalem was not likely to be a happy one. When the news got round that he was back, proclaiming himself a convert to this new belief, there must have been more than a little suspicion in all quarters. Soon after arrival he 'tried to join the disciples, but they would not believe that he was one of them and were all afraid of him'. This was hardly surprising in view of his previous record and his part in the stoning of Stephen. Again it was natural that he should be suspected of being a spy, and the news of his recent activities in Damascus would not yet have had time to reach the city.

The man who was first convinced that Paul was completely genuine was one who was later to become his travelling companion and, until they quarrelled, his closest friend. This was Barnabas, a Cypriot, a gentle and respected figure whom no one could suspect of any guile or collusion with an enemy of the Christians. It was Barnabas who proceeded to introduce Paul to the apostle Peter. Paul now heard from the lips of the rough Galilean fisherman the first-hand account of the life and sayings of his new Master. Peter was a married man and he took Paul into his house, where he and his wife looked after the convert for the next fortnight. The two men were very dissimilar, but they had something in common. If Paul had persecuted the Christians, Peter had three times denied his Master.

So Paul stayed with them, and 'went all over Jerusalem, preaching boldly in the name of the Lord'. After the experience on the Damascus road, after his three years of study and meditation, Paul's convictions, in any case, were complete. But now, to hear every day from Peter exactly what had been said and what had been done was an additional revelation. The oral tradition of Jewish teaching, the exactitude of memory which was required of them, meant that what Paul heard and what he later taught were in no way paraphrases. Modern men, accustomed to being bombarded with information from innumerable sources – let alone books – can scarcely conceive how exact was the information transmitted by perfectly trained memory. In some so-called 'backward' parts of the world even to this day whole genealogies, histories and sagas are transmitted by the oral tradition. Over the years some errors may creep in, but they are no more than the 'literals' to be found in printed books. What Paul was hearing from Peter was almost as exact as modern tape-recording. Now everyone knows that you can cut, edit and otherwise interfere with a tape-recording – but the words as spoken by Peter would have been completely authentic. He was not an old man in his dotage whose memory was failing, but a man about the same age or only a little older than Paul. The tragedy is that not more was later recorded in writing for, as John put it in the conclusion to his gospel: 'There are many other things that Jesus did. If every one of them were to be written I suppose the whole world could not contain the books that would be needed.'

Paul, who was quite convinced that he had seen the resurrected Lord in his vision, now daily spoke to the man who had lived with him and who had – in company with so many others – seen him after his crucifixion, death and resurrection. Paul claimed the same experience but unlike the others he had never known the Messiah when alive in the body. He was claiming to be an equal, but was he? It is an unanswerable question.

It was understandable that Paul with his vastly ambitious nature should demand equality. But ambition does not in any way necessarily imply a desire for wealth, or for worldly satisfaction and possessions. Many artists in every branch of art have starved and lived in conditions that would appear to most of the world completely miserable, and died as paupers, in order to record their version of beauty or of what they considered to be the truth. It is an aspect of idealism that sets the human race qualitatively apart from the animal.

There can be no doubt, in any case, that Peter completely accepted Paul's account of his experience. There was no reason why he should not. In that day and age scientific methodology had hardly invaded human consciousness, and any conception that things must be rigorously proved according to some analytical formula was unknown. It is only in recent years, nearly 2,000 years later, that the so-called scientific approach to objective phenomena is beginning to be called in question. The simple materialism of the eighteenth century – a most unreasonable 'Age of Reason' – or that of the industrial nineteenth century, with its confidence that man by the exploitation of the natural resources of the world could triumph over all obstacles, is being seriously challenged. The fire of the Renaissance, projecting man as an image of all things, is over. Soon the natural resources of the world, in terms of fuels at least, will be exhausted. The human race in some respects at least may find itself, in the phrase, 'back to Square One'. 'Square One' may well prove to be an area of psychic experience that in certain areas of the world has been largely forgotten. Professor Richard H. Bube of Stanford University, in America (a professor, it should be noted, of materials, science and electrical engineering) has gone on record as saying: 'One of the most pernicious falsehoods ever to be almost universally accepted is that the scientific method is the only reliable way to truth.'

Theodore Roazak in *Where the Wasteland Ends* has referred to the West's bleak 'mindscape of rationality' and, in regard to 'spiritual knowledge and power', comments: 'Here is a range of experience that we are screening out of our experience in the name of what we call knowledge.' Neither Peter nor Paul needed to be told of these things.

The only other apostle whom Paul seems to have met during this visit to Jerusalem was James, the brother of the Lord – a controversial figure. Speculation has been endless as to what is implied by the word 'brother'. There are two basic theories, the first being that James, as well as the three other 'brothers', mentioned in Matthew's and Mark's Gospels, Joses and Judas and Simon, were all the children of Joseph by a former wife. The other is that the brothers, and certainly James, were indeed the children of Joseph and Mary – real brothers, that is. Tertullian, one of the earliest and greatest authorities of the ancient Church, writing in the second century, seems to have had no difficulty in accepting this as a fact. Certainly there can be no doubt about the important place which James occupied in the church at Jerusalem. He was its recognized head, and on account of his righteousness was called 'James the Just'. Josephus tells us how, just before the siege in A.D. 70 when Jerusalem was destroyed, James was called before the high priest and asked to publicly recant his belief in the divinity of Jesus. Far from doing so, he made an open declaration of his faith, was condemned to death and hurled from a pinnacle of the Temple. He would seem to have been the first Bishop of the Church. According to Eusebius, the ecclesiastical historian and Bishop of Caesarea in the fourth century, James's episcopal chair was still shown at Jerusalem at the time that he wrote. In any case, Paul would have heard more first-hand details concerning Jesus from this 'brother of the Lord'.

Paul's passionate convictions knew no bounds, and the skill of his oratory and his ability to demolish opponents' arguments soon got him into further trouble. His special target was the Hellenists, or Greek-speaking Jews, whom he clearly undertook to tackle because of his fluent Greek – a language which most probably the apostles and many of the disciples did not know, or did not know as well as he did. Once again a plot was laid to murder him, and once again 'the brethren found out about it. They took him down to Caesarea and sent him away to Tarsus.' There can be little doubt that the Christians in Jerusalem breathed more freely after he had gone. They had been living quietly during his absence, continuing to make converts, and their cells had been spreading throughout the East. Then back he came and, even if he was now on their side, strife immediately broke out again. Paul had a habit of provoking trouble wherever he went. His life was a storm.

[15]

Alternatives

From 37 to 45 Paul vanishes once again from recorded history. There is some reason to suspect that he was in Syria and Cilicia, including of course his native Tarsus. It can hardly have been a happy return to the family home. He had left it a good Pharisee and he returned a renegade, who had embraced this new doctrine that must have been anathema to his father (if he was still alive), as well as to all his relatives and former friends. It is probable that during this period of his life either in Tarsus or elswhere he more than once suffered the horrible penalty of scourging – on account of his belief, and of his intemperate manner of proclaiming it. Writing a good many years later, in 56, he refers to having been punished on five occasions with the scourge, yet not one of these is recorded in Acts. It is reasonable to assume then that some if not all the scourgings took place during these missing years. Paul must have been extremely strong, quite apart from having an immense capacity for mental endurance, for the record specifically says that on each occasion he endured the full punishment, 'forty stripes save one'. More often than not the victim would faint long before the punishment was complete, or the judges, reckoning that the man had suffered enough, would terminate it. Paul, as in everything else, was determined to endure to the very end.

Quite apart from his profession of the belief that Christ was indeed the Messiah, another possible reason why Paul was disciplined so often is that he had undoubtedly already begun to consort with Gentiles. In Tarsus he cannot have failed to argue with them – something which in turn meant listening to their own beliefs. Philosophers abounded and so, quite apart from simple paganism and emperor-worship, did the mystery religions. Indeed these were all over Asia and the Near East (from which most of them had sprung) and, as has been seen, had even, to Tiberius's great annoyance, invaded Rome itself. How much if anything Paul absorbed from these cults is a subject which has proved a permanent battlefield for scholars, but it is most unlikely that he did not absorb – even if only by osmosis – something of the mental climate by which he was surrounded.

Out of a number of these mystery cults – 'mystery' because they required initiation into secrets which only the faithful might know – one of the most widespread was that of the Egyptian goddess Isis. In the first century A.D. her cult was in the ascendant, and temples of Isis were widely spread all over the Roman world. The fact that Isis, her husband Osiris and her divine son Horus formed a holy trinity between them satisfied nearly all the aspirations of the human heart. The attributes of the goddess are nobly described in a hymn to her, which has been translated by J. Lindsay:

> I am Isis, the Mistress of Every Land, and I was taught by Hermes and with Hermes I devised Letters, both the Sacred and the Demotic, so that all things might be written with the same letters.
>
> I gave and ordained Laws for men, which no one is able to change.
>
> I am the eldest daughter of Kronos. I am wife and sister of King Osiris. I am she who finds fruits for men. I am mother of King Horus. I am she that rises in the Dog Star, she who is called goddess by women.
>
> For me was the city of Bubastis built.
>
> I divided the Earth from Heaven. I showed the Path of the Stars. I ordered the course of Sun and Moon. I devised the activities of the Sea.
>
> I made man strong. I brought together woman and man. I appointed to women to bring their infants to birth in the tenth month. I ordained that Parents should be loved by children. I laid punishments on those without natural affection towards their parents.
>
> I made with my brother Osiris an end to the eating of man. I revealed Mysteries to men. I taught men to honour images of the gods. I consecrated the precincts of the Gods.
>
> I broke down the governments of tyrants. I made an end to murders. I compelled women to take the love of men. I made the Right stronger than gold and silver. I ordained that the True should be thought good. I devised marriage-contracts.
>
> I assigned to Greeks and Barbarians their languages. I made the beautiful and the shameful to be distinguished by nature. I ordained that nothing should be more feared than an oath. I have delivered the plotter of evil against other men into the hands of the one he plotted against. I established penalties for those who practise injustice. I decreed mercy to suppliants. I protect righteous guards. With me the Right prevails.
>
> I am the queen of rivers and winds and the sea. No one is held in honour without my knowing it. I am the queen of war. I am the queen of the thunderbolt. I stir up the sea and calm it. I am the rays of the sun.
>
> Whatever I please shall come to an end, it shall end. With me, everything is reasonable. I set free those in bonds. I am the queen of seamanship. I make the navigable unnavigable when it pleases me.
>
> I created the walls of cities. I am called the law-giver. I brought up islands out of the depths into the light. I am lord of rainstorms. I overcome fate.

Fate hearkens to me.
Hail, Egypt that nourished me.

Paul cannot have failed to meet many simple devotees of the goddess, as well as those who had been initiated into her mysteries. He will have seen her statue in processions through the streets – Mother Isis, holding her child Horus in her arms, her head inclined to look down with love at the holy child whom she had borne to her husband Osiris. She was the Madonna of East and West a long time before another Madonna would appear in Christian churches. It is significant, as R. E. Witt has pointed out in his *Isis in the Graeco-Roman World*, how many of the places that Paul was to visit in his travels were centres of Isis-worship. Echoes from it can possibly even be found in such famous passages as 'I am become as sounding brass, or a tinkling cymbal'. Tributes addressed to Isis include 'Shaking thy cymbals thou dost renew midwinter with thy sistrum [a musical instrument with thin metal rods, held in the hand]' and another reference 'the sorrowing waters of the Nile with its sounding brass'. By the first century Isis, who had been worshipped many centuries before in simpler guise, had become a mother goddess of universal attributes, not least of which was compassion and loving-kindness.

Isis appealed to women, for was she not the Universal Mother? Men, and especially the more aggressive and masculine, were less likely to succumb to her. Among the numerous alternatives – and there were enough cults for any man to find one that suited his nature – the most widespread was Mithraism. Temples to Mithras have been found all over the Mediterranean world, and even as far afield as London. Mithras was essentially the soldier's god and his cult travelled with the legions wherever they went. Like so many religions Mithraism stemmed from the East, its original home probably being Iran. It undoubtedly incorporated aspects of the Iranian national religion founded by Zoroaster. Among them was the belief in an eternal warfare between 'the Sons of Light and the Sons of Darkness' (a concept also to be found in Essenism).

Mithraism, like Judaism, had its sacred books, and its doctrines were collected into the Avesta or 'Law'. Mithras had been created by the good power in the universe, Ormazd, the Lord of Life. He was his faithful servant, who fought eternally against the evil power, the God of Death, Ahriman. Mithras had first created life upon the earth by slaying a sacred bull, and from its blood the first male and female human beings were born. His followers took a mystical communion together, in which they ate bread and drank wine. It seems possible also that the potent drug extracted from the black Hellebore was used in some initiation ceremonies to produce an illusory effect upon the worshipper.

His followers, called *sacrati*, passed through seven grades of initiation, corresponding to the number of the seven planets. Each grade had a masculine name, for Mithraism was confined to men. The third grade, *Miles* (soldier) was, as it were, the watershed between those in the higher ranks and those who were not fully in communion. The highest grade, *Pater* (Father) was a title that was later to be adopted by Christianity for its priests. Ascetism and celibacy were encouraged, certainly for the higher grades. This did not imply withdrawal from the world but a spartan, if puritanical, approach to the problems of life. Jerome in one of his letters refers to Mithraism as having, like Christianity, its celibate degrees and says that it offered communion with the Godhead in return for a pure and noble life. One of the concepts, the grade of *Miles*, corresponds very closely to the later 'Warrior of Christ.

Mithraism was encouraged by some of the later emperors, who saw that its hardy virtues were exactly what was needed to keep the empire together. The toughness of its initiation ceremonies, coupled with the Stoic qualities that Mithraism demanded of its followers, made it an admirable religion for soldiers. At the same time this was one of its weaknesses. Although it had many of the ingredients of a universal religion, and although it demanded a virtuous life and offered the hope of immortality to its followers, Mithraism had no place for women. Two further weaknesses were that it compromised with polytheism, and that its central figure was a mythical and not an historical personage. Christianity on the other hand was suffused with the influence of women, from Mary herself, right through the Gospels, and in the history of the early Church. It was also derived from an authentic historical figure. Furthermore Christianity would make no compromise with paganism and this was a great source of its strength. In this respect the influence of Judaism, with its determination to have no truck with idols or any of the pagan trappings, provided a core of steel.

Paul would certainly have encountered Mithraists all over Asia Minor. It had a firm hold in the Roman provinces in that part of the world, one of its principal centres being at Trapezus (Trebizond) in the north. A high percentage of the soldiers who policed and patrolled the provincial cities would have been followers of Mithras, and indeed there was something in the austerity of their creed that could hardly fail to appeal to the Pharisee in Paul's heart. At the same time there was one major element, above all else, lacking in this religion. It inculcated good ideas and a moral way of life but it lacked sympathy and tenderness. If there was no place in it for women, there was little for serfs and slaves. Although it did spread beyond the exclusiveness of the military it still remained pre-eminently designed for those who guarded the frontiers of empire, for the men whom, as Robert Graves puts it, cherished hardihood and the friendship that constant danger inspires:

> He who among us
> At full gallop, the bowstring to his ear,
> Lets drive his heavy arrows, to sink
> Stinging through Persian corslets damascened,
> Then follows with his lance – he has our love . . .

Another dominant cult was that of Attis and of Cybele, the Great Mother of the gods. Once again, as so often in these Eastern mystery religions, the basis of the belief centred round a divine youth who was killed and rose from the dead. Attis was born of a virgin who had become impregnated by eating some almonds from a sacred almond tree which had sprung up where the mortal son of a goddess had been emasculated by the jealous gods. The symbolism here is clear enough. Almonds – in the Mediterranean at least – sugared blue and pink, are still given to brides on their wedding days as emblems of fertility. Attis was both human and divine, and was so beautiful that the goddess Cybele fell in love with him. He, for his part, wanted to marry the daughter of one of the kings of Galatia and the goddess, infuriated at being spurned, drove him mad. He fled to the mountains and in his madness unmanned himself at the foot of a pine tree where he bled to death on the spot. Violets sprang up from his drops of blood. Violets, being typical flowers of spring, were always associated with Attis.

On 22 March each year a pine tree was ceremonially cut down by a group of eunuch priests, swathed like a corpse, and decked with violet wreaths. This 'body' of the dead god was then buried in a grave. On the second day of their vigil there was a great blowing of trumpets, presumably to rouse the sleeping god and call him back to life. On the third day, 25 March, there occurred the Day of Blood, the day when the god must be resurrected. The only way to achieve this was by shedding the blood of the worshippers. To the interminable sound of drum and cymbal, the clack of castanets, the blast of horns and the wailing of flutes, the worshippers worked themselves up to a frenzy. Insensible to pain, as they whirled about round the altar of Cybele, they gashed their bodies with knives and potsherds, bespattering the altar with their blood to give Attis strength to rise again.

Sir James Frazer in *The Golden Bough* observed that: 'The Australian aborigines cut themselves in like manner over the graves of their friends for the purpose, perhaps, of enabling them to be born again. . . .' The climax of this bloody scene occurred when the novices, those who intended to join the eunuch priesthood, sacrificed their virility, hacking off their manhood and hurling the bloody pieces into the lap of the goddess. Many, like the legendary Attis himself, must have died from this primitive emasculation. Then, in the small hours of the morning, the cry of a priest rings out and the worshippers run to the grave where the Attis-pine has been buried. There are lights hanging from the boughs of trees, priests waving flares – the grave is empty! Attis has risen! They, by their blood, and the novices by the sacrifice of their manhood, have achieved his resurrection. But they, too, are saved. They are promised salvation and in due course a resurrection, like the god.

Such cults and ritual orgies, reaching back into the earliest history of man, were to be found all over the East. In essence they were all the same, designed to ensure the fertility of man and the earth and, at a slightly higher and more symbolic level, the resurrection of man. It is unlikely that Paul can ever have seen this ritual, nor the somewhat similar rites (although without emasculation) that took place in honour of Dionysus. It would have been as much as an outsider's life was worth to be caught spying on them. But he cannot have lived and travelled as he did without knowing a great deal about them. At Hierapolis, only 100 miles north-east of Antioch, there was one of the major temples of that other eastern goddess Astarte–Astaroth–Aphrodite, goddess of love, also identified with the fish-goddess Atargatis. Sacred doves, symbolic of fertility, flew confetti-like above her shrine, while inside the temple sacred fish – for she was also the fructifying goddess of the sea – swam leisurely in special pools. Just outside the temple precincts lay the booths of the temple maidens, the prostitutes of the love-goddess. Similar temples were to be found in many of the places that Paul visited. There was one, for instance, just east of the Sea of Galilee, and another at Ascalon on the coast not far from Jerusalem.

Paul was to be the envoy to the Gentiles, and no man can successfully carry out an envoyship – be it spiritual or material – without having a very good knowledge of the people to whom he is going. He was later to write in his first letter to the Romans:

> Men say they are wise, but they are fools: instead of worshipping the immortal God they worship images made to look like mortal man or birds or animals or reptiles.[Here he was thinking of the Egyptian cults.] Because men are such fools, God has given them over to do the filthy things their hearts desire, and they do shameful things with each other. They exchange the truth about God for a lie; they worship and serve what God has created instead of the Creator himself, who is to be praised forever. Amen! Because men do this, God has given them over to shameful passions. Even the women pervert the natural use of their sex by unnatural acts. In the same way the men give up natural sexual relations with women and burn with passion for each other.

Paul knew his pagan world as few other Jews ever did. They averted their eyes when the swaying statues passed, and the flutes wailed and the cymbals clashed, and the eunuch priests cried out in their cracked trebles. Paul gazed steadily at the world that surrounded him. He fixed those piercing eyes on everything. He read their literature (Aratus, Epimenides, Menander, Aeschylus and Plato are all quoted by him). He was not going to hide himself like the Essenes. He was not going to turn his head away like the other Jews. He was going out into this world, and he needed to know the strength of the opposition.

[16]

The Man who was God

Because an obscure Jew called Saul, who was also a Roman citizen bearing the latinized name Paulus, goes unrecorded for about eight years some authorities treat this not inconsiderable passage of time as if time itself had come to a stop. The great world did not even know of Paul's existence, even if by his life and writings he was to enjoy a futurity that seems likely to last as long as man on this planet.

In 37 the event that had long been hoped for – indeed prayed for – throughout the Roman world took place. Tiberius, who had been on one of his rare visits to the mainland of Italy, died in his villa on the promontory of Misenum on 16 March. It was said that his successor Gaius Caesar had hastened the old man's end by smothering him in his bedclothes. He was seventy-eight. 'At the news of his death the people of Rome were so overjoyed that they ran about shouting: 'To the Tiber with Tiberius!' Others offered up prayers to Mother Earth and the Gods of the Underworld that he should have no home below except among the damned.' Thus Suetonius, who adds that some people who had been sentenced to death by him were executed nonetheless because, as his successor had not yet taken over, there was no court of appeal in existence. 'So the hatred of Tiberius grew stronger than ever. His cruelty, it was said, continued even after his death.'

Germanicus, the father of the new emperor, had been the nephew of Tiberius. A great soldier and universally popular, he was only thirty-four years old when he died at Antioch, that city which was to play quite a large part in Paul's life story. Rumour had it that he had been poisoned on the orders of Tiberius, because they wanted him as the next emperor after Augustus. Medical knowledge was then in its infancy and any death – especially of a powerful man – if it could not be immediately ascribed to some known cause, tended to be put down to poisoning. Germanicus had nine children by his wife Livia, three dying in infancy, leaving three girls and three boys. Two of the boys, Drusus and Nero, were arrested on trumped-up charges at the orders of Tiberius and were condemned to death. This left only Gaius, known as Caligula ('Little Boot'), because he grew up among the troops when his father was soldiering and they had made for him a miniature uniform including the *caliga*, or half boot, such as the Roman legionary wore.

As a young man Caligula had joined Tiberius on Capri, where the atmosphere of that extraordinary court-in-exile can hardly have improved his character. Tiberius himself had no illusions about him. 'I am nursing a viper in Rome's bosom,' he remarked on one occasion. 'I am educating a Phaethon who will mishandle the fiery chariot and scorch the whole world.' Tiberius's estimation of his successor's character was accurate, but the Roman people, remembering his father, greeted his accession with enormous enthusiasm. They hoped that in him they had found another Germanicus. His reign began auspiciously enough. Everyone felt that, after the iron horrors of the Tiberian period, Rome and indeed the whole empire were going to be blessed with peace and prosperity. Exiles were recalled, the Spintrian perverts were exiled in their turn, and many of the actions of his predecessor were annulled. Tiberius, for instance, had discontinued the practice of publishing an imperial budget, as Augustus had always done: Caligula revived it. He gave lavish spectacles and games to entertain the people, on one occasion having a bridge of boats built between Puteoli and Baiae on the Bay of Naples, a distance of some three miles. This was turfed over, and the Emperor and his courtiers, followed by the whole Guards division, put on a three-day entertainment, Caligula riding on horseback or in a chariot at their head. It was said that he did this because Thrasyllus, Tiberius's favourite soothsayer, had once said that Caligula had as much chance of becoming Emperor as of crossing the Bay of Naples on a horse. But, apart from such displays of pomp which the people loved, he did not neglect the more serious side of things, completing a number of important building projects that had been neglected under Tiberius, and restoring temples and other public buildings throughout the empire.

Unfortunately there was another side to his nature, a side that came more and more to the fore. There can be little doubt that Caligula was mad. It is said that his mistress Milonia Caesonia gave him a love-potion to secure his affections, which had the effect of driving him insane. It is more likely that he inherited that streak of insanity which seems to have run in his family. He forced his father-in-law to commit suicide, and regularly committed incest with his three sisters. Indeed, his sister Drusilla seems to have been the love of his life, and he was distraught when she died. On attending the wedding ceremony of one courtier, he decided he fancied the bride, and had her carried off immediately to his own quarters. His brutality, and his love of violence and sadistic spectacles, equalled, if it did not exceed, that of Tiberius. On one occasion at the Games, when the people cheered the wrong chariot team, he made the classic remark: 'I wish that all the Romans had only one neck!' In the words of Suetonius:

> He had absolutely no regard for chastity, his own or others', and was accused of homosexual relations active and passive with Marcus Lepidus, Mnester the actor, and a number of foreign hostages. A young man of consular family, Valerius Catullus, openly declared that he had enjoyed the Emperor, and that they were both quite worn out in the process.

At his banquets, if he took a fancy to the wife of anyone present, he would send for her at once and leave the room in her company. Upon his return he would openly discuss her good and bad physical points as well as commenting on her sexual performance.

This man, who even had his favourite racehorse, the Flyer, made a consul, was convinced that he was God. He established a shrine dedicated to his godhead, together with a school of priests, and a lifesize gold image of himself, which was dressed every day in clothes similar to those he happened to be wearing. Ordinary sacrifices like sheep or goats or cattle would not do for the divinity of Caligula. Before his statue, peacocks and grouse, pheasant, guinea hens and flamingoes were offered up. Convinced that he was Jupiter, the supreme god, he had a bridge built connecting his palace in Rome with the Capitoline Temple, publicly announcing that the god had asked him to share his home. When the moon was bright and full he would invite the Moon-Goddess to his bed. He had been an epileptic as a boy, and it is probable that the disease never left him. He suffered badly from insomnia, rarely getting more than three hours' sleep a night. Much of the time he would pace through the long corridors of the palace, his shadow leaping and jumping as he passed the lamps, the braziers and the brands held in the hands of his sentries. Terrifying visions haunted him. On one occasion he dreamed that he had a long conversation with the Mediterranean Sea. What the Sea told him he never revealed, but it can hardly have been comforting.

Caligula's conviction that he was the senior of all gods led to immense trouble in Palestine. He was determined that these irritating (and irritable) Jews should acknowledge his divinity – and in their principal temple at Jerusalem at that. Accordingly he sent orders for Petronius, the Governor of Syria, to have an immense statue of the Emperor constructed, which was to be erected in the Holy of Holies of the Temple. Prior to this Caligula had released from prison the grandson of Herod the Great, Herod Agrippa. The latter had been educated in Rome, had run into debt, and had been accused during the reign of Tiberius of treason. He was lucky not to have been killed out of hand, but he had merely been confined to prison. Clearly he had great charm, and he found his way into Caligula's unstable affections. He was presented by Caligula, in one of the latter's mad moments of generosity, with a replica of the chains he had worn in prison made out of solid gold, and handed back the tetrarchy, or subordinate rulership, of most of the territories that his grandfather had ruled. Later he was also awarded the tetrarchies of Galilee and Peraea and, after the death of Caligula, his successor Claudius added to Herod's control the dominions of Judaea and Samaria – a larger area altogether than even the famous Herod had controlled. He was not an inconsiderable man in terms of power, but he was of course always subordinate to the whims of the Emperor in Rome.

Petronius naturally temporized over the statue. He knew the nature of the Jews well enough, and certainly knew that to set up a statue of the Emperor in the Temple would cause something much worse than an ordinary riot. Even as it was, the Jews, who had heard what was projected, put on sackcloth and ashes and flocked in their hundreds to the place where the statue was being created. Petronius persisted in his diplomatic delay. But Caligula was determined that these infernal people, who would not recognize his divinity of their own accord, should be forced to do so, should be forced to kneel and acknowledge him as God. Finally, enraged that the work had not yet been completed, he sent an imperial edict to Petronius – to erect his statue in the Temple or commit suicide.

Fortunately for Petronius, the ship bearing the letter, which was dispatched in the winter of 40, was delayed by storms. And in advance of it he had further news. The word had gone round the empire like a lightning-flash – Caligula was dead. On 4 January 41 he was murdered by two Guards officers, one of whom Caligula had persistently insulted, and both of whom had been close enough to him to know that such a monster was not fit to rule a city, let alone the world. Approaching him they had asked for the watchword for the day and, when Caligula said 'Jupiter', Cassius Chaerea and Gaius Sabinus cried, 'So be it!' (Jupiter was the god who brought sudden death). Caligula, stabbed in the head and neck, fell to the ground, where he called out, 'I am still alive!' His assassins struck again and again, 'including sword thrusts through the genitals'. God was dead. At the same time a centurion who was in the plot killed Caesonia, while Caligula's daughter, Julia Drusilla, had her brains dashed out against a wall. Caligula was twenty-nine when he died. He had ruled for just under four years.

He was succeeded by Claudius, grandson of Augustus's wife Livia by her first husband – although rumour had it that he was in fact sired by Augustus. He was unprepossessing to look at, and he stuttered; a man whom his own mother had called 'something that Mother Nature had begun to work on but then flung aside'. Yet the fact remains that Claudius was no fool, he was sensitive and an excellent scholar. During his reign the empire knew a kind of tranquillity that had not been seen since the death of Augustus. One of his first actions was to countermand the setting up of the statue in the Temple of Jerusalem. He also gave instructions to Petronius to do nothing that could in any way offend the religious susceptibilities of the Jews, and ordered all his subjects to discontinue the practice of worshipping at shrines to Caligula. It is noteworthy that Paul's emergence from obscurity coincides with the mild and relatively peaceful reign of this Emperor. Nearly all his missionary journeys took place while Claudius was on the throne. Under Tiberius and under Caligula they would hardly have been possible, or would have ended in disaster. When Claudius died in 54, and Nero succeeded him, Paul himself was not to have very long to live.

[17]

The Golden City

At about the time that Paul was summoned to Antioch to preach to the growing community there, Herod Agrippa moved down to Caesarea, the residence of the Procurator of Judaea. In his determination to prove that his Roman years had not alienated or corrupted him, and that he was as good a Jew as any, he had turned upon that natural scapegoat, the breakaway sect of Christ-followers. It seemed clear to him that the best way to tackle the problem was to cut off the apostolic head. Accordingly he had James executed and Peter imprisoned – with a view to having him killed after a formal trial, in which he may possibly have hoped to expose Peter's belief to ridicule. Peter, whether by miraculous intervention, as the story is told in Acts, by convincing his guards of his innocence of any wrong, or by a simple bribe, managed to escape. (It is even possible that the guards themselves secretly shared his faith.) Herod was furious at the loss of his star prisoner and had the guards executed.

While Herod was in residence in Caesarea the news came through of Claudius's startling successes in Britain. He was the only emperor of the first century to visit the country and his policies were to lead within four years to the annexation of a large part of Britain. Herod proceeded to make elaborate preparations for games and a festival to celebrate the Emperor's triumph over this misty island so remote from his own sunny Judaea. One day during these festivities he received a delegation from Tyre and Sidon. Herod addressed them and the assembled populace with rhetorical eloquence, the sun shining on his elaborate robes and causing sparks like fire to glitter from his crown. Well versed in the adulation that Eastern potentates expected from their subjects the crowd cheered, and some in front called out, 'It isn't a man speaking, but a god!'

No sooner had Herod sat down than he was seized with terrible pains, the reason being, according to Acts, because he had accepted this gross piece of flattery and had not given the honour to God himself. He died, 'eaten by worms', five days later. Whatever disease it was that killed him it was certainly providential for the Christians. The three rulers who had been a menace to the spread of the sect – Tiberius, Caligula and Herod Agrippa – were all dead. A comparatively benevolent emperor ruled the world. The time was ripe for expansion.

Throughout these years, despite Herod and despite the antagonism of both Romans and Jews, the faith was in fact flourishing throughout Galilee, Judaea, Samaria and Syria. It had taken root in the great city of Antioch and was even spreading beyond the Jewish community and making converts out of former pagans. Peter's dream of the vast net let down from heaven containing all sorts of unclean beasts which no strict Jew might touch is very significant at this moment. When the voice told him to kill and eat he naturally replied that, according to the Law, he must not do so. The voice gave him the answer: 'Do not consider as unclean anything that God has declared clean.' The symbolism of this was obvious: those who were outside the Law, Gentiles and pagans alike, might be embraced within the faith. The time was fast approaching when Paul might begin to set out on the path for which he had so long been searching – the conversion of non-Jews.

The mother church in Jerusalem, hearing of the growing number of converts in Antioch, and probably fearful of the news that Gentiles were being accepted, sent Barnabas, a sound and reliable character, to investigate matters in the city. The latter, although his devotion was unquestionable, probably found himself rather at sea in dealing with Greek-speakers, and with men and women born pagan who now wished to join a church which, though it was in dispute with orthodox Judaism, was nevertheless based on respect for the Law. It was natural that he should think of Paul. Antioch in some ways was not so unlike Tarsus: it was a melting-pot of races and creeds, with Greek the predominant language. Paul's knowledge of such peoples, his eloquence and his ability to communicate with all types made him an obvious choice. He had lived among pagans, he was a fluent Greek-speaker and he was familiar with their customs and rites. Yet he had never in any way become contaminated, or – despite his miraculous new belief – lost the strictness of a Pharisee, or the skill at debate that he had acquired in Jerusalem under Gamaliel. Barnabas took ship for Tarsus, found Paul, and explained his mission. There can be no doubt that it sounded extremely attractive to a man of Paul's temperament. After his conversion, after the first dazzling fire of enthusiasm (which never left him), he had nevertheless for a good many years now been working in something of a backwater.

Antioch provided just the right challenge. It was the third largest city in the Roman world, only Rome itself and Alexandria surpassing it in population, riches and in splendour. Tarsus after all was somewhat provincial, but Antioch was the centre of Roman government in the East. As Antioch the Golden, it had been visited in 47 B.C. by Julius Caesar, who had confirmed its freedom. Ten years later, Caesar's avenger, Mark Antony, had spent the winter there in company with Cleopatra, prior to his disastrous Parthian campaign. Both Augustus and Tiberius had shown their imperial favour by adorning it with public buildings, and the city, quite apart from its many temples, boasted all the attributes of a great Roman metropolis: theatre, gymnasium, circus, public baths, aqueducts and cool colonnaded walks. Standing on the left bank of the river Orontes, about twenty miles from the sea, Antioch was set in a green and fertile plain. Guarding it to the south was Mount Silpius with its citadel on the peak, and with one of its limestone bluffs carved into a giant head of Charon, the ferryman of the dead.

As Paul and Barnabas and their fellow travellers sailed up the Orontes they would have passed by the sacred Grove of Daphne. This commemorated a nymph whom Apollo had unsuccessfully attempted to rape in Thessaly – unsuccessfully because Daphne had called out to Mother Earth to protect her, and had been immediately changed into a laurel tree. Apollo made a wreath for his head from its leaves, thus originating the tradition of the crown of laurel. Whether Paul knew this legend or not is immaterial; he is certain to have heard now, if not before, of the uses to which the famous Grove was put. Dominated by a giant statue of the god, the Grove of Daphne was sacred ground and provided sanctuary. This meant that criminals, escaped slaves, debtors and the like, could not be seized while within the ten-mile circumference of the woods. Since the whole area, with its many streams and fountains, was dedicated to Apollo and the memory of unravished Daphne, it had become, by a curious reversal, dedicated also to the celebration of the pleasures of sex. Male and female prostitutes from all over the East thronged the woods, paying a tithe of their earnings towards the upkeep of the temple and other buildings. To mention the Grove of Daphne to a Roman was to provoke a leer, a chuckle or a sneer. In much the same way other famous centres of prostitution have passed into history and folklore in later centuries.

They came to the city itself, shining white, built in imitation of the town plan of Alexandria – the Hippodamian system of broad streets cutting one another at right angles. The two principal colonnaded thoroughfares intersected at the town centre. This meant that Antioch was a city of four quarters, for which reason it was sometimes know as Tetrapolis, 'Four Cities'. Like the Alexandrians, the Antiochenes did not enjoy a good reputation in the ancient world, or with the Romans in general. If, in Edward Gibbon's words, the Alexandrians 'united the vanity and inconstancy of the Greeks with the superstition of the Egyptians', the Antiochenes united every vanity, every superstition and every sensual excess from all over the Eastern world. They were also renowned for their ready wit and their sense of satire. They had no illusions about anything or anybody and, like the children of other great cities today – London, Berlin, New York – they were quick-tongued and sceptical. But because they were mainly easterners, living in an indulgent climate, their character was easy-going. They were notorious for their eating, drinking and sexual licence. This was probably one reason why Antony, who was similarly inclined, had chosen the town for his winter headquarters.

Paul, familiar with dissolute Tarsus, was now confronted with one of the most profligate cities in the world. Even the Romans, a people not noticeably given to puritanical attitudes, felt that the Antiochenes really carried things a bit too far, that they were indeed, to use the modern jargon, somewhat 'over-permissive'. It is hardly surprising that Paul was constantly to warn his converts against the sin of *porneia*. *Porneia*, literally fornication, but covering in ancient thinking every form of sexual excess and deviation, was something to which his converts, whether Jews or Gentiles – but especially Gentiles – were exposed every day of their lives. It was not, as old Romans like Cato had known, that the East threatened Rome and Roman virtues with a sword. It threatened with its luxury, languor and vice. It threatened with its extravagant oriental cults, its orgiastic mentality, and its total sexual licence.

As time was to show, Cato the Elder was right, and those who opposed him with their arguments in favour of freedom and self-indulgence were wrong. Paul for his part has often been maligned in the modern Western world as a puritan and kill-joy. He was no more so than many thinking Romans of the republic, or pre-empire days, and indeed even later, who had seen that the influence of the Orient upon what had once been a race of hardy farmers would prove fatal. The decline and fall of the Roman empire was not entirely occasioned, as some would have us believe, by matters of economics. Morale, or the lack of it, also played a considerable part. It is customary for many nowadays to argue that men like Paul were wrong; that they were repressive. On the other hand, looking round at many of the more 'advanced' and 'free' societies today, it is possible to discern something a little similar to the state of affairs that prevailed in Rome in the first century. Societies once renowned for their hardihood and vigour, as well as morality based on the family unit, have lost both former virtues – along with their morality. On the other hand, perhaps there is no connection between these things. Human societies may possibly (and the evidence from the past seems conclusive) follow the same rhythms as Nature herself – flower, fruit and fall.

While Paul was augmenting the congregation at Antioch, converting Gentiles such as the Greek Titus, the news reached the Church that a famine was threatening. A group of prophets, as they are described, came to the city from Jerusalem warning of this impending disaster. It would hardly, however, have required the gift of prophecy to see that a bad grain shortage was imminent. They would have had ample opportunity on their journey to observe the state of the crops in the areas through which they passed, to have got the word indeed from the farmers. Palestine in any case was already in distress, and the Emperor Claudius was taking special measures to relieve it. The Jewish mother of a pagan king, Queen Helena of Abdiene, had even sent officials to Egypt and Cyprus to buy corn and figs for distribution among the people of Jerusalem. The news was received at Antioch with dismay, but the organizations of the early Church immediately went into action. Although many of the Christians – and it was in Antioch that this Greco-Latin term was first applied to them – were poor, there must undoubtedly have been quite a number who were merchants, tradesmen and manufacturers. 'They decided that each of them would send as much as he could to help their brothers living in Judaea. . . .' No doubt they made extra subscriptions to the poor fund to which, in the normal Jewish manner, they contributed every Friday. The men chosen to take this relief money to Jerusalem were Barnabas and Paul.

[18]

Aphrodite's Island

Paul and Barnabas did not travel alone. They took with them Paul's Greek convert Titus. He was evidence of their success in Antioch of bringing Gentiles into the new Church, but he was far more than that. Some commentators have used phrases such as 'They were so ill-advised as to take with them a Gentile Christian'. On the contrary, the action can only be seen as a very deliberate one, designed to bring to a head the controversy that was raging as to whether it was only Jews who could be accepted into this sectarian branch of Judaism, or whether 'the others' could also be admitted. Paul was never any man's fool and to suggest that he unthinkingly took Titus with him is to underestimate his intelligence. Titus was a test case. He had been born a pagan, he was a Greek and he was uncircumcized. These three factors put him completely outside the Law. If Paul could get him accepted, then he had won his case, that the doctrines of Christianity could be taken throughout the empire to all and sundry. The most important statement which Paul wanted to make was something that had not previously been accepted: that the Messiah of the Jews was the Messiah of the whole world.

The presence of Titus was bound to cause a row with the Pharisaic group, which was clearly what Paul intended. The whole matter had to be brought out into the open and debated, and some form of settlement reached. Paul's confidence that if he could convert Gentiles and former pagans – which he had already done – then he could come to some accommodation with his fellow Jews was well justified. The conclusion was finally reached that Paul was as much the apostle as those whom Jesus himself had designated, but that, while Peter was the apostle to the Jews, Paul was to be the apostle to the Gentiles. 'So they shook hands with Barnabas and myself and agreed that as partners we would work among the Gentiles and they among the Jews. All they asked was that we should remember the needy in their group, the very thing I have worked hard to do.'

It is unlikely that Paul met Peter on this occasion, for the latter would very likely have still been in hiding after his escape from prison. But he would certainly have met James the brother of Jesus who, in his position as head of the Church, was the man above all from whom Paul needed official approval of his future course of action. James appointed a young man to go back with them to Antioch to act as amanuensis. He would also have brought with him documents containing authentic accounts of the life and sayings of Jesus. This was John Mark, a cousin of Barnabas, the son of a widow who was prominent in the church at Jerusalem. It seems possible that John Mark was the young man who had followed Jesus into the Garden of Gethsemane 'dressed only in a linen cloth' and who, when the soldiers tried to arrest him after all the other disciples had escaped, left his garment behind in their hands 'and fled away naked'. If this supposition is correct then it is very easy to see why James would have appointed him to go up to Antioch along with Barnabas and Paul. At a time when oral tradition was so strong and vivid, he could tell the members of the community there what he personally knew of the life and sayings of Jesus. He could reinforce what the documents said out of his own memory.

If Tarsus had served as the base for Paul's operations during the missing years he had now transferred his headquarters, as it were, to Antioch. It was from Antioch that he set out on the first important journey of which we have any record, however slight that may be. During the winter of 46 a conference was held consisting of the church elders, teachers and prophets (the latter being concerned with the interpretation of the scriptures and inspirational exhortation of the faithful). It was decided, and no doubt this decision was based on the results of the Jerusalem meeting and instructions sent by James the Just, that Barnabas and Paul should go to Cyprus along with John Mark as soon as the sailing season opened in the spring. Among those who are mentioned as being principal members of the Antiochene community were Simon Niger (the Black), probably though not necessarily a Negro, Lucius of Cyrene, who may well have been a Greek, and Manaen. The latter was clearly of a distinguished family, for he had been brought up either as a foster brother or close companion of Herod Antipas, the Tetrarch. A mixed company then, it was indicative of the fact that this new faith was one which broke clean through all current stratification of society.

'Having been sent by the Holy Spirit', as we are told in Acts, Barnabas, Paul and John Mark sailed for Cyprus. Any decision taken in those days by the believers was naturally enough ascribed to some divine word or impulse. But there was a perfectly practical reason for their going to Aphrodite's island, and one which must surely have been debated in some considerable detail well in advance. (It sometimes seems to be forgotten that the Christians did not just live in some cloud-cuckoo-land of dreams, visions and voices, but that all or nearly all of them were practical hard-working artisans, tradesmen and merchants.) Barnabas had been born in Cyprus and must therefore have had friends and relatives there, as also probably his cousin John Mark, and Paul was a fluent Greek-speaker. Another good reason for making Cyprus their target was that it had a large Jewish community, stemming from the time when Augustus had leased the copper-mines of the island to Herod the Great. There was also the nucleus of a Christian community for, during the persecution following the death of Stephen, in which Paul had played so large a part, a number of them had fled to the island for safety. Cyprus, one of the largest islands in the Mediterranean, was also a good communications centre. Roughly equidistant between the coast of Asia Minor to the north and Syria to the east, its greatest length is about 140 miles and its greatest breadth about sixty miles. It had been celebrated for its fertility since earliest times and had been colonized by the Phoenicians and the Greeks, and was subject to the Egyptians, Persians and Romans. It was now a Roman province. Quite apart from Barnabas's personal connection with the island it was clearly a good starting-point for any attempt to get the movement into the main arteries leading westward to Greece, and beyond that into the heart of the empire, Italy itself. It was easily reached from the port of Seleucia in Syria, where the three men embarked. The easternmost point of Dinaretum was only about seventy miles away and the mountains of the island were clearly visible on a fine spring day.

The three men had been escorted down to their original departure-point by a delegation from the church, for it was as customary then as now for groups of friends to come down and see travellers aboard their ship. They dropped down the river and, after leaving the mouth of the Orontes, turned north. A few miles away lay the main port for Antioch, Seleucia. It was here that all the large ocean-going cargo vessels loaded and unloaded, and that passengers embarked for overseas voyages. Paul and his companions would have taken a standard sea-going freighter of about 100 tons, one that ran between Syria and Cyprus, going out with manufactured goods and returning with copper, salt, wine and fruit. With a favourable wind they should have reached their destination, the port of Salamis, within twenty-four hours. Salamis, near modern Famagusta, was the centre of the salt-mining industry and an important commercial port, the principal city in the eastern half of the island. Here they knew that they would find a fair-sized Jewish community. They could quickly find accommodation, and equally quickly start about their business of contacting the Christian members and speaking to the other Jews in synagogues.

Cyprus at this time was peaceful under the rule of Rome. Its stormy history, when it had passed between one conqueror and another, for the moment was at an end. After the Battle of Actium in 31 B.C. it had come into the hands of Augustus, but less than ten years later its administration had been transferred to the Roman senate. It is for this reason that Sergius Paulus, who was governing the island at the time that the missionary party visited it, is accurately called by the author of Acts Proconsul, not Governor. He seems to have been a man of culture and there is some slight, but inconclusive, evidence that he contributed information to the historian Pliny the Elder on the antiquities of Cyprus. He was also, like so many in his day and age, a devotee of astrology and an intimate of a renegade Jew, one Bar-Jesus. Jews and other Easterners were often to be found in Roman circles, for the science of astronomy, then inextricably mixed with the pseudo-science of astrology, had come out of the East. Juvenal, for instance, in his Sixth Satire records a palsied Jewess coming round soliciting alms:

> In a breathy whisper. She knows, and can interpret,
> The Laws of Jerusalem: a high-priestess-under-the-trees,
> A faithful mediator of Heaven on earth. She too
> Fills her palm, but more sparingly: Jews will sell you
> Whatever dreams you like for a few small coppers.
> (translated by Peter Green)

Similarly Apuleius in his *Golden Ass*, written in the second century, recounts the story of a Syrian astrologer with whom a rich merchant deposits the required sum for him to cast a horoscope concerning a sea voyage that he wants to take if the stars are propitious. While the astrologer is making his calculations a young man runs up. He and the astrologer greet one another, the latter asking how his voyage went. The young man cannot contain himself and cries out that he was shipwrecked, lost all his property, and only just escaped with his life. On hearing this the merchant snatches his money from the tables and makes off into the laughing crowd. Such incidents were common enough in those days. Even emperors—Tiberius on Capri for instance—took no major decisions without consulting soothsayers. The lack of real belief in any power except Fate or Fortune made people of all classes disposed to listen to charlatans and rogues, as well as to those who were genuinely convinced that they could read the stars. The situation is not so dissimilar today, when businessmen, actors and actresses, truck-drivers and tycoons regularly read their horoscopes in newspapers or consult their own favourite astrologer.

Having strengthened the faith of the Christian community, and having preached it in the synagogues, Paul and his two companions made their way either on foot or, more probably, on muleback, right along the south coast of the island to Paphos. This was the great centre of the cult of Aphrodite–Venus which had been established in the old city on a hill a few miles above the port. It would have been enjoyable enough travelling through the Cypriot spring, the mountains of the Troodos range capped with snow and screening Paphos to the north and east, forests of pine-trees dense along their slopes, the country enamelled with wild flowers, and the Mediterranean sparkling below them to the south.

The world-famous shrine at Paphos had, according to Herodotus, been first established by the Phoenicians, although it is quite possible that long before them there had been a local cult of a fertility goddess. The principal image, the sacred Aphrodite, was not a sophisticated Greek statue but a simple phallic cone. Similarly shaped stones have been found at a number of other cult sites in Syria, Pamphylia and as far west as Malta, and Eryx in Sicily. The Aphrodite of Paphos, as probably the others of their time, was clothed in a woman's robes. No bloody rites disfigured the cult of the goddess of love and fertility, except the blood of virgins. For here, as in many other centres of her worship, it was customary for young women before their marriage to prostitute themselves to strangers at the sanctuary. (A somewhat similar custom had obtained in parts of ancient Egypt, the theory behind the latter seeming to have been that the pain of defloration would be associated with a stranger, and not with the future husband.) In Paphos, where the act was considered a holy sacrifice to the divine principle of fertility, the money obtained from this prostitution went to maintain the sanctuary. Quite apart from these future brides, the precincts swarmed with the official temple prostitutes, the handmaidens of the goddess who, as in the Grove of Daphne, paid part of their earnings to the temple. Since Paphos was a busy port, and Aphrodite was considered the patroness of sailors, there was never a shortage of customers. A brisk trade was also done in silver amulets modelled in the shape of the Aphrodite figure, which were considered lucky charms that would preserve mariners from shipwreck and drowning. Similarly, to this day, in some Sicilian and Italian ports (including Tiberius's Capri) phalli of carved coral are sold as charms. Few visitors who buy them have any knowledge of how ancient is the cult they celebrate.

Even if the three missionaries avoided like the plague the shining temple on the heights, where the sacred doves wheeled and the incense fumed, they cannot have ignored the evidence of the cult in the port, the sailors with their amulets and the prostitutes who swarmed the docks waiting for incoming ships. It was while they were in Paphos that an unexpected summons reached them. Sergius Paulus, the Proconsul, wished to meet these visitors whom, he had heard, preached a new form of religion. A man of curiosity then, eager for a sign, or eager to test the wisdom of these Jews against the wisdom and power of his own magician, Bar-Jesus. They accepted with alacrity – it was in any case equivalent to an imperial summons – and made their way up to the palace which stood on the hill, a little above the city. The interview that followed is recorded in some detail in Acts, for it turned out to be so important that it marked the highlight of their Cyprus tour.

Bar-Jesus, 'Son of a Saviour', was called in Greek Elymas, or 'Sage'. He was undoubtedly, as has been seen, typical of many of his time, with some skill in interpreting the stars as suited him, proficient also in magical tricks of the conjuring type and, being possibly a member of the court entourage, probably well-off from the sale of tips and information to locals eager for official information and favours. He was certainly far from pleased when he saw that Sergius Paulus was listening with considerable attention, and even apparent approval, to the message that this bearded, weather-beaten Jew was giving him. It is interesting to note that it was Paul, and not Barnabas or John Mark, who was selected to give the good news of the Messiah to this important Roman official. The others stood by ready to assist with further evidence of Christ's life and Resurrection. They were not needed.

Bar-Jesus stood it as long as he could and then, seeing perhaps his lucrative position as friend and counsellor slipping from him, interposed his own arguments. 'He tried to turn the Proconsul away from the faith.' Paul's temper was never far below the surface; he had a low tolerance threshold. Here was this renegade expatriate, not even a practising orthodox Jew such as others with whom he had argued, and a lying scoundrel at that, daring to speak against the truth of God and of mankind's Saviour. Paul exploded. He looked Bar-Jesus straight in the eye and said: 'You son of the Devil! You enemy of all goodness! Full of every evil trick and deceit, isn't it time you stopped trying to turn the Lord's truth into lies? Look now! the hand of the Lord falls upon you: you will be blind and not see the sun for a season!'

'At once Elymas felt a dark mist come over his eyes and he staggered about trying to find someone to take him by the hand.' In this battle of two will-powers Paul had demonstrated his complete ascendancy. Sergius Paulus was dumbfounded. He had already been deeply impressed by Paul's teaching but now, after so extraordinary a demonstration of power, he became a believer. For those unwilling to accept the miraculous, one must immediately ask the question – what exactly happened? It is more than likely that Bar-Jesus as an Oriental mage believed implicitly in magic: his own and other people's. Overwhelmed by the dynamism of Paul's personality, and outstared by his piercing eyes which transmitted like a lightning flash the passion of belief, he was completely convinced that what his opponent had said had come true. It is possible that he too in due course became a believer in this new faith – for from whom else could the historian have got the information about what he felt at the moment of losing his sight? The circumstances are not so extraordinary as they may seem to a twentieth-century city-dweller. We have plenty of evidence from anthropologists and others, working for instance in remote areas like New Guinea, of contests between 'witch-doctors', or what we might call faith-healers, that sound not so dissimilar to the encounter between Bar-Jesus and Paul.

Bar-Jesus disappears from the story, so also does Proconsul Sergius Paulus, but that this incident was considered very important is shown by the fact that the author of Acts has transmitted it in such vivid detail. One salient point is that from now on Saul, as he has previously been called, is always called Paul. The reason for this is not so hard to find. Sir William Ramsay put it clearly some years ago:

> After his years of recent life as a Jew, filled with the thought of a religion that originated among Jews, and was in his conception the perfected form of Jewish religion, did he reply [when asked by the Proconsul those standard questions of the time 'What is your name and where do you come from?'] 'My name is Saul, and I am a Jew of Tarsus'? First let us see what he himself says to his method of addressing an audience (1 Cor. ix, 20f.), 'to the Jews I made myself as a Jew that I might gain Jews; to them that are without the law as without the law; I am become all things to all men; and

> I do all for the Gospel's sake.' We cannot doubt that the man who wrote in this way to the Corinthians replied to the questions of Sergius Paulus, by designating himself as a Roman, born at Tarsus, and named Paul. By a marvellous stroke of historic brevity, the author sets before us the past and the present in the simple words: 'Then Saul, otherwise Paul, fixed his eyes upon him and said . . .'

It is noticeable also that after this famous episode Paul, who has previously appeared as junior in the Christian hierarchy to Barnabas, is nearly always mentioned first. Although the thirteenth apostle, although the last as it were into the fold, he had made himself by his intellect, faith and ambition one of the foremost. James the brother of Jesus was still the head of the church in Jerusalem, but from now on it was perfectly clear that, in all the lands that lay beyond that comparatively narrow sphere in the East, Paul was to be the dominant figure.

[19]

News in Asia

In the port of Paphos the three travellers found a merchantman bound for Pamphylia, a district of Asia Minor, about 150 miles' sail to the north-west. Although there is no mention of how long they had stayed in Cyprus it is reasonable to assume that, arriving in the spring, having spent some time in Salamis, and then the longish route along the southern coast, followed by their stay in Paphos, it would now be early summer. This was a pleasant enough time to make the crossing, the winds blowing mainly westerly past Rhodes and the province of Lycia, and giving them a beam wind all the way into the gulf at the head of which stood Antalya, the principal port of the province. They did not stop, however, for the merchantman in which they travelled had cargo to deliver, and possibly timber to collect, at the smaller harbour of Perga lying eight miles up the Cestrus River to the east. Although it has now vanished, and the river is silted up, Perga was then a centre of trade between Greeks and the natives from the interior. For the first time in his life, as far as is known, Paul was confronted with a culture that was predominantly native, in the sense of being non-Greek. The Pamphylians were a mixed race of aborigines, Cilicians and Greek colonists. Their language, the basis of which was probably Greek, was disfigured and corrupted by barbarian elements. Hardly a good ground, one would have thought, to preach the gospel. . . . Futhermore, the summer heats were now burning over the Pamphylian plain, and the whole area, locked within the Taurus mountains, was like a giant frying-pan. Furthermore again, the plain, low-lying and with stagnant waters left behind in pools from the Cestrus River's spring overflow, was a perfect breeding-ground for the malarial mosquito.

Paul was now in his middle or even late forties, an unremarkable age today, but in the first century, and especially for a man who had lived as hard as he had, almost the beginning of old age. And yet he was now intending to set out with a caravan across the Taurus mountains to reach Antioch in Pisidia. The prospect would be daunting even to a young and healthy man – and at some point during his stay in Perga Paul fell ill. Reams of paper and gallons of ink have been expended over the centuries on the nature of the mysterious malady referred to as his 'thorn [stake] in the flesh'. Did he, as happened to Julius Caesar, become more prone to epileptic attacks as he grew older? This seems quite likely, and the midsummer heats and enervating nature of Pamphylia would hardly have helped the condition. Some authorities, and in particular Sir William Ramsay, have come down heavily on the side of recurrent malaria being Paul's sickness, which Paul later refers to in his letter to the Galations as the 'messenger sent to buffet me' and a 'messenger of Satan'.

It is quite true that recurrent malaria might be described in such terms and would certainly prostrate the victim at unexpected times and in a most unpleasant way. On the other hand nothing is more alarming than an epileptic fit, in which the seizure is often preceded by a loud scream or a cry, after which, to quote J. A. C. Brown,

> all the muscles of body go into spasm . . . after about half a minute this 'tonic' phase is followed by a so-called 'clonic' phase in which

> the limbs rhythmically contract and relax, the bladder or bowels may be emptied, or the tongue may be bitten until the contractions gradually cease and the patient lies breathing heavily and unconscious for a varying length of time.

Christian historians and churchmen, as has been said before, have often been reluctant to consider Paul as having been epileptic, feeling perhaps that there is something shameful about the disease and that it would in some way invalidate his life, his work and his writings. This is simply not true, and where could one find a better description of Paul than that already quoted of the epileptic character 'with its violence, its love of mysticism, its persecutory beliefs and impulsiveness'?

Certainly something strange happened in Perga that caused John Mark to abandon both Paul and his cousin Barnabas, and take ship back to Caesarea for Jerusalem. Homesickness, a dislike of their change of programme in heading inland for Pisidian Antioch, a resentment of the fact that Paul had now assumed the position of leadership which had formerly belonged to Barnabas, personal illness – many theories have been advanced. The record says no more than that he 'left them there and went back to Jerusalem'. Was he perhaps a witness of an epileptic fit – quite frightening even today, when something (if little) is known about the malady – but which at that time would have been inexplicably terrifying? John Mark's desertion, which was how Paul viewed it, was not to be forgotten. On his next missionary journey he refused to take the young man with him, and this was to lead to a major quarrel between himself and Barnabas.

Of the next stage of their travels the author of Acts says in his laconic way: 'They went on from Perga and came to Antioch of Pisidia. . . .' Whether it was Luke or not, whoever wrote Acts would have made a brilliant journalist today, but never a 'colour' or feature writer. He is concerned solely and totally with the objective of his story – the spreading of the gospel – and eliminates with a razor-stroke whatever does not immediately contribute to this. One has also to remember that in those days of papyrus scrolls, simple quills and ink, a writer could not afford time or space to dally on extraneous events. Basic facts were all. Had a modern historian or travel writer been along, one can imagine with what monotonous thuds volume after volume would have landed on the reader's table. We would like, of course, to know a great deal more, but perhaps in the end we are lucky. No excessive verbiage, no landscape or other portraiture obscures the incised and simple detail of the record.

The journey must, in any case, have been a hard one, across the burning plain and then, as the caravan trekked up through the gorges and ravines of the Taurus mountains, they may well have needed fires at night to keep them warm. Always with them there was the fear of robbers. Although the Emperor had made considerable efforts to stamp out banditry in Asia Minor no one could possibly police the whole wild and mountainous area (it would be difficult enough today). At night the travellers would have had to take turns in watches, swords or staves by their sides, scanning the slopes above them, waiting anxiously for the dawn. With first light, after some olives, a bit of bread or biscuit, and a mouthful of cold mountain water, the groaning camels, snorting horses and braying donkeys would have been forced to their feet. Quite apart from travellers like Paul and Barnabas many of the people would have been merchants, bringing up to Pisidian Antioch the products of the coast as well as imports from overseas. It was no doubt with the memory of this journey, as well as many others in mind, that Paul would later write in his second letter to the Corinthians of what he had endured to promote the faith: 'In journeyings often, in perils of waters, in perils of robbers . . . in weariness and painfulness, in watchings often, in hunger and thirst, in fastings often, in cold and nakedness.'

After harsh days through the mountain passes the caravan emerged upon the high plains of central Anatolia. The clear air, the scattered settlements, the good farmland interspersed with beautiful lakes – in particular the one called Limnai (modern Lake Egirdir), blue, shining and freckled as lapis lazuli under the turning wind – were enough to lift up any heart. After the stifling heat of the plain, and the winds and harshness of the mountains, the beautiful uplands awaited them. And beyond, a little northeast of the lake, on a hill overlooking the plain of Anthius, lay the city. Colonia Caesarea Antiochaea was its full name, or Antiocha ad Pisidiam, literally 'Antioch towards Pisidia'. It had been founded by Greeks and had been made a Roman colony under Augustus, who had settled legionary veterans here to provide a Roman nucleus, a core as it were to the strange mixture of Greeks, nomads, aborigines and Jews who formed the main body of the population. It was a frontier town. From here the squadron of cavalry stationed in the city went out on sporadic forays against bandits, and from here was maintained the system of regular patrols that guarded the mountain passes. The Romans also had other military bases connected with Antioch by the great highway, Via Sebasta, which ran west through the town of Apollonia and east through Misthia, whence a small road (later to be taken by Paul) went on to Iconium. Even as far afield as these remote uplands of Asia Minor the hand and sword and sandaled foot of the legionary were evidence of the power exerted from the marbled palace in Rome where the Emperor received dispatches from every part of the known world. Paul was in Antioch to promote an unknown world, to assert against all the evidence of imperial might that a small handful of Jews, in schism with the main body of their people, were bent on changing everything.

As visitors to the Jewish community, and as visitors who made it quite plain that they had a special message to deliver, they were asked to speak in the synagogue. It is noticeable that in this somewhat remote provincial city there were a number of converts or 'God-fearers' from among the local, formerly pagan, peoples. Paul began his famous address with the words: 'Fellow Israelites and all Gentiles who worship God. . . .' He was heard with attention and, after a brief historical sketch of the origins of Judaism, inserted presumably for the benefit of the Gentiles present, he went on to make the momentous statement that the Messiah whom the prophets had predicted had already come, that he had been rejected by leaders of Jerusalem and by the Jewish people there, and that it was at their instigation that the Romans had put him to death. This was harsh enough for Jewish ears, even if excitingly interesting to Gentiles who may have long chafed at being as it were second-rate citizens in the Jewish faith. Paul now went a great deal further. He declared the evidence of this Messiah's resurrection from the dead. He further declared that 'through him remission of sins is being announced to you, and that in him every one who has faith is justified from all the things for which there was no acquittal in the Law of Moses'. This was a completely revolutionary statement. This visiting preacher was saying that a new Law had been established, superseding the old, and what was more it clearly included non-Jews, for in his peroration he addressed them all together as 'Brothers'. It is more than evidence of Paul's astounding powers of oratory and blinding sincerity that the orthodox Jews heard him through to the end – more than that, invited him and Barnabas back to the synagogue on the following Sabbath. They wanted to hear a great deal more about this Saviour.

Jews and Gentiles alike, but one suspects more of the latter, were agog to listen to the next exposition of this news which seemed too good to be true: that all men might be saved by this hitherto unheard of man who had risen from the dead. It is not surprising that on the next occasion when Paul rose to speak, the synagogue was crowded to overflowing and, no doubt to the great disgust of the orthodox, there were more Gentiles than Jews in the audience. Such a thing was unknown, was indeed unlawful. Gentile converts they could stomach, but to have outright pagans coming into the holy place to hear a heretical, indeed blasphemous statement was almost too much to bear.

'Nearly every one in the town came to hear the word of the Lord. When the Jews saw the crowds, they were filled with jealousy. . . .' This was not surprising. Judaism was, still is, an exclusive religion with, whatever may be said to the contrary, an accent laid upon racial superiority. What gave Christianity, at least as it evolved through Paul, its unique quality was that it embraced all men and women, slave and free, rich and poor, noble and peasant, and of every race under the sun. If it had not been for this extraordinary man it is quite possible that the life and teachings of this Jewish Messiah would have provided no more than a splinter sect of Judaism to be found in Palestine and a few other related parts of the Near East. Paul changed the world.

[20]

'Through many troubles . . .'

How long Paul and Barnabas stayed in Pisidian Antioch is never indicated. It must certainly have been a matter of months, not weeks, and it is quite clear that Paul was ill for some time while he was in the city. There can be no doubt of their success in promoting this new belief in a risen saviour, destined for all mankind. Paul aptly quoted the words of Isaiah: 'I have set you to be a light for the Gentiles, to be the way of salvation for the whole of the world.' Such sentiments were naturally attractive to all the non-Jewish people who came to listen to him, but to the orthodox they must have been more than irritating. The trouble was – and it always was – that Paul's excellent training under Gamaliel, coupled with his acute intellect, meant that he could meet the Jews on their own ground, outquote them and demolish their arguments at source. Irascible and prone to argument, the Jews were hardly likely to enjoy this experience.

The basic attraction of Paul's message was that all people were acceptable. The saviour had died in the most ignominious way as a condemned criminal in the company of two proven criminals, leaving the promise that all human failures – and everyone was a failure – were redeemable by this scapegoat of God. It was an astounding statement, and it remains so to this day. No one, without skipping the hurdle of disbelief, can quite cross into that special ground where fact, reality, and on the surface of it unreality, become one. Paul could do this. He could also convince thousands of hearers during his years of travel and endurance that there truly was another life – one beyond the whips of slave-dealers, the extortion of money-lenders, the avaricious and sensual desires of the human animal and the petty life of man on this planet. Whatever he was, whatever his physical condition was, he was a genius of a unique degree.

The news that Paul and Barnabas between them brought to Antioch was not confined to the city itself but 'spread everywhere in that region'. Antioch was not only the military, but the administrative centre for the whole of the region called Phrygia, the western area of the province of Galatia. How much Paul may have known of the city's importance in this respect before making it his target is open to conjecture, but undoubtedly he will have heard about the city in his previous travels, and have come to the conclusion that it would be an excellent centre for disseminating the faith. It is clear that his optimism was justified. Almost inevitably, however, the orthodox Jews were not going to tolerate for long what they now saw quite clearly was the dissemination of a heretical branch of Judaism, and one which contravened the Law in accepting into its worship uncircumcized Gentiles and former pagans. The Roman administration, for its part, was unlikely to be concerned about theological disputes among the Jews. As far as they were concerned, certainly in these early stages of the spread of this new doctrine, these Christ-believers must have seemed little more than some obscure branch of Judaism. Every man to his own favourite god, let them settle their religious arguments amongst themselves.

The Jews were hard workers, good merchants and craftsmen, and usually good citizens. There was only one real fault to be found with them: they had to drag religion into everything, instead of just keeping it aside for the necessary feasts and festivals. The Jews themselves could not take any action against these other two members of the race, so there was only one recourse to them, and that was to get word to the Romans that the men were troublemakers. They were causing the spread of a revolutionary doctrine which was likely to endanger the peace of the city. Gentile women 'of high social standing', who had become converts to Judaism, were among those who brought the activities of Paul and Barnabas to their Roman husbands' ears. As in any colony, the first reaction of the ruling class is always to stamp out whatever seems to threaten the peace; particularly so when that colony is composed of a hotchpotch of races and the rulers are distinctly in the minority.

Paul and Barnabas were expelled not only from Antioch but from the whole surrounding region. It is quite possible that this was one of the occasions when they were formally beaten by

Roman lictors after a public trial. Paul as a Roman citizen – and no doubt he had some document to prove it – could not be beaten without trial although Barnabas, a Jew, could be. Following the command that Christ had given to his first messengers that 'if any place will not receive you and refuses to listen to you, shake off the dust that is on your feet as a testimony against them', the two registered their formal disapproval against the treatment they had received. The fact remained that they had been long enough in the city, and had convinced enough of the people to share their belief, that they left behind the nucleus of a flourishing Antiochan church.

It was probably the early autumn of 47 when the two men set out on the imperial highway that led to Lystre, about 130 miles to the south-east. This time it is unlikely that they went with any caravan. They were two discredited travellers in sun-bleached cloaks, staffs in their hands, a wallet containing all their worldly possessions slung over their shoulders, and heavy leather sandals on their feet. The author of Acts, while practical in so many ways, often tends to ignore a certain very basic fact – economics. Paul, Barnabas and John Mark had shipped to Cyprus, lived there some weeks, shipped again to Perga in Pamphylia (where Mark had left them), travelled a long way inland to Pisidian Antioch, stayed there several months, and were now once again on the road. Even accepting the fact that they no doubt lived as frugally as many peasants do to this day in the eastern Mediterranean, they must still have needed some money. Undoubtedly the home church of Syrian Antioch, which had sent them out, had provided what was considered enough for the journey, but it can hardly have been envisaged that the men would be away for so many months. They would of course have lodged free with sympathizers in many places but one must also assume that converts contributed cash enough to see them on their way from one centre to another.

Iconium, the next major target of their route, was the chief city of Lycaonia, the central area of Asia Minor. There can be little doubt that the news of what happened in Pisidian Antioch was not slow to reach Iconium, even if it did not precede the travellers. Now their current destination was still within the sphere of Antioch, and they must therefore have had some suspicions that to start once again proclaiming what they had been forbidden would certainly lead to further trouble. In this they were not mistaken.

Their reception was much the same as before – they were invited to preach in the synagogue, listened to with interest but hostility by the orthodox, but with fervent attention by Gentiles and Gentile converts to Judaism. It was not very long before exactly the same situation arose, a division between the followers of the Law and those, whether Jews or not, who saw in this new faith a hope that had never seemed to exist in the world before. Paul probably wintered in Iconium. 'The apostles stayed there a long time. . . .'

A man might travel in spring, summer and autumn along the Asian uplands, but he would be hard put to it to do so when the winter set in. It was probably not until the following year that the blow fell. It might have seemed sensible to promote his revolutionary doctrine to a limited few, to avoid giving offence to those who would certainly dislike it, and do everything they could to undermine him. Such was not Paul's way, nor indeed that of Barnabas – for it must never be forgotten that this brave and reliable companion suffered as much as Paul did, and without any possibility of redress under Roman law. They were warned by sympathizers, for they had made a number of converts, that there was a plot afoot to have them stoned. The administration was presumably prepared to turn a blind eye. In any case these two men had both been instructed to stop their troublemaking within the sphere administered by Antioch, and they were still within it. Paul and Barnabas, aware also that the yeast of their convictions was already rising within the city, decided to move on yet again. This time their destination was Lystra, another town in the link that Augustus Caesar had built to maintain the Roman Peace throughout Asia Minor.

The inhabitants of Lystra spoke their own Lycaonian dialect, but the language of trade and cultured conversation would have been the demotic Greek of the day, a language with which Paul had been familiar since a boy. There were few Jews in the town, no synagogue, and indeed probably the only Jews regularly to visit the place were merchants coming in the autumn to buy grain for Iconium and Antioch. Paul and Barnabas stayed either in a hostel or with some Jews to whom they had been recommended by previous acquaintances on their route. They spoke privately with people and probably used the forum or market-place for addressing such members of the public as could understand their Greek, or were prepared to listen to the extraordinary statements made by these two itinerants who seemed to have nothing to do but talk. And how Jews could talk! It was amazing that they ever got any work done, and this couple did not seem to be earning their living in any visible way. However, all the East was familiar with inspired madmen, followers of this, that or the other. At any rate these two seemed to be whole men, not like the priests of Cybele and Attis; although as far as they could follow it, this belief in a man-god who had died in the spring and been resurrected after three days did not sound so very unfamiliar.

What turned the scales in Lystra was the extraordinary event that occurred one day when Paul was addressing what was probably a largely sceptical crowd. He happened to notice a man sitting among them – he may have seen him on previous occasions being carried about by friends or relatives – who had been born a cripple. The power flowed through Paul, the same power that had confounded the magician in Cyprus, only this time it was healing. He was made aware that this man believed in him, believed in what he said, and without the reciprocity of belief the power could never operate. In the same words as are used to describe his encounter with Elymas at Paphos, Paul 'looked straight at him'. He shouted out: 'Stand up straight on your feet!' The effect was electric. The man jumped up and began to walk around.

The cripple was healed. The people of Lystra were completely overcome. They had known the man since his childhood, could testify to the fact that he had never been able to walk, and now here came this strange wandering Jew, who was always holding forth about his salvation-man, and cured him in some completely incomprehensible manner. It was hardly surprising that in Lycaonian Lystra the memory of one of their town's chief myths, the chief claim to fame indeed of Lystra, immediately sprang to mind.

Far, far back in time, in the days when the gods took to frequenting the earth more than they seemed to do nowadays, Zeus and his messenger Hermes had come down to this part of the world to see what the humans were up to. Disguised as poor travellers, they had been far from hospitably received. They had been scorned, insulted and turned away from the houses of both rich and poor, until they had finally come across the cottage of a poor old couple, Philemon and his wife Baucis. These two had taken pity on the travellers and had entertained them with such as they had in the way of food, coarse bread, an egg or so, and rough country wine. Before going back to Olympus the two gods turned all the Lycaonians who had insulted them and refused them hospitality into frogs in a lake. Philemon and Baucis, however, were rewarded by having their cottage transformed into a magnificent temple of white marble adorned with gold. They themselves were reincarnated as two noble trees which guarded the temple. It stood just outside the city gates, as did all temples to Zeus, and was the glory of Lystra. The temple was pre-Roman, and must certainly have been built in the early days of Greek colonization of the area, but to the simple locals it embodied the truth of the story about Philemon and Baucis.

Looking at the tall Barnabas, the one who expressed power and dignity but left most of the talking to the electrical little man who was his companion, they seemed to see incarnate in them Zeus the King, and Hermes his messenger. That was it! 'The gods have come down!' they shouted. 'The gods have come down like men!' They were not going to be turned into frogs this time; no, they were going to show them the respect that the earlier Lycaonians had failed to do. The news of what had happened quickly reached the head priest in the temple of Zeus. Sacrificial oxen were prepared, their horns gilded and garlanded, and an impromptu procession was formed. Preceded no doubt by flute-players, the priest and his attendants, the oxen and the crowd streamed back in Lystra, to offer sacrifice to Zeus and Hermes.

Barnabas and Paul had retired to their house, completely unaware of what was being prepared in their honour. But when the whole procession stopped outside, either they or their host must have gathered the import of the whole thing. Nothing could have been more calculated to upset and distress them – this was exactly the kind of superstitious rubbish that they were trying to weed out from the world. Tearing at their cloaks in repudiation of the blasphemy, Paul and Barnabas stormed out of the house. The hermetic spokesman shouted out: 'Men, what are you up to? We too are only men, just like you. We are here to bring you the good news – and that is that you should cease from follies like these and turn to the living God, who made heaven, earth, sea, and everything in them.' The crowd was silent under this harangue, silent as Paul went on to say that this God had previously allowed all nations to go their own way, but that He had always shown a proof of Himself in the rain from heaven, the annual crops, and given them food and happiness.

The priest and the people, who had come to pay the greatest tribute that they possibly could to these men whom they had believed to be gods, were dumbfounded. The rejection of their intended sacrifice was bad enough, but now to be shouted at and reproached was insufferable. They had only hoped to pay respect, to make a sacrifice, and then to turn the whole occasion into a happy festival with meat and wine, singing and dancing. Now this man whom they had mistakenly believed to be Hermes – and it was quite clear looking at him now that he was no more than a bearded, bald-headed little Jew – was insulting them. All right, if these weren't gods, then who were they? Some of the Jewish grain merchants from Iconium and Antioch who were in the crowd were quick enough to seize their opportunity. They told everyone that the men were notorious troublemakers who had clearly been expelled from their own cities, and that the best thing the people of Lystra could do was to get them out of the town. Soon after the stones began to fly.

It is very noticeable from the account that Barnabas does not figure in the stoning. He was presumably pushed contemptuously aside while the crowd vented their disappointment, hatred and anger on Paul. He now stood, though not for quite the same reasons, in the same place as Stephen had done on that faraway day outside Jerusalem. As he was later to write in his second letter to the Corinthians: 'Once too I was stoned. . . .' Battered and bleeding, Paul crumpled to the ground under the hail of stones and hatred. Assuming him to be dead some of the mob dragged him out through the city gates, so as not to have a corpse within their walls. They realized they had made a terrible mistake. They had believed that this broken piece of wreckage was a god. There in front of them, in his marble and gold temple, stood the real god, Zeus King of the Heavens, Lord of Olympus. The sacrifice should go to him, the libations of wine should be poured to him, the flutes should sound in the twilight, and the people should know the real happiness that this man had falsely said his false god could bring them.

[21]

Endurance

Astonishingly enough Paul was still alive. But he was to bear the scars to the end of his life. It is possible – whether the epilepsy or malaria theories are discarded or not – that some of his later physical troubles may date from this day in Lystra. Barnabas, friends and converts gathered round Paul's blood-soaked body, got him to his feet and took him back into town. At first sight this might seem a remarkably dangerous thing to do, but it must be concluded that the mob had all dispersed. They would have made for their homes to avoid any trouble with the authorities who, whatever their feelings, could not openly condone attempted murder. Under the circumstances the dangerously ill man should have been allowed days or even a month in which to recover, but it is clear that Lystra was now too hot to hold them. On the very next day Barnabas and Paul were on the road again. It is almost certain that some sympathizers gave or lent them a donkey. After the agonizing experience of stoning Paul would certainly have been in no condition to walk. They made their way to Derbe, a small town which has been identified as the modern Daevri

Sehri. It lay just across the border of the Roman province in an area administered by King Antiochus of Commagene, a vassal of the Emperor.

Derbe can never have been anything other than a dull frontier town, but as such it was not a bad place for a man to recuperate. It was probably a long time before Paul was anything other than a very sick man recovering from innumerable wounds, either in a travellers' hostel – primitive enough in parts of Asia to this day – or in a house recommended as that of a friend or relative by one of the converts made in Lystra. He was scarred for life. He was later to write to the churches in this area that he was branded (as were runaway slaves) to prove that he was the slave of Jesus. He displayed the same qualities in his fight for health as he did in everything else. Nothing – floggings, stonings, imprisonments, hardships of all and every kind – was ever going to stop him from promoting this revolution in human life. He would tell the Jews, but especially the non-Jews of the Roman empire, that they could all attain a life that was beyond their existence in time, that they could be 'delivered out of the body of this death'.

The most understanding quality possessed by Paul was that he was under no illusions as to the difficulties of living a good life. He was constantly aware that a life under the rule of virtue, or according to the laws of God, as he understood them from his Pharisaic training, reinforced and illuminated by his belief in the Messiah, was the most difficult thing on earth. It required a discipline far in excess of that of the Roman soldier in some lonely land holding the frontier against Parthians, Asian horsemen or wild Teutonic tribes. Other men before him, notably Socrates, had well understood how hard was the virtuous life, and Socrates, in a very different way from Paul, was an equally unusual man. Plato records how in a hard winter when Socrates was serving as a soldier on campaign, at a time when everyone else was muffled up in sheepskins against the cold, he carried on in his ordinary cloak and walked barefoot over ice and snow. He was abstemious by nature but, if he felt in the mood, he could drink other men under the table.

An example of his physical strength combined with his will-power is recorded in Plato's *Symposium*, a meeting of friends to eat, drink, and talk:

> Aristodemus said that Eryzimachus, Phaedrus, and others finally went away – he himself fell asleep, and as the nights were long took a good rest: he was awakened towards daybreak by a crowing of cocks, and when he awoke the others were either asleep, or had gone away; there remained awake only Socrates, Aristophanes, and Agathon, who were drinking out of a large goblet which they passed round, and Socrates was discoursing to them. Aristodemus did not hear the beginning of the discourse, and he was only half awake, but the chief thing he remembered was Socrates compelling the other two to acknowledge that the genius of comedy was the same as that of tragedy, and that the true artist in tragedy was an artist in comedy also. To this they assented being drowsy, and not quite following the argument. And first of all Aristophanes dropped off, then, when the day was already dawning, Agathon. Socrates, when he laid them to sleep, rose to depart; Aristodemus, as was his manner, following him. At the Lyceum he took a bath, and passed the day as usual. In the evening he retired to rest at his own house.

Socrates's self-discipline and his physical endurance were probably equal to that of Paul. There was a salient difference between them, however, and it is a difference that sets these two geniuses of the human spirit quite apart. Socrates, who said that 'virtue is knowledge', maintained that provided a man in any situation knew what was the right and virtuous thing to do he would necessarily do it. Paul knew better. 'I know that good does not live in me – not, that is to say, in my human nature. Even though the desire to do good is in me, I am not able to do it. I do not do the good I want to do: instead, I do the evil that I do not want to do.' Socrates with his iron self-control could truly say that if he knew what was the good and right thing to do, then he would do it. Paul with his more sensitive perception, his perception of the dichotomy of human nature, was aware that a man needed more than the knowledge of what was good, he needed spiritual assistance in order to practise it. He himself had found this in his belief, and he promised it to all others who would follow him. His experience at Pisidian Antioch and Iconium, culminating in the disaster at Lystra, had only reinforced a determination to endure all things for the sake of what he believed to be the truth. 'Paul and Barnabas preached the Good News in Derbe, and won many disciples.' It was probably the people of Derbe he had in mind when he later wrote in his message to the church throughout Galatia that 'You did not reject or despise me, even though the state of my body might have engendered scorn or disgust. . . .'

One might have expected that when the spring came and the snows melted he and Barnabas would have made their way south through the passes of the Taurus mountains to Tarsus, and so on to Syrian Antioch. Far from it, they went back the way they had come: through the city where Paul had been stoned, and the cities from which they had been ejected. They were determined to see that the nucleus of believers whom they had left behind had not fallen into error, and to correct it if they had. It seems almost certain that in all the places where they stayed any length of time written documents concerning the life and sayings of the Saviour were left behind with whoever seemed the most trustworthy of the new believers. If Jews were highly trained in the oral tradition the same was not so of Gentiles, a few of whom might have known long passages of Homer by heart – but little else. It is possible that they risked going back because they knew that the city magistrates would have changed with the new year of 48. But this meant little, the records were still there, the men who hated them were still there. It was an act of astounding courage, foolhardy indeed if both men had not been convinced that they were under divine protection.

Acts as so often is laconic: 'They strengthened the believers and encouraged them to remain true to the faith. They told them that "We must pass through many troubles in order to enter the Kingdom of God."' In each place that they visited they talked with those whom they considered most reliable and correctly informed. Later, in what seems to have been a show of hands, almost certainly influenced to some extent by Paul and Barnabas, they were appointed in the Jewish fashion, elders or presbyters of the local congregation. When they had first come into this remote area of the Roman empire they had brought a completely new message to pagan and Jew alike. When they left after their second visit they left behind them soundly constituted cells of believers, which were steadily expanding all the time. It was an incredible achievement. Two men alone, in the face of many established creeds and considerable general hostility, had planted the seeds of religious revolution in a large section of the eastern Roman empire.

Leaving the territory of Pisidia during the spring they made their way once again down to Perga. Here no doubt the procedure was identical, strengthening early converts, making sure that new ones had received the message correctly, and appointing trustworthy leaders of the community. Like so many of the later saints of the church, it is noticeable that, despite dreams and mystical experiences, Paul was eminently practical when it came to matters of organization. He had a businesslike character. Possibly there was no ship available at Perga to take them on to Seleucia *en route* for Syrian Antioch, or they had already decided to go down to the main port of Antalya to make new converts before leaving Asia Minor. The latter seems more likely. Antalya was an important town and a large commercial port – an admirable place from which the message could be disseminated by sailors, merchants and other travellers.

It was in the summer of 48 that they finally got aboard a ship bound for Syria. They had been away for two years. This was their third sea-voyage and, uncomfortable though it most probably was, it was nothing compared to the discomforts of that first summer in Pisidia, the perils of the mountain passes, or the even greater dangers and violence that they had faced in the cities. They had covered at least 1,000 miles, mainly on foot, in Cyprus and Asia Minor. It would be a remarkable achievement even for a modern traveller, intent perhaps on coming back with a travel book or documentary. Much as a man might try to do it the hard way, it would be impossible to emulate the conditions that Paul and Barnabas encountered. But they were not doing anything so simple as to produce an entertainment, they were trying to convert the world. Faced with contemptuous or hostile officials, they were also confronted with worse hostility from many Jews as well as pagan ignorance from Gentiles.

It is doubtful whether they could ever reach the peasant level of the peoples. There were too many problems of dialect and language. Their message must necessarily have been transmitted in Greek: the one language used in the places they had visited by educated and semi-educated for all matters of business and general conversation. Many of the Jews even, who had long been settled in Asia Minor, had probably forgotten their own language and had certainly adopted Greek as a *lingua franca*. Paul and his companion were coming back now over the summer sea to report to those who had sent them out the extent of their work, both failure and success. But there was greater success than anyone might have expected. It was an auspicious beginning.

[22]

Divisions and Dissensions

Thin, marked by privation, two Jews in travel-worn cloaks entered Antioch the Beautiful, Antioch 'The Crown of the East', one summer's day in 48. The city at that time had a population of nearly half a million, an immense figure in the ancient world. Among so many, of so many races and creeds, no one would have cast a glance at these shabby travellers and if they did would probably have thought that they looked like a pair of merchants who had come to grief in some venture, shipwrecked possibly. The shorter, bald one certainly seemed to have enough to say, and to judge from his appearance he had recently been through some hard times.

Paul and Barnabas, after a wash and a change of cloaks in the house of one of the Christians, went straight to a full meeting of the church. The news had flashed around that they were back. It would have seemed almost unbelievable after so long a time, for many must have thought that after leaving Cyprus they had perished somewhere in those wild Asian uplands. Now they heard the splendid news, news which definitely proved that God had blessed their project in sending these two envoys to the pagans, and to the Jews who had not heard of the resurrected Messiah. It was comforting too to feel that they were less alone than formerly, and that hundreds of miles away in cities from Cyprus to Pamphylia and even in remote Lycaonia there were now others who believed as they did. The tide of faith, it was clear, was already making up into far away estuaries. What probably heartened them more than anything was the amazing news that Sergius Paulus, Proconsul of Cyprus, had become a believer. If a man of such consequence, and a Roman, could join their ranks it did indeed seem that nothing was impossible.

When all the news was told, later to recirculate throughout the city bringing in further converts, Paul and Barnabas 'stayed a long time there with the believers'. Once again there is no mention of how they supported themselves. Either the community fed and clothed them for their services or, in the tradition of Jewish rabbis, they went back to their respective trades or professions – though what Barnabas was proficient at we do not know. As a Levite, but 'a man of Cyprus by birth', he may have owned land there, or been a merchant or a craftsman as were so many Jewish Cypriots. In any case, to the author of Acts such questions are irrelevant. All that matters is what these men did in the service of establishing the church.

It cannot have been long before the news of what the Antiochenes were doing – and had, it seemed, achieved – reached the mother church in Jerusalem. Although it had been agreed before the departure of Paul, Barnabas and John Mark into the world of the Gentiles that they were free to make Christians out of those who were not Jews, it would seem that many of the congregation there had not fully understood what this meant: accepting into the faith men and women who had not been trained in the Law, and men who had not undergone that simple tribal ritual of circumcision. While the orthodox Jews, who had in general been so much against Paul and Barnabas, as they had found out to their cost during their travels, were unwilling to acknowledge Christians at all, there were plenty of Jews who had opted for this new offshoot of their faith. But they would not tolerate the fact that Gentiles, who had not even embraced the Law, might be received. One cannot help wondering whether John Mark's desertion was not occasioned by the fact that he found Paul, and even Barnabas, prepared to accept Romans, Greeks and Asiatics, who had no knowledge of the Law whatsoever. For many of the Jewish members of the early church Christianity must have seemed only a purified form of Judaism. It entailed no more than an acceptance that the Messiah had already come, that he promised salvation to all Jews who believed – but that he was still the Messiah of the Jews alone.

The news that these two converters had been working among pagan Cypriots and remote Asiatic barbarians, and receiving them into the church without demanding full conformity to everything that had gone before, came as an unpleasant revelation. It appeared that this man Paul, once so ardent a Pharisee and persecutor of Christians, was now saying that the whole world could come within the embrace of *their* church, not only without being Jews but without accepting Torah. This was unthinkable and highly undesirable. When they had come to believe in Jesus as the true Messiah they had not envisaged that he would become a Messiah for Gentiles as well, unless of course those Gentiles did the same as converts to Judaism did. It is easy to understand their outlook. Their country was in Roman hands, they paid their taxes to Rome, they had been prepared to believe that the promised kingdom was not of this world, but they considered that the Messiah had been born a Jew and had come to preach salvation to Israel. Were they also to believe that even their oppressors might enjoy the benefits of the Kingdom without coming under the discipline of the Law, and without bearing the caste mark of circumcision?

It all seems somewhat trivial today, this argument about a relatively minor operation on the male member but, as has been said before, it was a matter of great significance at the time. Judaism did not recognize uncircumcized proselytes. Therefore, those who were now prepared to believe in a Jewish Messiah must conform first of all to this basic law. Unimportant though it all may seem at first glance, a great deal hinged upon it. It would determine whether Christianity was an advanced form of Judaism, or whether it was something very different. Paul, to judge from what had been reported about his speeches in Galatia, had taken things a great deal further than had been expected – or wanted. There was a smack of Oriental mysticism, a smell of the pagan mystery religions, about his emphasis on the crucified Christ and on the Cross, and especially his argument that men could be immediately forgiven upon proclaiming their belief in Christ as Saviour. Something had to be done about it. Certainly an investigation must be made as to what exactly was being transmitted to foreigners far away from the mother church in Jerusalem.

Peter had already declared his position after his dream about the great net let down from heaven, as well as by his association with the centurion Cornelius when he had said that, although it was against the Jewish Law for a Jew to associate or eat or drink with Gentiles, God had revealed to him that no man must be considered common or unclean. When Peter came to Antioch to see Paul and Barnabas, he made no secret of his convictions. In this city, the only one in the East where Gentile and Jewish converts met on equal terms, he also mingled like the others with former pagans. Then the Pharisaic Christians arrived on the scene, the delegation sent from Jerusalem to investigate charges of laxity or even an element of pagan heresy in what was being promulgated in Antioch.

No doubt the city itself shocked them. It was the kind of place where, if he must earn his bread there at all, any good Jew or Christian would keep strictly within his own group.

Then they found out that the Gentile converts had definitely not been circumcized. But what troubled them as much as anything was that Jewish Christians were eating and drinking with these former pagans. Possibly even eating 'the other thing'? Peter felt the whip of their argument and ceased to associate with uncircumcized converts. He had, after all, been known to deny his cause before. His action in doing so inevitably made a deep impression on Barnabas and other Jewish Christians. Paul saw at once what all this was leading to – the division of the church. Unless prompt action was taken it would be split straight down the middle and there would be two branches of Christianity, one for Jews and one for Gentiles. This surely could not be the intention of Jesus's brother James back in Jerusalem? They had shaken hands in agreement before he and Barnabas had departed for their first missionary tour. It had been established then that he was to take the message to the Gentiles, but it had never been said that he must first of all make, as it were, pseudo-Jews out of them. He could discount the investigating delegation (he could always deal with *their* arguments), but what he could not discount was Peter's back-sliding, and it was Peter's behaviour above all that very naturally influenced others.

Peter was not an intellectual. He could not see that the current dispute might easily destroy the embryo church. He was a great, good man of entire simplicity – the reason why he had been chosen by Jesus. Paul destroyed his position as well as that of the investigators in one short, sharp public encounter, probably before the assembly of the whole congregation. 'If you,' he said, 'who are a Jew, live like a Gentile and not like one of your own race, how can you possibly insist that Gentiles live like Jews?' In view of Peter's previous conduct, in view of his real convictions, the question was unanswerable. He accepted the force of Paul's logic immediately and never afterwards showed any resentment at what almost amounted to a public humiliation. He was too big a man to feel any rancour, and he was a man who could always recognize what was right even if he could not always do it. He knew, in fact, the Pauline predicament. As far as Antioch was concerned the matter was almost at an end. Paul had saved the church from division, but it was still important to get the approval of Jerusalem. James the Just, that mysterious figure who looms powerfully but obscurely over all this early history, must be consulted. A final decision must be given.

Paul and Barnabas and a number of other unknown delegates were now dispatched to Jerusalem to get the exact ruling on this awkward, and all-important, subject. Peter, it would seem, had already preceded them to Jerusalem. He had undoubtedly gone straight to the house of James. He himself might be the first of the disciples, certainly the most prominent in the testimonies of the four Gospels (mentioned by Mark twenty-three times, by Matthew twenty-four times, by Luke twenty-seven times, and by John thirty-nine times), but it was the brother of Jesus who seems to have been accepted as the head of the church. Close on Peter's heels came the delegation from Antioch, astonishing the Christian communities through which they passed by their tales about Asia Minor, and about the establishment of the church in such remote places as Lystra and Derbe.

The delegation from Antioch was received in Jerusalem by a full council of the apostles and elders of the Church. Paul and Barnabas were listened to with growing attention as they described their missionary activities in these distant lands. Clearly their account of this spreading of the good news must have been disposing the audience in their favour, for a group of Pharisaic Jews, probably the same as had visited Antioch, stood up and interrupted. 'The Gentiles have got to be circumcized,' they declared. 'They must be told to obey the Law of Moses.' Instant chaos followed, everyone arguing on this, that and the other point; some pointing out that Christ on occasions broke the Law, particularly in regard to the Sabbath, and others denying it. Paul no doubt had already had a conference with Peter to find out whether he would support him, and had also very probably sounded out James's views on the subject. In the middle of all this confusion Peter rose to speak. 'Brothers,' he said, 'you well know that God appointed me a long time ago as the one who should take the Good Word to the Gentiles. . . .' He went on to point out that God had given the Holy Spirit to the Gentiles just as he had done to the Jews. No distinction had been made between them. 'Why then,' he went on, 'are you trying to put a burden on them, a burden which neither we nor our fathers have ever been able to support? It is only through the grace of Lord Jesus that we have the faith to be saved, and the same applies to them.'

Peter's intervention had the desired effect and everyone quietened down, allowing Paul and Barnabas to carry on with their story. Paul may possibly have been annoyed that Peter was claiming to be premier envoy to the Gentiles, for it had been agreed on his meeting with James before he had set off for Cyprus that Paul was to be for the Gentiles and Peter for the Jews. However, Peter's brief but telling words had achieved the desired effect. For hour after hour no doubt, and possibly at more than one assembly, the story of their activities was unfolded. At the conclusion James alone stood up – evidence enough of his position in the church – and defined what was to be the attitude towards the Gentiles. He quoted the prophet Amos to good effect, how the Lord had said that apart from restoring the fallen house of David the time would come when 'all other peoples will seek the Lord, all the Gentiles whom I have called to be my own'. There was no contradicting the prophet, nor indeed James who, quite apart from having been the brother of Jesus and having seen him after his Resurrection, was a man of such ascetic life that he was universally called the Righteous.

He laid only one main injunction upon the Gentiles who were to be received into the church – and it had nothing to do with circumcision. The converts must follow the Mosaic Law in so far as their eating habits went and in their sexual behaviour. They must not eat any food that had been offered to pagan gods. (A steady source of revenue to the temples was the sale of slaughtered animals, only special parts of which had previously been burned before the smiling faces in the darkness.) They must not drink blood, for blood, again according to the Mosaic code, was life itself. They must not eat strangled animals. The latter may sound strange but it was based on humane principles, an objection to the unnecessary pain inflicted upon the animal by slaughtering it in this way – one, incidentally, which some epicures maintained produced a better-quality meat. The last injunction, to abstain from immorality, was clear enough. It meant that they must keep away from places like the Grove of Daphne, from the heights of Paphos, from those Groves of Astarodth which had for centuries been a temptation to the children of Israel – the incense fuming among the trees, the harlotry and sodomy and the monetary payment that went to support the cults, the idols, the temples and the priests.

The judgement of James was confirmed by the general council, and a letter was drafted for dispatch to the church in Antioch as well as to those in Syria and Cilicia, embodying these principles. It was a triumph for Paul, but it must never be forgotten how large a part Peter and James played in the whole affair. Without them the Pharisaic party would probably have won the day. Having now acquired the necessary instructions and sanctions from the head of the church and the main body in Jerusalem Paul and Barnabas went back to Antioch, to read the letter to the whole congregation. With them went two emissaries from the city, sent possibly to see that the meaning of the instructions was understood and also, almost certainly, to prepare a report for the council on the exact state of things in Antioch and its offshoot churches. These two men were Judas Bar-Sabbas and Silas-Silvanus, the latter like Paul a Roman citizen. It was an intelligent choice, since Judas was a Jew (possibly the brother of Joseph Bar-Sabbas who had been an unsuccessful candidate for the place that had been left vacant among the disciples by Judas Iscariot). Silas, on the other hand, as a citizen could deal with local authorities as well as coping with the special problems of Greek or Roman converts. The message was read, and the relief was obvious: they did not have to burden themselves with the wool-winding sophistries of Jewish Law. They were free, they may have felt. In fact, they were far more burdened than those who twined their limbs under the dark-green laurel leaves in the grove outside the city.

[23]

Roads

It was agreed by the church at Antioch that Paul and Barnabas should revisit the scene of their recent labours, reinforce the communities and, above all, make sure that there was no backsliding. Throughout the whole of Jewish history, as the denunciations of so many of the prophets show, the children of Israel were very prone to follow after strange gods, to fornicate and commit adultery, to over-indulge in wine and, in fact, to break all the commandments. If it was so difficult to keep Jews who had been trained and educated in the Law on the straight and narrow path it was easy to imagine how great would be the concern about Gentile converts to Christianity, men and women who had been born pagans, had sacrificed to idols and had probably indulged in every sort of immorality. It was important furthermore that the new orders from the mother church at Jerusalem should be transmitted to these people far away. It was rumoured that some of the Pharisaic group were already active, trying to get them to obey the whole of the Law. If that was almost impossible for Jews, it would certainly prove so for Gentiles. It would probably deter them sufficiently to turn them back to their old ways and beliefs. Paul and Barnabas must get to them quickly and tell them about the new dispensation.

The expedition was due to set out from Antioch in the spring of 50. Then a violent quarrel broke out between Paul and Barnabas. The latter once again wanted to take John Mark along with them. The exact reasons why Mark had left them before in Pamphylia and gone back on his own will never be known, but there can be no doubt that Paul viewed it as an act of unforgivable desertion. Mark, as has been said before, may have had some good excuse but as far as Paul was concerned he had failed in the field. It is quite possible that Mark disliked Paul personally (he was hardly the easiest of characters), or disliked his interpretation of Jesus's life and works. It might have been expected that Barnabas would accept Paul's judgement and dismiss Mark, but he was determined to revisit his native Cyprus. So 'they separated from each other'. Barnabas and Mark went to Cyprus, and Paul accompanied by Silas went through Syria and Cilicia *en route* for Lycaonia. The fact that Silas was also a Roman citizen was an advantage. In case of any trouble with the governing authorities both of the men could claim citizenship and therefore a fair trial. The quarrel in effect proved beneficial, for instead of one expedition setting out to cover the same ground there were two, which meant that the work could be done more thoroughly. All the same it was not the happiest way for previous travelling companions, who had been through so much together, to part. If Paul was right in his refusal, he was at the same time somewhat lacking in that charity, or loving-kindness, which was at the core of his message.

After visiting the churches on their way through Syria and Cilicia it is probable that Paul and his companion also visited Tarsus. Paul would certainly have wanted to see the state of the believers in his native city. Tarsus in any case lay on their route through the Cilician Gates which would lead them to the uplands of Asia Minor. The longest and one of the most difficult passes in the world, the Cilician Gates in some places were little more than thirty feet wide. They had witnessed the passage of many armies, and of many men much more famous than these two obscure travellers. Among others, Alexander the Great with his army had passed this way *en route* for the conquest of the East. Paul was destined to go West, bound for another and quite different kind of conquest. Even if it was late spring when they went through that fearsome rocky landscape, even if the snows had already melted, they would have been wet and cold, struck to the bone by the dark dampness of the cliffs towering above them. With sighs of relief they must have greeted the uplands as they took the Roman road westward for Derbe. After seeing the converts and reading the instructions from the church at Jerusalem (which will have been received with considerable satisfaction) they moved on again to Lystra. Here, where he had been stoned and left for dead, Paul found a thriving community. He and Silas stayed in the house of a widow and her son, a young man called Timothy, both of whom had been converted on his previous visit.

Timothy's mother was Jewish but his father had been Greek. Such intermarriages would have been fairly common in the East, but it would appear that Timothy was generally regarded as Jewish, and that he wanted to become a full member of the community as well as being a Christian. Paul arranged for him to be circumcized. In doing so he was in no way contravening the instructions from Jerusalem. These merely said that it was not necessary for Gentiles to be circumcized but clearly if a convert wanted it, then the church would more than approve. Timothy was later to become Paul's most trusted companion and fellow worker. He at once showed his desire to prove his worth by volunteering to come along with Paul and Silas as they made their way to found further churches and to visit others which had sprung up in their absence.

It is clear that Paul's ambition was to go to the ancient Ionian city of Ephesus. It was on the coast, a little north of the beautiful island of Samos, and commanding considerable trade as it was on the great river basin of the Cayster, and within easy reach of two other important rivers. Ephesus was an ideal place in which to begin a new community, in contact with all the hinterland and a major centre for communications with Greece. Paul was ambitious: Greece lay next in his mind, and beyond Greece, Italy and Rome. For years he had been, as it were, on the periphery of things, but the experiences of his first expedition had convinced him that he had the capability of changing the world. Greece was still the intellectual centre of this world, but beyond that lay Rome, the seat of power. Throughout his life Paul showed an astute knowledge of the world and its machinations. He knew where power lay; some of it of course in Jerusalem – though little of that was political – some in Antioch in Syria, less in Pisidian Antioch, less still in his native Tarsus, and naturally far, far less in remote places like Derbe and Lystra. If he was not ambitious for himself (and he certainly was not in material terms) he was overweeningly ambitious in the cause of his belief. Paul, throughout all his privations, troubles and physical torments, was always capable of imagining success. In this he had no doubt, and his flaring determination could cut through the uncertainty of others. Most people, and it is as true today as it ever was, do not know what they really want – except maybe a quiet or relatively untroubled life, with some reasonable security for themselves and those they care for, and a peaceful exit from the world. The great dreamers are not like that.

It is a curious fact that certain types of men even have physical similarities:

> [His] outward appearance was distinguished by simplicity and strength. He was below the middle height, with the plebian features of the Slavonic type of face, brightened by piercing eyes; and his powerful forehead and still more powerful head gave him a marked distinction. He was tireless in work to an unparalleled degree. He put the same exemplary conscientiousness into reading lectures in a small workmen's club in Zürich and in organizing the first Socialist State in the world. . . . The simplicity of his daily habits was due to the fact that intellectual work and intense struggle not only absorbed his interests and passions but also gave him intense satisfaction. His thoughts never ceased to labour at the task of freeing the workers.

Those words were written about Lenin by his great compatriot Trotsky, and it is not difficult to see that if one substitutes 'Derbe' for 'Zürich' and 'the Christian Church' for 'the First Socialist State' there are considerable similarities. There remains, however, one vast distinction. Lenin was concerned only with freeing the workers from the chains of a certain type of materialistic society and substituting for this what he considered to be an infinitely better and more efficient one. Lenin certainly wished to change the world but this was, one might say, in a relatively limited way, and of necessity he was concerned first and foremost with his own country, Russia. Paul wished to change the world entirely. He was always concerned that the followers of his belief looked after the poor and sick, and that they worked hard at their trades, but he was asking something of them far harder than that they must be good-living workers in a social community. He was certainly asking them that, but he was also demanding that they become members of a completely timeless community where neither trade nor profession nor race mattered compared with a love and compassion for all fellow men. Paul was not responsible for the death of anyone in his life – except that, before his conversion, he did acquiesce in the death of Stephen. Can the same be said of Lenin? Paul wrote much, but he never wrote anything called *In Defence of Terrorism*, as did Trotsky. He was prepared to die for his belief but not kill for it, nor ask any others to do so.

This was the man who now contemplated from the mid-summer uplands the prospect of going to Ephesus. As so often, his commonsense got the better of him. Ephesus was a malarial area and, whether he had had malaria before or not, his health was not strong enough to risk the hot coastland at that time. It is noticeable on this and other occasions that 'the Holy Spirit did not let them go'. Bithynia, well to the north, with a Black Sea coastline as well as a coast that faced Byzantium and Propontis (the Sea of Marmara) suggested itself to them. But again 'the Spirit of Jesus did not allow them'. This was logical enough for, apart from Byzantium, the area was primitive, with few towns of any importance, and although well-wooded and fertile had little else to commend it from their point of view. Paul's real interest lay in the West, in Greece and Italy, where he could communicate his message to peoples capable of understanding it and of disseminating it on fertile soil. So they travelled on steadily westward through Mysia, the north-western corner of Asia Minor, until they reached the port of Alexandria-Troas.

The city had been named in honour of Alexander the Great and was so called to distinguish it from Alexandria in Egypt. Apart from its connection with the great conqueror, Troas was also famous for being situated on the coast near the site of ancient Troy. Strabo tells us that Romans making the 'Grand Tour' of Greece regularly came here to inspect the site of the Trojan War, no doubt quoting to one another passages from Homer as they mentally reconstructed the scenes. Troas was almost in the shadow of Mount Ida, whose north-western spur ran practically to the coast. Paul cannot have failed to have heard of Homer but will almost certainly never have read him – all those adulterous gods and their strumpet wives and mistresses! With despondency, or with scorn, he may have contemplated the tourists and the guides as they left the city to spend a day at Troy or a night on the sacred mountain. On the peak of Ida, where Zeus had sat to watch the fluctuating fortunes of war, or on one occasion lain in the arms of Hera covered by a golden cloud, there grew an immense pine over 200 feet high According to Strabo, the Roman or the Greek would carve his name on its bark to record his ephemeral presence – like visitors to all such famous sites throughout the centuries.

West and north from Alexandria-Troas lay Macedonia, home of Alexander, home of those hardy mountaineers who had conquered Greece before going on to conquer Asia and the East. There would have been many Macedonians in the streets of the city, men quite different from the Greeks whom Paul would have met before, speaking a broad dialect, wearing large-brimmed hats and heavy woollen cloaks, and looking as if they could give a good account of themselves in a tavern or dockside brawl. It was not so surprising that Paul should have had a vision one night that he saw a man of Macedonia standing before him and saying: 'Come over to Macedonia and help us!' Macedonia was the obvious place to arrive in Greece, and Troas an equally obvious point of departure from Asia.

Midsummer, and the *Meltemis* were blowing, those winds from the north that are almost the only winds in the Mediterranean that even approximate to the trade winds of the great oceans. They could be expected to blow from between north-west and north, reaching force six or seven, usually falling away towards evening; although on occasions they might blow undiminished throughout the night. Now a wind of this force, classified as strong, is not one which can be regarded lightly and it is one which, if the vessel is trying to go to windward, will cause her to make a large degree of leeway – and ancient sailing-ships were not well-designed for this kind of work. The destination of the boat which they were going to join was Neapolis, a Macedonian port lying something over 100 miles to the north-west of them, dead in the eye of the prevailing wind. It is probable that by the route they finally took the distance was about 150 miles. It is equally probable that they had to wait in Alexandria-Troas for a number of days before the captain decided that the wind had moderated enough, or that it had veered sufficiently into the north for the passage to be feasible.

It is very likely that it was during this time of waiting that Paul and his two companions first encountered Luke, who was later to be called by Paul 'the beloved physician'. Luke was a Greek, and tradition makes him a native of Antioch in Syria. Even if he was, it is clear that his meeting with Paul must have been quite fortuitous, for the latter had had no original intention of going to this Mysian port. On the other hand, there is a reasonable argument that Luke was a Macedonian who was converted in Alexandria-Troas and consequently accompanied the party on the expedition into his native Macedonia. Speculation has been rife over the ages as to the identity of the author of Acts. Luke certainly was a physician and, as Julius Caesar had given Roman citizenship to all physicians in Rome, Luke may well have inherited this status. He was certainly the one real man of letters among the Gospel-writers, with an inquiring mind and a regard for scholarship that may have come from his physician's training. As Dr Bartlet has put it: 'His was indeed a *religio medici* in its pity for frail and suffering humanity, and in its sympathy with the triumph of the Divine "healing art" upon the bodies and souls of men.' Ernest Renan called the Gospel of Luke 'the most beautiful book ever written'. Certainly Luke was one of the most remarkable men of all time and, whatever his ancestry or background, he was an ideal companion for a man who often seems to have been ill. Furthermore, against Paul's passionate temperament he posed a cool logicality, a sense of humour and a born historian's demand for exactitude. With the addition of Luke the party had now swollen to four men – little enough one might have thought to undertake an attack upon the beliefs of sophisticated Greeks and less sophisticated, but considerably more powerful, Romans.

Finally the day came when the captain of the merchantship considered that the wind was suitable and that he could risk the beat across to Neapolis. Travellers in their hostels were told to get their gear ready. Those who were in the taverns took a last draught of the local Trojan wine. Sailors cast off the warps that had secured the ship to the quayside. There was no need to use the longboat to give them a pluck out of the harbour for the wind was still northerly. With the mainsail-yard braced right round until it ran from bow to quarter, they were under way on a north-westerly heading. It would not be too extreme to say that the invasion of Europe had begun.

[24]

Into Europe

It can hardly have been a comfortable crossing with the wind funnelling down from the north, spray leaping and the travellers hunched in their cloaks on the tilted deck. The captain made first for the little island of Tenedos, which he could see quite clearly in the bright Aegean air as they left harbour. It was many centuries before that the Greek fleet had hidden under the lee of Tenedos, causing the Trojans to think that the invaders had left their land, while the giant wooden horse was slowly rolled into Troy. The captain was adopting the normal Aegean practice of island-hopping, when possible always keeping another one in sight. Then they saw ahead of them wooded and hilly Imbros, with its two anchorages where the ship could wait if the wind came up too hard from the north. They seem to have been lucky, for the record reads that they 'sailed straight to Samothrace'. It is quite likely that they stopped here to let some passengers disembark, for it was now mid-summer and in August the great festival of the mysterious Samothracian gods, the Cabeiri, took place.

Paul and his party, even if unwillingly, must have heard talk aboard about the Cabeiri, talk which will have quickened as they came up abreast the island's massive mountain, over 5,000 feet high and dominating all the northern Aegean. The Cabeiri were fertility gods and had been worshipped in Samothrace since pre-Greek times. Their name probably derived from the Phoenician *Qabirim* meaning 'the Mighty Ones', and their rites were kept strictly secret from all but initiates. They were, above all, propitious to seafarers. The Christians and any Jews who may have been travelling on the ship averted their heads as the Greeks and others aboard kneeled in worship or burned incense in the shrine that was customarily mounted at the stern of a ship. Some of the sailors no doubt wore a purple amulet or sash. This showed that they were initiates and under the protection of the Cabeiri, who would see that they did not suffer shipwreck or death by drowning. As the ship turned to port, rounding the northern end of the island, the capital came on their beam. Beyond it, in a deep narrow valley, lay the shrine where the Samothracian gods lived and where incense fumed in front of the stone phalli that were their symbols.

On the next day they made the crossing to Thasos, northernmost of all the Aegean islands, an island famous for its marble, its wine and nuts. Its mountain slopes were thickly wooded with chestnut trees, while the lower land bustled with the turning leaves of olives. A rich and beautiful island! How much attention Paul and his companions paid to it is conjectural. Acts is not concerned with scenic beauty, but it is doubtful whether even the most inwardly obsessed man could pass Thasos on a fine summer day without a lift of the heart. Soon after, the Macedonian coastline sliding past them, the sailors trimming the sail or hauling on the brailing ropes to shorten it when gusts of wind spun off the hills, they saw the port of Neapolis dead ahead at the end of the bay. Due south of them the pyramidal peak of Acte, soaring up over 6,000 feet, made its sharp statement of power. Centuries later it would be called Mount Athos, and dozens of monasteries would celebrate the faith that was now for the first time reaching these shores.

From Neapolis a Roman road ran to their destination, Philippi. It climbed the Pangaean range of mountains, Neapolis behind them fringed with crisp waves, and then at the top they looked down on to the plain where the city sweltered under the sun. Although it no longer exists, Philippi was then an important military colony, with a great fortified barracks atop the ancient Acropolis, stone walls surrounding the city, and a massive triumphal arch through which the Via Egnatia led on to Rome. Named after Philip of Macedon, father of Alexander the Great, Philippi liked to call itself 'the first city of Macedonia', although this title was disputed by Amphipolis, the capital of the eastern section of the country. Philippi however had become a symbol of empire for it was near here, so rewritten history said, that Augustus had triumphed over the murderers of Julius Caesar – Brutus and Cassius. There had been two battles, in the first of which Cassius was killed, while the remaining troops under Brutus had been routed in the second. Brutus, whom Shakespeare was wrongly to describe as 'the noblest Roman of them all' (he was possibly the son of Caesar and he was certainly a traitor) survived the second battle and was urged by a companion to make his escape from the field. He had his moment of nobility. 'Fly?' he answered, 'Yes, fly we must, but not with our feet – with our hands,' and fell on his sword. The legend, now sanctified by the great triumphal arch at Philippi, was that the victory was that of Augustus. Such it had been made to seem after the latter had defeated Antony and Cleopatra and taken the whole of the Roman world for himself. In fact, the victory over the dissident Republicans that was won at Philippi was almost entirely due to Antony, a brilliant general, even if in his private life he was exactly the kind of Roman that Paul would have disliked intensely. Nevertheless it had been Antony's victory, and all else was fiction. Octavian (his name before he acquired the title of Augustus) had been too ill at the time to take much part in the battle or in its co-ordination. Little or none of this will have meant anything to Paul and his companions as they came down the fine paved road and saw the arch that commemorated only another falsehood.

Philippi was essentially a colonial town, a kind of miniature Rome set down in Macedonia to administer and to dominate. The Jewish colony was so small that there was not even a synagogue, only a meeting-place outside the city walls near the small river Gangites. Here on the Sabbath, Jews and a few Gentile converts would gather together for the ritual washing of their hands before prayer and a reading of the Law and the Prophets. Paul, Silas, Timothy and Luke, who had probably settled themselves into some local lodging-house such as were to be found in all similar Roman cities – a compendium usually of tavern, bawdy house and hostel – soon found their way to the Jewish community. Paul took the first opportunity that came to hand to announce the news of the Messiah, of his resurrection, and of the promise that was now extended to all people under the sun, if only they would believe.

In view of what followed later at Philippi and elsewhere it is important to see just how this message, which might have seemed to have no more relevance to politics than the cults of Isis or Attis, could be misunderstood. The Greek words that Paul used, as well as all other Christians, to talk about the resurrection were 'Anastasis Christou', 'The resurrection of Christ', but 'Anastasis' could also mean 'an uprising'. Whereas the Christians constantly incurred the hostility of orthodox Jews for their proclamation that the Messiah had already come and had died like a criminal on the cross, they were destined to suffer at the hands of the Romans because of several misunderstandings. First of all 'an uprising of Christ' suggested a Messianic insurrection, something which the Romans naturally feared, as also did orthodox Jews who had come to terms with Rome and lived under the protection of Roman Law. These Christians, then, were revolutionaries. They inferred also from this talk of 'Christ the King' that they were proclaiming another monarch on earth, whereas there could only be one, and he was the Emperor in Rome.

There were other factors, as R. H. Barrow has pointed out in *The Romans*:

> In the first place, Christianity was particularly vulnerable to misinterpretation: secondly Christians appeared to hate the human race. They looked forward to the early return of Christ when all but themselves would be destroyed by fire as being evil; and in this disaster to 'Eternal Rome' and to the hopes of mankind they seemed to glory. In the second century and onwards this attitude of mind expressed itself in a different way; Christians went out of their way to provoke enmity that they might win a crown of martyrdom. Christians came from the lower order of society, and their teachings seemed to aim at social revolution.

At a later date, when the church that Paul had helped to establish throughout Europe had become widespread and well-organized, other complications were to follow. First of all the Christians did not hold their prayer meetings in public as did the believers in other gods (with the exception of certain aspects of the mystery religions). This easily laid them open to charges of strange immoral practices and even of cannibalism. What, for instance, would a Roman make of these words written by John, that spiritual descendant of Paul?

'Then Jesus said unto them, verily, verily, I say unto you, Except ye eat the flesh of the Son of man, and drink his blood, ye have no life in you. Whosoever eateth my flesh, and drinketh my blood, hath eternal life; and I will raise him up at the last day.'

All this lay in the future, but the seeds of misinterpretation had already been sown. The stoning of Stephen, although committed by Jews, had produced the first martyr, while Paul in his career to date had never gone out of his way to placate the opposition or to come to any form of accommodation with people of other beliefs. At first all went well in the small community at Philippi, the first convert to Christianity on European soil being a woman, Lydia of Thyatira, a city in Lydia in Asia. As was common at that time she probably took her name from her native province and she used it as her business name. She was the overseas agent for the sale of the famous Lydian dyes which were as much in demand throughout the ancient world as those of Phoenicia. Lydia had already become a convert to Judaism, 'a God-fearer' as such were termed, but now she found in the message preached by Paul something far more appealing than Jahweh and the strict tenets of Jewish Law. There was, and indeed is, in Christianity something that is particularly affecting to the female heart – an implicit tenderness not to be found in any other religion before or since.

Lydia was undoubtedly a woman of some wealth and at once invited Paul and his friends to stay in her house. But before that, she herself was baptized in the Gangites, along with 'the people of her house'. It is significant that at a later date the small church at Philippi supported Paul financially on several occasions, as well as sending him money when he was in prison in Rome. Most of this, one suspects, must have come from Lydia and was therefore an offshoot of the Lydian dye industry. This was mildly ironical, for Lydia was an area long known for sumptuousness and wealth, for having invented the game of dice as well as the art of coining money, and Lydian music was notorious for its soft voluptuous strains. But there was no doubting the genuine nature of Lydia's conversion, and Paul and the others, happy to leave the unsalubrious atmosphere of their lodging-house, accepted the hospitality of their Lydian convert.

If Paul had now established the nucleus of a church in Philippi – no small achievement in view of the fact that he had so few Jews to provide a central core – he was not to be without some of the usual troubles. In this case, however, they started off from an unusual cause. One day, as Paul and the others were going to the river to pray, they were followed by a slave-girl who had clearly listened on previous occasions to some of their conversation and preaching. No ordinary slave, she was 'inhabited by an evil spirit that made her predict the future'. Fortune-tellers, mediums, soothsayers, they are still with us today and they were extremely common, as has been seen, in the first century.

They had an ancient and highly respected ancestry in Greece, going back for instance to the priestesses of Delphi, whose interpreted utterances had swayed the destinies of Greeks over centuries. The text has it that the girl had a python, literally a spirit, but *python* also had a connection with the giant serpent that Apollo was reputed to have killed at Delphi (thus acquiring his epithet 'the Pythian God'). This girl, like the Delphic priestesses, seems on occasions to have fallen into cataleptic trances during which she raved in a strange voice. These utterances were interpreted by her masters, for she was owned by a syndicate, as it were. No doubt in business matters, in love affairs, and in other issues the syndicate with their local knowledge could interpret the girl's cries as best suited them, at the same time pocketing a handsome fee. She now took to haunting the meetings of Paul and his friends, dogging their footsteps, and calling out, 'These men are slaves of the Supreme God! They announce to you the road to salvation!' She had of course heard Paul and others preaching to the small congregation on the river bank, and it is not insignificant that she is reported as using a phrase popular with Paul 'the slave of God' or 'of Jesus'. The name Jesus would have meant nothing to the girl but *Theos*, God, would have been perfectly familiar. Apparently she became so irritating by constantly following them, and by the eternal reiteration of these words, that after a number of days Paul, whose tolerance threshold was never very high, finally lost his temper. (Anyone who has ever been followed, or more or less adopted, by a lunatic beggar in the East will understand his reaction.) He rounded on her and said: 'I order you in the name of Jesus Christ to come out of her!'

As on the occasion with Bar-Jesus in Cyprus, as with the crippled man in Lystra, so now the effect of the words was like a concentrated charge of electricity flashing through the air. 'The spirit went out of her at that very moment.' It is quite clear that on these three occasions one factor is constant. Bar-Jesus, the soothsayer, believed in the powers of magic – he had faith in them – the cripple had faith in Paul, and the slave girl of Philippi, whether she had faith in Paul or not, certainly believed in the powers of magic. Belief was always the link in all these extra-material happenings.

The reaction of the girl's owners was very understandable. They had been the possessors of a valuable capital asset, and now all they had was a slave-girl like millions of others. Like anyone suddenly deprived of a good source of income they were more than indignant, they were furious. It would appear that only Paul and Silas were present, for 'they seized Paul and Silas and dragged them before the authorities'. The praetors were seated in the forum dispensing judgement on the affairs that were being brought before them in the normal course of the day's work. But the sudden arrival of a mob hustling along and kicking a pair of foreigners caused them to put aside routine and attend to what seemed to be urgent business. The slave girl, incidentally, disappears from the story but one cannot think that Paul really did her a good turn. From being an important and well-fed possession she no doubt became a 'hewer of wood and a drawer of water'.

Paul and Silas were accused of being foreigners, Jews, disturbers of the peace, and of attempting to subvert the laws of Rome. At this point both men should have declared their Roman citizenship and demanded a formal trial, to which they were fully entitled. But mob rule prevailed and, if Paul and Silas ever said anything, their voices were overwhelmed in the clamour of their enemies and the pack-yelp of those who will follow anything so long as it provides a spectacle to ease the tedium of their lives. Both may well have shouted out that they were Roman citizens, but even if the magistrates had wanted to give them a fair trial it was clear that the easiest thing to do to keep peace in the forum was to have them sentenced and penalized on the spot. Paul and Silas were stripped of their clothes and the lictors set about their task. Lictors were the officers who attended upon magistrates, bore before them a bundle of rods flanked by an axe (for capital punishment), and carried out the judgements of the court.

A flogging was an experience never to be forgotten. Richard Wurmbrand who wrote about his life in communist prisons (New York, 1968) said that 'the blows burned like fire. . . . It was as if your back was being grilled by a furnace, and the shock to the nervous system was great'. There is no reason at all to imagine that in the savage first-century world the pain of a flogging was any less than that described by an anonymous sailor who served in the British navy in the early nineteenth century: 'The cat-o'-nine-tails is applied to the bare back . . . [which] soon resembles so much putrified liver, and every stroke of the cat brings away the congealed blood. . . .' All this Paul and Silas suffered. If they screamed, there is no record. Paul, certainly, was expiating his guilt in the murder of Stephen, and both of the men were enduring for their belief the far greater pains that their Saviour had endured. The resilience of the human frame is almost unbelievable, as any examination of recent war records will show. Even the most materialist-minded, if they care to read history carefully, will find that men and women have endured what seem intolerable tortures and privations for the sake of a belief. Animals, caged in their simpler reactions to the universe, will concede more easily – and certainly will not die for an abstraction. Those (like Dr Morris in *The Naked Ape*) who would equate human beings with their biological ancestors make a mistake. The difference is not quantitive but qualitative.

Bloody and probably almost insensible, Paul and Silas were dragged from the forum of Philippi and thrown into jail.

[25]

Earthquake

Paul and Silas were taken to the innermost cell of the city jail, and their feet confined in stocks. Other prisoners had watched them hustled through – clearly a beating by the lictors! Well, there were worse things than that. For some time they lay there, feeling the aches and pains of their torn backs, too weak to have protested at any point that they were Roman citizens, and that an offence had been committed against them. After some time they revived sufficiently to make the only form of protest – though it was more than that – that was available to them. 'About midnight Paul and Silas were praying and singing hymns to God, and the other prisoners were listening to them.' One can easily imagine some of the comments, a town drunk perhaps with a splitting headache imploring them to shut up and let people get some sleep.

And then it happened. Philippi, like so much of this part of the world, lies on an earthquake zone, and earthquakes can be expected at any time over at least three months of the year. Housed in the strong stone jail the prisoners would not have felt the first early-warning waves, although animals would have. Dogs, cats and birds especially would have caught the signals, and an oppressive and uneasy silence would have engulfed Philippi. Then, after the unnoticed preliminary tremor, there came that deep underground rumble, quite unmistakable, as the main wave hit the city, the vibrations occurring every one or two seconds. The cell rocked, the whole jail rocked, the bar securing the door from the outside fell to the ground as the doorposts vibrated with the shock. The prisoners in the outer jail, who were probably fettered to one main chain secured to the wall, found to their amazement that the bolts holding it had pulled out. They were free! The main door of the jail swung crazily on its hinges, and the night air swept in. The jailer who had been sound asleep jumped up and saw that all the doors were open. He knew the Roman law – to lose a prisoner entrusted to your care meant death. He assumed at once that there had been a mass breakout. Ignorant of what had woken him, he probably thought it was the noise of the prisoners assaulting the doors and making their escape. They, in fact, were still too bemused and frightened by their experience to have made a dash for freedom, and lay prostrate on the floor. The jailer drew his sword and called out that he was going to make an end of himself. Then Paul intervened. At the top of his voice he shouted, 'Don't harm yourself! We are all here!'

The bemused jailer sheathed his sword, called to his slaves for lights, and then rushed in and fell at the feet of Paul and Silas. An earthquake is a terrifying experience, a reminder of natural forces beyond man's control, but at that time it was still surrounded by mystery, and by all the elements of superstition. Poseidon, God of the Sea, was also known as the Earth-Shaker. His palace was not so far from Macedonia, in the depths of the sea near Aegae in Euboea. When he rode out – as he must have done just now – he would sometimes shatter rocks with his trident or shake the earth as a proof of his power. The jailer felt sure that these two men were in some inexplicable way connected with what had just happened. The gods sometimes still revisited the earth in mortal guise, to see what was happening among men. And the behaviour of these two prisoners was inexplicable. Why had they not made a dash for freedom when the door of their cell had so magically flown open? He led them out into the main body of the prison where his slaves would by now have had olive-oil lamps lit and brands flaring at the main door. The other prisoners were once more secured. They were all agitatedly talking to one another, and congratulating themselves that the stone roof had not fallen on them. But the extraordinary calm of these two prisoners seemed to prove that they were not like other men. He heard from what was being said around him that, just before the walls had rocked with the passage of the god, these men had been singing and praying. The jailer, still trembling from shock, said: 'My lords, what must I do to be saved?' The fact that he addressed them in such terms – two bruised and beaten men in blood-stained cloaks – is evidence enough of the power and personality of Paul and Silas. 'Believe in the Lord Jesus,' they answered, 'and you will be saved – both you and your family.'

Clearly he showed his incomprehension. He had heard of many gods, but never of this one. In the small hours of the morning, he and his family and household slaves clustered around, Paul and Silas gave them the basic outline of the Saviour's life, of his Resurrection, and of the hope that was now extended to all men. Still shaken by fear of the unknown, still somewhat mystified, the jailer and his people listened to the account of this god who was also a man, but who was also the one and only god. There were no others. Almost as an afterthought he took Paul and Silas to the well in the outer courtyard, where he himself washed their lacerated backs and attended to their wounds. They had told him that he must be baptized, a purificatory washing, as he understood it, which would remove the stain of his previous wrong beliefs and which would awaken him to a new form of life. The jailer would not have been unfamiliar with the idea behind this ritual, for a symbolic death followed by purification by water was not unknown in other Eastern religions, notably that of Isis. (Apuleius describes how an Isiac initiate had to undergo a sanctification ceremony followed by salvation through prayer.)

He and all his family were baptized at once, probably at the well-head. It is unlikely that they would have gone down to the river at that hour and when Philippi was still in a state of shock after the earthquake, and above all when Paul and Silas were still technically prisoners. Then, once again, the practical came to the fore. Paul and Silas were taken to their new convert's house and given some food; olives most probably, yesterday's bread, goat's cheese and almost undoubtedly some wine. When they were hurled into jail after their summary condemnation they would have been in no state to receive the usual simple rations allotted to prisoners. Their wounds treated, in so far as the elementary medical knowledge of the time permitted, and some food and wine – wine which Paul was later to commend to the far from robust Timothy as good for his stomach – the two apostles were not in danger of dying. They were in any case reinforced to such an extent by the passion of their convictions that they could survive under conditions where many men would have collapsed for weeks altogether. It is, incidentally, even if it has no particular relevance to this occasion, always worth bearing in mind that men of this age and time were considerably tougher physically than moderns. They were the product, even if unintentionally so, of selective breeding. Whereas, in the twentieth century, the sickly and malformed may be kept alive – in their turn to breed – in the first century only the hardiest passed childhood and reached puberty, let alone arrived unscathed into adult years. It is ironical that so much of the sentiment and technical skill which is now expended in the Western world on keeping the sick alive derived from the belief propagated by Paul. If he had not been incredibly robust, kippered by the sun and the sea, inured to every kind of physical hardship and discomfort, it is doubtful whether his news would ever have reached Europe.

It is probable that the jailer, however reluctantly, now took his two charges back and bolted them in once more. Whatever they may have said to him, and however much he had been convinced by their argument, they were still Roman prisoners and it was as much as his life was worth to let them out of custody. 'The next morning,' as the record has it, 'the Roman authorities sent the lictors down with the order, "Let these men go".' There can be no real reason why they should have done this if they had not been informed that both Paul and Silas were citizens. This information could well have come from Lydia of Thyatira, who would have known the facts and who was a not unimportant member of the community. It is likely though, that the information came from the unnamed jailer, who will certainly have been informed by both the men that they had citizenship status. He must have been horrified to find out that they had been flogged without a formal trial, and that he had thrown them into the inner cell and placed them in stocks. It is extremely doubtful whether he himself, in his humble capacity, was a citizen. He may even have been a Macedonian Greek with no claim to anything except that he had been born in the Philippi area. Citizens! They were members of the august minority who were entitled to a say in the running of the empire....

When the lictors came to the door of the jail they told the keeper that the two Jews should be set free and sent on their way. He in his turn passed on the message to the prisoners. 'The officials have sent word for both of you to be released. You may leave now, and go in peace.' What a night he had had, earthquake, conversion, discovery that these two men were superior in status to himself, and now at last the happy knowledge that the authorities had realized their mistake and wanted no more than that they should be allowed to leave Philippi! But if he thought his troubles were at an end he had made a great mistake. The older of the two, the citizen Paulus of Tarsus, had no intention of leaving. He would not, he said, quit the jail until he had a full apology from the town authorities. He and Silas were brought before the lictors – almost certainly the very men who had beaten them the day before – who repeated the orders of the praetors. They both might go free, but they must leave the city limits. Despite his wounds, despite an earthquake, despite a highly emotional night in which he had added another cell to the church of Macedonia, Paul was in no mood for such an easy dismissal as was being proposed. No doubt at this point he and Silas produced from their wallets documents that proved their citizenship.

'We were never found guilty of any crime,' said Paul. 'Yet they whipped us in public! See! We are citizens! Then they threw us here into prison. Do they now think they can send us away secretly? Not for a minute! Let the authorities themselves come right here in person and take us out.'

Few incidents show more characteristically the fire and passion of this man who, if he had not been one of the greatest religious leaders of the world, would have made a superb politician. He knew he had the praetors of provincial Philippi over the proverbial barrel. They had made a gross error, had condemned two citizens of Rome to be flogged (something forbidden by at least three operative laws except after full trial, formal conviction, and still with the right to final appeal). The lictors withdrew and went back to the forum. Silas possibly suggested to Paul that it would have been better to go quietly and not to have made a further scene about the matter. Paul was adamant. His blood was up and, in the same way that he would insist that members of the church should keep the laws of God, he was equally determined that the administrators of the laws of Rome should keep them too. After all, what was Philippi? A provincial garrison town – and he was a citizen of Tarsus, a place long honoured before Philippi had acquired any real status. Paul had the Jewish temper, the same one that endured to the end of the siege of Jerusalem in 70, the same that three years after that led the Zealots of Masada to commit suicide rather than surrender their fortress to the Romans.

This ultimatum – an ultimatum issued by a beaten man held in the town jail – was now delivered to the praetors. They saw at once what a storm they had inadvertently sailed into: they could be reported to higher authorities, they could even be reported to Rome and then they might well be ruined. All they had thought they were doing was punishing a pair of Jewish vagrants! Best, they wisely decided, to eat humble pie and apologize. The last thing they wanted was trouble from above, or trouble in the city, come to that. The sooner they got rid of these two, however humiliating it might be, the sooner Philippi could return to its normal sleepy colonial status, with the wine-parties of officers and their wives, and everybody's acknowledgements of difference in rank and in social position and simple competitiveness about who had the finest courtyard, the best cook or the best wine-cellar.

Paul had won the day. The town officials arrived and apologized, at the same time begging them to leave the town because they could not guarantee their safety if the mob got stirred up again. Paul and Silas, not without some condescension, agreed to this, but first of all they had to pay a visit to Lydia's house and address the congregation. Luke, it would seem, who in any case had not been involved in the trouble of the previous day, decided to stay behind. He would not only be a mainstay of the new church in Philippi but he would also be able to practise his profession in the city. He does not seem to have met Paul again until six years later, when the latter was once more in trouble with the authorities, this time on his way to prison in Caesarea. His last action before they left would have been to attend to their wounded backs, no doubt giving them a herbal salve to take with them. Lydia of Thyatira, Luke and the others of the small congregation watched them go. Paul, Silas and Timothy set foot on the Egnatian Way, through the hot, swampy plainland – headed westward.

[26]

'Orpheus with his lute . . .'

Autumn. Many centuries later Rimbaud was to write words that could well have escaped from Paul as he and his two companions made their way south-west through Amphipolis: 'Autumn already! – But why regret an eternal sun if we are engaged in the discovery of the divine light – far from people dying by the seasons. Autumn. Our boat floating on the motionless mists turns towards the port of misery, the huge city with its sky stained with fire and mud.' He might also have echoed other lines from the same poem: 'Sometimes I see in the sky boundless shores covered with white and joyful peoples. Above me a vast golden ship waves its multicoloured flags in the breezes of morning. . . .'

The trio passed through Amphipolis, also known as the 'Nine Ways', a city which was almost encircled by the serpentine river Strymon. Once one of the most important Athenian possessions in the north of Greece, it had been a bone of contention between Athens and Sparta in the fifth century B.C., finally falling to the brilliant Spartan general, Brasidas. He had been killed in the battle which gave his state the victory and his body was buried within its walls. Even when Paul visited it, only a few centuries later, Amphipolis had become no more than a small neglected colonial town – so short-lived are the values of places and of people in the limited human span.

'They passed through Amphipolis and Apollonia. . . .' Apollonia on waters of Lake Bolbe also goes unmentioned in the history of the church. Their destiny was the great sprawling city, Thessalonica, named by the Macedonian general Cassander after his wife, the daughter of Philip and sister of Alexander the Great. Formerly it had been called 'Warm Bath', and whether this referred to its natural springs or to its situation the name was accurate enough. Modern Salonika, standing at the head of the great Salonikan gulf, is largely sheltered from the northerly winds and tends to swelter with heat in summer and autumn. South-west of it across the gulf rose the awe-inspiring peak of Mount Olympus, nearly 10,000 feet high, its summit covered in eternal snow – the home of the gods. Here they had their palaces and from here they watched dispassionately the follies and the passions of mankind.

The Thessalonica that Paul walked into after his journey of about 100 miles from Philippi was an important port, a natural outlet for all the products of the mainland as well as an importer of goods. It was also a free city, the residence of the governor of Macedonia, and a centre of industry and trade. As such it had naturally attracted a fairly large Jewish population, and Paul knew well in advance that he would find a synagogue. He must also have known that he would find the same troubles as in similar places elsewhere – hatred from orthodox Jews and trouble with the authorities because he and his message aroused dissension. After his recent experience in Philippi it took a great deal of courage for him and his two companions once more to put their collective head into the lion's mouth.

Paul's immediate concern was naturally to address the congregation in the synagogue, and the elders courteously invited him to do so on the first Sabbath that he was in the city. His method as usual was to demonstrate by quotations from the prophets that Jesus had in all respects fulfilled every condition required of the Messiah. Again he told them what almost inevitably annoyed the orthodox, that their Messiah was not the great conquering king who would make Israel the ruler of the world but that he had already come, had been crucified by the Romans at the instigation of the Jews, and that he had risen from the dead. He was now the salvation of the whole world and Gentiles were as welcome as Jews into the Kingdom. As we know from his later letters to the church in Thessalonica, Paul was particularly absorbed in the doctrine of the Second Coming. Christ's return was imminent and everyone should live as if each day was the last before the Judgement. This was a heady brew to put before Jews, Gentile 'God-fearers', and even pagans. The Gentiles and pagans, it is clear, including a number of important women in the city, did not find it as difficult to accept Paul's teaching as did the Jews. After all they were familiar enough in Thessalonica with risen gods who promised salvation. The cult of Dionysus was prominent in the area as was that of the singer Orpheus.

Since the devotion to Orpheus had assumed a number of mystic undertones it is important to know something about it in order to understand what would be the reaction of a pagan to Paul's preaching of the resurrected Jesus. Orpheus was the legendary founder of the cult which had become known as Orphism, or the Orphic Way of Life. It seems very probable that, many centuries before, Orpheus had been the name or title of a series of Thracian priest-kings. Certainly, as the story was told, Orpheus himself was the son of a Thracian king (or Apollo) and his mother was one of the Muses. After his return from the Argonautic expedition he married the nymph Eurydice, who died from the bite of a snake. Inconsolable, Orpheus made his way down to Hades with the lyre which had been given him by Apollo, and so enchanted the gods of the underworld by his music that they allowed Eurydice to return to the world above. There was one condition, however, that as he made his way up to the sunlight, he should not look back upon his wife. At the very last moment, when they were about to pass beyond the fatal bounds, Orpheus could not resist one glance over his shoulder to see that Eurydice was really there. Immediately she was whirled away from him, to become once more a ghost. His renewed anguish at this second loss of his wife led Orpheus to treat all other women with coldness and contempt, with the result that the women of Thrace on one of their Bacchanalian orgies tore him to pieces. His head was thrown into the Hebrus river, whence it floated across the sea to Lesbos (thus establishing that island's claim to be one of the first great centres of the music of the lyre). The other fragments of his body were collected by the Muses and buried at the foot of Mount Olympus. All this is a familiar type of Greek myth, but it was closely allied with the worship of Dionysus, that Thraco-Phrygian god in whose orgiastic rituals *omophagia*, the eating of raw flesh, played an important part. Walter Pater says in his *Study of Dionysus*:

> And now we see why the tradition of human sacrifice lingered on in Greece, in connection with Dionysus, as a thing of actual detail, and not remote, so that Dionysus of Halicarnassus counts it among the horrors of Greek religion. That the sacred women of Dionysus ate, in mystical ceremony, raw flesh, and drank blood, is a fact often mentioned, and commemorates, as it seems, the actual sacrifice of a fair boy torn to pieces, fading at last into a symbolic offering.

Sacrifice was at the core of Orphism, sacrifice followed by renewal of life. The original mythical story, or possibly not mythical but referring to an annual human sacrifice to ensure the return of spring, became gradually overlaid by a far more intellectual and indeed spiritual way of thought. Man, it was considered, was part divine and part wicked. The main aim of life was to expel the wickedness, and this was achieved through a series of incarnations so that finally, completely purified, the soul would be set free from the 'circle of birth'. The sense of sin, then, was prominent in Orphism, as was the need of atonement, the belief in the suffering and death of a god-man, and finally the belief in an immortality when the soul would be freed from all evil and united with the divine. Philosophers like Plato and Pythagoras were influenced by Orphism and it spread all over the Greek world, as well as into Italy, 500 years or so before Paul arrived in Macedonia. The austerity which his creed demanded would also have been familiar to his Greek audience. Even the Jewish laws about food and purification would not have seemed surprising to people familiar with Orphism. Their belief included abstinence from animal food of all kinds (except possibly at the mystical banquet), avoidance of all actions that might be considered polluting – such as being present at a birth or a death – the wearing of white garments by initiates and, in general, an ascetic life. Gold tablets which have been found in tombs near Rome, Sybaris in southern Italy and in Crete have shed some further light on the cult. These contain fragments of a sacred hymn, and were clearly buried with the dead to secure protection and an entry into the divine world. Such lines occur as 'I am dying from thirst, give me to drink of the waters of memory', 'I have paid the penalty of unrighteousness', 'I come from the pure' and 'I have fled out of the weary, unhappy circle of life'. In return for his devotion the Orphic initiate is assured that all will be well: 'Oh happy and blessed one, thou hast put off thy mortality and shalt become divine.'

One immense distinction from the mysteries in the faith which Paul preached was that Christianity was more than just a club designed to ensure the salvation of those very special members who had been admitted to it. It was open to all of every race. It did, of course, have its points of similarity as is perfectly clear, and its later development (secrecy and catacombs inspired by imperial persecution) shows parallels with some of the mysteries. On the other hand, none of them enjoined kindness to one's neighbour or love for all mankind. They did indeed promise salvation but – devil take the hindmost! Paul, Silas and Timothy were standing up and saying that their god had really lived on the earth (no mythical figure like Attis or Orpheus) and that he extended to *all* unrestricted love and kindness. This was the revolution. It was this emphasis on everyone being acceptable that basically affronted the Jews. No on else, without conforming to all their rituals and customs, was going to be accepted even as a second-rate citizen into the promised kingdom. The end of Paul's stay in Thessalonica was inevitable.

[27]

Expulsions

A short time before Paul, Silas and Timothy had been sent on their way out of Philippi the Emperor Claudius had come to the decision which was to have a considerable bearing on Paul's future. He had expelled the Jews from Rome. Why, one might ask? They were thrifty, hardworking and usually behaved themselves better than most other foreigners. True, they stuck obstinately to their belief in their most peculiar god, but otherwise they were good citizens. The reason is to be found in Suetonius's life of the Emperor Claudius: 'He expelled the Jews from the City because the Jews in Rome made continual disturbances in the name of Chrestus. . . .' This is the first Latin reference we have to Chrestus (Christ), and the first reference to the explosive quality of the doctrine. Paul, in fact, was forestalled in his desire to be the first to take the message to the heart of empire.

How this early community of Christians actually established themselves in Rome remains a mystery. They might have come out of any of the great trading ports of the East, merchants, peasant immigrants, sailors even – though the Jews were never prominent upon the sea. At any rate it is quite clear that they had become an irritant in Rome and, although Suetonius does not elaborate, one may reasonably suspect that the 'disturbances' were caused by orthodox Jews reacting, just as they did in the case of Paul, against what seemed to them a blasphemous assumption based on a misunderstanding of the Prophets. It was always the same problem. How could the Jews, a proud and very touchy people, accept that their Messiah had come and had died like a criminal? The one thing that gave them strength during the occupation of the country by the Romans, and the one thing that had given them strength over the centuries of deportations and the dominion of foreign overlords, was the belief that the time would come when the promised Messiah would establish his chosen people and would confound all their enemies. Their faith was being drastically undermined by these followers of 'Chrestus', people who consorted with pagans, did not adhere to the strict tenets of Law and who admitted uncircumcized Gentiles into their worship. There was nothing to cling to if their conquering Messiah was demoted in such a violent fashion, nothing to hope for, and no reason for them to feel that the Roman, the Greek and all other foreigners were basically inferior. What the Christians were saying in effect was that the Jewish race was not a special élite, chosen of God since the beginning of time.

The disturbances must have been serious, for the Emperor Claudius was not prone to take actions of this nature without good cause. Indeed, in the next few sentences of his biography Suetonius comments on his treatment of other foreign nationals.

> When the envoys from Germany visited the Theatre for the first time they took their place among the common people. But then, seeing that the Parthian and Armenian envoys were seated with the Senators in the orchestra [the semicircular space in front of the stage] they went to join them. For, they said, were they not just as brave and as nobly born? Claudius admired their straightforwardness and allowed them to remain there.

This was not a man then who was inspired by xenophobia, something in any case not so common among the Romans. The latter, with all their love of power, were at the same time fairly tolerant of other races and other creeds. They did not care what gods a man worshipped so long as he conformed to Roman custom, which now included emperor-worship, and of course so long as he paid his taxes. The Jews, generally speaking, had been prepared to accord ritual tribute to Caesar and, although they were a difficult people to handle, they had been acceptable within the capital. But now it seemed that they had a splinter group within their framework, a group who maintained that some king or other (superior to Caesar) had been upon the world and promised the imminent extinction of that world, the destruction of Rome and all it stood for, and the triumph of his followers. It was all very difficult for a Roman to understand, and decidedly unpalatable. It seemed also that most of the Jews themselves were against this particular religious belief, and the conflict between the majority and this strange minority was causing trouble in the city. The simplest thing was to expel all Jews – except perhaps those who had clearly shown themselves as conforming to Roman customs. After all, it was extremely difficult to differentiate between the Jews who believed in this Jahweh of theirs, this Zeus, or Jupiter-like King of Gods, and those who believed in this 'Chrestus'. Out with them!

Claudius's expulsion of the Jews was, as has been seen, far from characteristic of this quiet and scholarly man. Even Suetonius, one of the great gossips of history (a title which takes some earning), could not find a great deal to say against him. True, he appears to have been a glutton and to have been constantly cuckolded by his wife Messalina. The latter is a misfortune that has happened to many men, and Messalina – who liked to disguise herself and serve as a common whore in a brothel, 'emerging unsatiated' – was something of an exception among the female of the species. Many of Claudius's actions show a tender heart:

> Discovering that a number of ill or worn-out slaves had been deliberately abandoned by their owners on the Island of Aesculapius in the Tiber (so as to avoid looking after them or giving them medical attention) Claudius immediately freed them all. He furthermore declared that any who should recover should never return to their former owner. He added the rider that any slave-owner who killed a sick slave should be charged with murder. . . . The provinces of Greece and Macedonia, which Tiberius had made, as it were, his private property Claudius restored to the Senate. The Lycians [a mountain-dwelling people of southern Asia Minor whence Paul was to catch his vessel at the port of Myra on his final journey to Rome] he deprived of their national independence in order to punish them

> for their passion for violent vendettas. On the other hand, he restored the independence of the Rhodians in order to show his appreciation of their recent improvement in behaviour.

He granted the Trojans, the supposed founders of the Roman race, permanent exemption from tribute. At the same time, while Augustus had been content with prohibiting Roman citizens from taking part in the Druidic cult found in Gaul and in Britain, Claudius decreed that it should be abolished altogether. This was because of his dislike of the practice of divination by the slaughter of a human victim and most probably, as recorded by Julius Caesar, of their custom of burning men alive in wicker cages. Claudius hardly sounds the kind of man who would have banished the Jews from Rome without some very good reasons.

It is important to look at other aspects of his reign, since it was under him that Paul made so many of his travels. It is evidence enough of the smooth administration and efficiency in communications that Paul and his associates could travel so widely and – though punished in various cities for what were considered misdemeanors – without let or hindrance, violence or robbery, over vast territories not all of which are entirely safe to this day. Indeed, it was not until the nineteenth or even the twentieth century that travel throughout the Mediterranean or the lands bordering it was as well-organized as it was in the first century A.D. Claudius, although unfortunate with his ill-health and his inborn timidity (not surprising in one who had grown up during the reigns of Tiberius and Caligula), was in many respects a good and enlightened ruler. He extended citizenship to many provincials, settled the eastern frontiers, successfully began the conquest of Britain and expended the imperial treasury wisely in such projects as the Claudian Aqueduct. Mauretania (the area of North Africa now more or less corresponding to Algeria) was added to the empire during his lifetime. In his dealings with the provinces, despite opposition from the Senate, he continued the liberal policy that had first been evolved by Julius Caesar. Unlike Caesar, however, he did not – perhaps because he did not have to – resort to the wholesale violence and massacre that had accompanied Caesar's conquest of Gaul.

The one great fault that characterized the reign of Claudius was his increasing dependence upon talented and rich freedmen. This was a development in the Roman empire which not unnaturally disgusted the nobly born Romans, but which was made almost inevitably by their proven unreliability, and by their basic hostility to the whole concept of the Emperor. By the time that Paul was in Thessalonica, and Claudius had only a few more years to live, the influence of the impartial freedmen such as Pallas and Narcissus had become paramount. The Emperor preferred to devote his time to his studies, to his historical works and to his autobiography. All of these, sadly, are lost; they would have told us a great deal that one would have liked to know about this century in which Paul was living and travelling. The virtual rule of freedmen, like that of the eunuchs in the later Ottoman empire, was not so much inefficient as destructive of the pride of the people who should have been ruling Rome. Decimated by the Civil Wars, by Tiberius and Caligula, the upper classes clung to the outward show of power while never holding its reins between their hands. The construction of a new harbour at Ostia (the harbour of Rome), the draining of the Fucine Lake, the building of two new aqueducts, all these were on the asset side of Claudius's reign. On the debit side were his increasing dependence on his personal servants who owed their power and position to him alone, and his fatal capacity for picking the wrong women to share his lonely life. Messalina has rightly passed into history and legend as the outstanding example of a corrupt and sexually insatiable woman, whom Claudius finally had executed. But his next choice was no better. Agrippina had been twice married before she became the wife of the Emperor. By her first husband she had had a son, later to become the Emperor Nero, whom she compelled the weak and study-bound Emperor to make his heir in preference to his own son Britannicus by Messalina – to be poisoned by Nero, a year after his succession. Agrippina was also Claudius's niece, something that upset the more old-fashioned Romans, since the relationship was considered incestuous. It is doubtful whether Paul was at all familiar with the intricacies of Rome and its power complexities – although he must have got a certain amount by hearsay, especially after he went to Corinth and met some of the Christians who had been expelled. Whatever he heard, it would in any case only have reinforced his determination to bring another kind of order into the world.

Despite his initial success in Thessalonica, where he may possibly have hoped to settle for some time and establish the keystone to the church in Greece, he was to encounter the familiar trouble. The Jews of the synagogue detested his message. Sometimes, one feels, Paul, although he was proud of his Pharisaic training and of his Jewishness, must have disliked his race and mentally clung to his Roman citizenship. Nearly all his troubles stemmed from the Jews. Gentiles might not necessarily accept his message, but in general they showed more tolerance than his own people. That, as the Romans had already found out, was the real trouble about the Jewish race: they were the least tolerant of all those within the wide bounds of the empire. They themselves could be tolerated so long as they kept within their own community – as they had always done in the past. But this was a new departure; these 'Chrestus' followers seemed to be a menace to the state. There was a *Crimen Maiestatis*, crime against the Emperor, which seemed to cover the situation for it was a crime against the Emperor to proclaim another king. The orthodox Jews proclaimed another god: this was acceptable for there were many gods, and every man was entitled to his own belief. But this new sect, which included not only Jews but members of other races, was saying that their Christ was due to arrive on the earth at any minute and that he would set up another kingdom. There can be little doubt that Paul and most of the other early Christians did literally believe in the imminent arrival of the Messiah. Paul's words, furthermore, as he later wrote in his first letter to the community at Thessalonica, were hardly likely to go down well with orthodox Jews. He described them as the people 'who killed the Lord Jesus and the prophets, and persecuted us. How displeasing to God they are! And how hostile to all men!'

It was hardly surprising that not long after Paul and his two companions had been in Thessalonica, 'the Jews became jealous, gathered some of the worthless people from the streets, and formed a mob'. They attacked the house of a Jew bearing the Greek name of Jason, because the three 'disturbers of the peace' had been lodging with him. Either by chance, or fore-warned, none of the wanted men were in the building. Jason, however, and some other Christians were dragged before the magistrates. The charge was that 'They are all breaking the laws of the Emperor, and saying that there is another king, called Jesus'.

The charge in effect was true. That was exactly the message that Paul was proclaiming, and his proclamation of the Second Coming suggested to simple minds a great king shortly to arrive from the East, who would overthrow the Roman empire. In Thessalonica, unlike Philippi, the magistrates were cautious. (News of the Roman status of Paul and Silas may well have reached them.) All they wanted, like almost all the authorities with whom Paul came in conflict during his life, was peace, progress and normal trading within the area of their authority. Who can blame them? That was exactly the purpose for which they had been appointed. Then along came this Jewish troublemaker, with some crazy story about another Jew, who apparently had been crucified and survived it (impossible!), and who was going at some time in the near future to become ruler of the world. Jason was a well-known citizen, so were a number of others including some 'women of good standing', who also shared this absurd but also dangerous belief. The best thing to do was to make them all put down a bond to ensure that they would in no way break the peace. And, of course, the promoters of this seditious nonsense must be got out of the city – as quickly as possible.

[28]

Rejections

The small town of Beroea lies in the foothills of Mount Olympus, popular then as now for its indulgent summer climate, where cool winds fan the mountainside while the plains and the coastal strip below are baked with heat. About twenty miles from the sea, it was one of the most ancient towns of Macedonia and like many others had its Jewish colony. Jason and the converts in Thessalonica had no doubt suggested it as a suitable retreat for Paul and Silas, and as having a community in the local synagogue who were receptive to new ideas. Timothy, it would appear, stayed behind in Thessalonica, to rejoin them in Beroea later. Neither he nor Luke seem to have been as predisposed to getting into trouble as Paul and Silas. But it is noticeable throughout his life that, no matter who was with him, Paul ran into trouble. He sought it out, one might say, as determinedly as the pilot of a meteorological aircraft who is investigating storms or hurricanes. His was not the nature of the solid Barnabas to take people by reason or gentle argument, nor of Luke the quiet observer. Wherever Paul was, there was the storm centre. So, 'as soon as night came, the brothers sent Paul and Silas to Beroea'.

It was pleasant there, the river racing out cold from the mountain above them, and the people friendly and sympathetic to travellers from foreign lands. A parochial place! The Masters of the Synagogue listened with pleasure and attention to this stranger who brought them even stranger news. There was hospitality here, a quickened interest at something unfamiliar coming from the outside world. So the Messiah had really arrived, and would come again, and all would be changed. Good news indeed! 'They listened to the message eagerly. . . . Many believed, including many Greek women of good social standing as well as many Greek men.' The appeal of Paul's style of preaching to the Greeks is significant. He couched the story of a Jewish Saviour in such a way that it was intellectually acceptable to people who were familiar with Dionysus, Demeter and Orpheus, and who could identify with the whole conception of resurrection and rebirth.

Even the Jews seem to have treated this addition to their history with tolerance; Beroea was not a place where passions ran high and, whether one believed this wandering Pharisee or not, there was no reason for being disrespectful to him. He was a Roman citizen furthermore, respectable indeed even in that, as well as in his impeccable background – taught by Gamaliel and none other.

Beroea was a charming backwater. Paul had no doubt long been hoping to take the Via Egnatia and head for Rome across the Adriatic. Rome was always what he sought, the heart of power, the heart of darkness, where he could set fire to the aspirations of millions. Once again he had been deflected and, pleasant though this provincial town was, he burned to go westward. But even Beroea soon proved too hot to hold him. Word got back quite naturally and very soon that there were two new Jews in the community, with a most unusual message. It suggested that all the writings of the Prophets had been fulfilled in a man called Joshua–Jesus, and that the Second Coming of the Messiah was imminent. A dangerous doctrine, and one which could well imperil the lives of all Jews within the empire. After all, as was now known in most Jewish communities (except perhaps a few provincial townships like Beroea), the Emperor Claudius had recently expelled the Jews from Rome, for the very reason that these 'Christ-believers' were a danger to the state. The trouble may probably have originated from the Sanhedrin, which exercised a powerful discipline throughout the ranks of the synagogues and, as Jews were always coming and going upon the peaceful highways of the empire, there was no difficulty in keeping in communication with one place and another. At the same time, this theory of Sanhedrin intervention which has been widely canvassed – thus laying the blame upon the leaders of Judaism – needs some consideration. From it derives some of the later Christian condemnation of the Jewish race, something quite as illogical as the Hitlerian persecutions which had absolutely no foundation in Christian belief. Jews irritated people. They said that they were different, chosen by the God of the whole universe, and destined to be the only ones admitted to some divine kingdom when the rest of humanity would be swept away into outer darkness. Another irritating factor was that, for some still unexplained genetic reason, they seemed undoubtedly more clever than most other races. No one could deny that the Jew was better at business even than the Phoenician – another Semite – and no one could deny that their private lives were quieter and more dignified than those of other nationalities. They did seem to have some extra quality, and this was hardly likely to make them popular with their neighbours. Then along came another but very different sect of Jews, who admitted foreigners into their cult, but who proclaimed that they were even more 'special' than the Jews themselves.

When the news reached Thessalonica that Paul and Silas were in Beroea the reaction was immediate. It is always easy, in any community in the world, to hire a crowd of ne'er-do-wells who care nothing for the issues concerned but who will promote a demonstration for the sake of money. Once again there was trouble, mob violence, and once again Paul had to fly for his life. It is notable that both Silas and Timothy (who had now joined them) 'stayed in Beroea'. It was Paul whom the authorities were after – constantly. This is proof enough that he was the outstanding advocate of the belief in 'Chrestus', and that his belief was seen as a revolutionary one.

Although the author of Acts gives us no details except that 'the brothers sent Paul away to the coast', and that he subsequently arrived in Athens, it is almost certain that he went there by sea. A number of authors have stated that he reached Athens by the overland route, but this seems quite illogical. Beroea was about twenty miles from the sea, and Methone on the Thermaic Gulf was the direct centre for communications with all the major ports of the Aegean world. (Philip, the father of Alexander the Great, had lost an eye during a siege of the town.) It was certainly from Methone that Paul took ship for Athens. The usual coastal route awaited him, but through some of the loveliest scenery in the Aegean. One cannot believe that, obsessed though he was with the vision of another world, Paul was not moved by the magnificent coastline of Greece. His letters prove him a poet, one of the greatest who ever lived, and there is in his imagery something not entirely Hebraic, something reminiscent of the strange clarity of Greece. He was alone now, alone for the first time in his known missionary activities, although clearly he had often been alone in the 'missing years'. One doubts whether it troubled him very much, for he was never, in a sense, lonely. Whatever had happened to him on the road to Damascus had changed his life totally, and had given him a constant sense of the omnipresence of God.

The vessel would most probably have turned west to come under the lee of Euboea, the long fish-shaped island that gives protection against the northerly winds of the Aegean. Paul's coaster would undoubtedly have had oars as well as sails, for the passage between Euboea and the mainland of Greece would have been practically impossible for a ship dependent on sails alone. In the Euboea channel he would have seen the roaring tide whose streams can run at as much as seven or eight knots. He will have seen, too, the shoreline race by near the town of Khalkis where the distance between Euboea and Attica is no more than 130 feet. There is no indication that Paul was familiar with Homer, but his fellow passengers would certainly have been. He must have heard as they passed the Bay of Aulis how it was here that the Greek fleet bound for the siege of Troy had had to wait for a favourable wind. It was here that Agamemnon's daughter, Iphigenia, was supposed to have offered herself as a sacrifice to the goddess Artemis in order to ensure that the fleet had a successful passage across the sea to Troy. (The traditional site of her death is now commemorated by a small whitewashed chapel dedicated to St Nicholas.) On his right hand lay the district known as Boeotia, whose name has come down to us in the word 'Boeotian' as being synonymous with peasant-like stupidity. That is because the Athenians wrote the literature. The Boeotians were not so much stupid as astute and cunning. Christopher Wordsworth says:

> It was the policy of Boeotia, contrived with more than Boeotian shrewdness, to make Euboea an island to everyone else but themselves. . . . They locked the doors of Athenian commerce, and kept themselves the key. This was the channel by which the gold of Thasus, the horses of Thessaly, the timber of Macedonia, the corn of Thrace, were carried to the Piraeus.

But all this was long in the past, long before the rise of Rome, long before the domination of Greece by the legions from Italy.

Paul lived in eternity, in a timeless world, obsessed with the end of time, and with the beginning of a new era when, in the words of Shakespeare 'time must have a stop'. Ancient legends would have meant little or nothing to him. But the sight of Athens, of the fabulous buildings capping the great rock of the

Parthenon, of the immense statue of Athene – that landmark to sailors – cannot have failed to shake his nerve. Little towns, Beroea, Lystra, Tarsus or even Antioch cannot have prepared him for the astonishment of Athens. There she stood, the monument of all the ages, the home of the greatest intellects that the Mediterranean world had ever known, the source to which – even five centuries after her Periclean glory – every Roman who could afford it sent his son in order to make of him a truly cultured man. The Acropolis, rising some 180 feet above the plain, flashed with the glorious marble that the Athenian genius had turned into some of the greatest architecture in the history of the world – buildings which were emulated by the Romans then, as they are emulated to this day. The city staggered the eye. Paul suffered a loss of confidence. It is notable that his later encounters with the men of Athens do not show him at his most formidable.

'Even a Jew cannot make a living in Athens'; so runs a local saying. Certainly the quick-witted Athenians had little to learn about commerce or craftsmanship or indeed almost anything from other nations. There was though, as would be expected, a Jewish community complete with its synagogue. Paul as usual made straight for the heart, 'arguing with Jews and Gentiles who worshipped God'. The account does not show him as having made any converts at this early stage. The city's smiling indifference angered him. Everywhere he turned he was confronted with marble gods and goddesses, many of them painted in vivid primary colours. Altars smoked, incense billowed out of temples, people made private offering at little shrines. Priapic statues with erect penises (lovingly and jokingly touched by passers-by) stood close to statues of naked women – heathen idols! The whole air vibrated with a splendid disbelief in practically everything, except in life itself. It is curious perhaps that Paul, brought up in Tarsus and familiar with paganism from his earliest years, should have reacted so strongly against these surroundings. One may conclude that even his certainty was somewhat undermined by all these other certainties.

Paul like many others, philosophers, scholars, students, and men with time on their hands to do little 'but hear the latest new thing', got into discussions, debates and arguments in the *agora*, the market place, where transactions were intellectual as well as material. Inevitably he met with Stoics and Epicureans, for they were the predominant leaders in philosophy at this time. Indeed, it might well be said that Stoicism and Epicureanism still remain at the core of much human thought. Stoics, although like later Christians they came in a variety of shades, basically maintained that man has an invisible quantity, a soul, whose true home is not on this earth but in the remote universe, in the light of the sun, or in the eternal silence of the stars. Man must not fear death, for either it is no more than absorption into the universe – into the absence of consciousness which, as far as he knows, was his condition before birth – or it is a new birth into the consciousness of the God who made all things. E. H. Blakeney in his *Classical Dictionary* summarized the Stoics:

> They derived their name from the Painted Hall at Athens, called the 'Stoa' (lit. *porch*) . . . Stoicism is mainly a great ethical system. Philosophy takes the place of religion in that system; and this philosophy is the exercise of virtue, the setting forth of wisdom as a truly practical interest. According to the Stoics, virtue consists in (1) absolute judgement, (2) absolute mastery of desire, (3) absolute control of the soul over pain, (4) absolute justice. The key-note of the system is duty. . . .

There is nothing that Paul would have been unfamiliar with here, and little, except in his proclamation of a Man-God, that Stoics would have found unfamiliar in Paul's Cristo-Judaic ethics. Admirable though Stoicism was, however, there was one vast and salient difference between this philosophy and the religious belief preached by Paul. Stoicism meant acceptance. It had much in common with the 'Kismet' of the Moslem, the acknowledgement of the fore-ordained pattern which a real man should look straight in the eye and not try to evade. Paul's message was that the world could be changed, that man through faith in Christ had a power over his destiny. Over and above all that, permanent and perpetual compassion was the quality that God desired of the human race. Stoicism was noble, but somewhere at the core there was an emptiness.

Epicureanism on the other hand was, though far from as simple as some later commentators would have us believe, basically centred around the idea that the prime object of life was happiness. Mistranslated by numerous of the followers of Epicurus, and constantly mistranslated in later centuries, the teaching of this very remarkable man had practically nothing to do with the delights of sensual pleasure. Born in the fourth century B.C. in the island of Samos, Epicurus took up permanent residence in Athens in 306 B.C. The highest good, he taught his followers, was happiness, something which could only be achieved by peace of mind resulting from the cultivation of virtue. Whereas the Stoics made virtue an end in itself, Epicurus saw it as a means. 'Quietude of mind and a steadfast faith' he enjoined, adding that 'a right conception of pleasure conduces to right living, since it is not possible to live pleasantly without living wisely and well and righteously'. He had died in Athens in 270 B.C., aged seventy-two.

It was the latter-day descendants of these two principal schools of thought with whom Paul was now to dispute, announcing his 'resurrection of Jesus'. He was of course misunderstood. They were all prepared to discuss the nature of man, his place in the universe and the existence of an all-powerful God. They were not ignorant idol-worshippers – that was for the general populace, for the peasantry who needed obvious and simple reminders of the natural forces that shaped the world. But what on earth was this strange little Jew talking about? The idea of the physical resurrection of the body was ludicrous. Everyone had been to funerals, everyone knew that whether interred in the earth or burnt on a funeral-pyre the material body returned to the earth, was reformed into the atoms of which everything was made. At that moment in Rome the Stoic philosopher Seneca was saying that every right-thinking man was 'a pilgrim in search of the good'. He was endeavouring to put this kind of wisdom into the mind of a pupil who unfortunately was not to do him much credit – the future Emperor Nero.

Paul's passionate advocacy of his belief did not make much impression upon these scholarly and cultured Athenians. 'What,' they asked, 'is this ignorant *spermologos* trying to say?' A *sperm-*

ologos meant literally a seed-snapper, a man who picked seeds from the gutter in order to keep alive or, as in this case, a man who grabbed the seeds of other men's ideas and then, without really comprehending them, hawked them about as his own. Who was he to come to Athens, the home of philosophy, and try and tell them about some completely obscure figure, and what exactly was his message? 'He seems,' said some of them, 'to be talking about foreign gods.' They were well used to new cults and mystery religions coming out of the East, but few of them would stand the scrutiny of a trained mind. Yet it is evidence of the extraordinary personality of Paul that the Athenians took him seriously enough to invite him to a public meeting on the hill of Ares, the Areopagus.

In former times this had been the criminal court of the city, where murderers or men accused of crimes against the state were taken to state their case before the Council. It is doubtful at this time whether the Council ever met, but the Hill of Ares still meant in Athenian eyes the seat of judgement. This was where the truth was established. Two prominent white stones marked the place where accused and prosecutor took their stands, one the Stone of Shame and the other the Stone of Ruthlessness. It is more than doubtful that either Paul or any of the interrogators actually stood upon these ancient symbols of the days when Athenians had been the proudest citizens of Greece, and had conducted all their own affairs. Nevertheless the implication was still there and, if not fully understood by Paul, would certainly have been understood by his audience. This foreigner with his Cilician Greek who maintained that all their philosophers were wrong, and that he had some magic key to the universe, was being put on intellectual trial. If he was right and they were wrong, then let him prove it. They at least were showing that Athenian liberalism was extended to all, even to obscure wandering Jews: provided, of course, that they were prepared to defend their opinions and to argue them rationally.

Paul began well enough. 'Gentlemen of Athens, I see that in every way you are very religious. . . ' They accepted that, although it somewhat smacked of patronage coming from a stranger and being addressed to the heirs of Socrates, Plato and Aristotle – to mention but a few names out of their vast intellectual heritage. Now he was talking about an altar dedicated to 'An Unknown God'. There was nothing particularly uncommon in that; there were many in the world with a similar dedication. All it meant was that people did not want to offend any deity who might possibly have been forgotten during the erection of altars throughout this or other cities. He worshipped this unknown god? How very peculiar! And now he was going on to say that this god of his had made the world and was ruler of the universe.

This was nothing new. He must have been reading Cleanthes's great hymn: 'Most glorious of immortals, O Zeus of many names, almighty and everlasting sovereign of nature, directing all in accordance with law. . . .' They did not need to know that 'God does not live in temples'. Their distant ancestors might have thought so, but they knew well enough that temples were only visible symbols of belief, and that the statues and paintings in them were a comfort to the masses. Let him get to the point – what exactly was it that he had to tell them that was new? Ah now, at last it came. There was going to be a day of judgement when the whole world would be judged with justice by a man whom this god of his had chosen. Unbelievable, and even more unbelievable this judge had already lived on earth and had been raised from the dead! This was too much. Those who had merely been yawning began to laugh. They had really wasted their time coming to listen to this ignorant, arrogant and quite absurd mountebank. But still, they must not forget that they were Athenians. They must extend the normal courtesy to a visitor, even if they would never again bother to listen to him: 'We would like to hear you on the subject some other time. . . .'

Surprisingly enough, in view of the intellectual climate of Athens, not all were sceptical. As Paul left the Aeropagus a number of people followed him, who wanted to hear a great deal more about this belief. Among them was a member of the Areopagus Council, Dionysius, as well as a woman named Damaris. His opportunity to talk to the wise in the wisest city in the world had not been an entire failure. But it had not been a great success either. If it had been a success, there can be no doubt that he would have stayed on in Athens but, 'after this, Paul left Athens and went on to Corinth'. The brief statement is testimony to a rejection.

[29]

A Tent-Maker in Corinth

Corinth, the ancient rival of Athens, was in mythology the home of the sorceress Medea, of Sisyphus, who was condemned for his rapacity in life eternally to roll a huge marble stone up-hill in Hades, and of Bellerophon who attempted to fly to heaven on his winged horse Pegasus. Traditionally the birthplace of navigation and commerce, and the originator of the trireme, it had once been the greatest trading power from the gulf that bears its name to the islands of the Ionian Sea, Sicily and Italy. The Corinth Paul saw was a new creation.

In 146 B.C., the year that Rome defeated and sacked Carthage, the same treatment had been handed out to Corinth. Infuriated by a series of insurrections in Greece, the Romans had decided to make an example of this powerful and famous city. Lucius Mummius, the Consul in charge of the operation, had done his work with devastating thoroughness. Corinth had been razed to the ground. The home of philosophers like Diogenes (who had once openly rebuked Alexander the Great), the home of some of the greatest craftsmen and gifted artists in Greece, was obliterated. Its men were killed, its women and children sold into slavery, and the vast accumulation of art treasures in the city were transported to Rome. Mummius then proceeded with typical Roman canniness to ensure in his contract with the shippers of all this loot that if any of the art treasures were lost in transit they must be replaced by others of equal value. His own values were those of the victorious *nouveau riche* conqueror, ignorant of the refinements of life. The city had been refounded in 44 B.C. by Julius Caesar, in the very year of Caesar's assassination. By this time Greece had become a Roman protectorate and Corinth was now made a colony. It became the capital of the province of Achaia and was resettled by Roman veterans and descendants of freedmen.

Paul may have reached the city by the overland route from Athens, although it is equally likely that he took a coaster from Peiraeus, the main commercial harbour of Athens, and went to Cenchreae, the port on the eastern side of the isthmus of Corinth. It was this narrow strip of land, dividing the Aegean from access to the Ionian Sea, that had first given the city its commercial importance. Boats were transported across the isthmus on a system of rollers to Lechaeum, the harbour of Corinth. The long sea-route round the southern point of Greece was thus obviated – as well it needed to be. Cape Malea is one of the most dangerous points in the Mediterranean, and an old saying had it that the man who rounded Cape Malea might as well forget that he ever had a home.

Corinth was above all a sailors' city, renowned for its drunkenness and debauchery. It had been the home of the famous Lais, a courtesan of beauty and wit whose most famous lover was Aristippus, the Cyrenaic philosopher. She, as it were, set the tone for the city, and it was to Corinth that businessmen from Athens came when they wished to escape from the eyes of their neighbours for a week or so of old wine and young mistresses. Above the city, soaring out of the plain to a height of 1,900 feet, rose Acro-Corinthus, where the citadel of Corinth gave it dominance over all the neighbourhood. Strabo, who gives a detailed description of the city, tells us that the peak of the mountain was not only devoted to war. Here, as on Mount Eryx in Sicily and at Paphos in Cyprus, there was a temple dedicated to Astarte–Aphrodite–Venus, the goddess of love, that was served by a thousand priestess–prostitutes. Although the ancient glories of Corinth had long gone and been replaced by pure commercialism when Paul came walking down the dusty way, where the slaves hauled the ships to east and west, the atmosphere must always have been much the same. Here money talked, money could buy you anything and everything. It was a far call from quiet Beroea, or even from Athens, come to that, where intellect was still prized above all else.

Paul was in for a surprise. He knew of course that there was a flourishing Jewish community in Corinth along with its synagogue, but what he can hardly have counted on was finding that in advance of him there were some Christians in the community. Only two are mentioned, although there may possibly have been others. These were Aquila, a Jew born in Pontus on the southern shores of the Black Sea, and his wife Priscilla (a diminutive of the Roman name Prisca), both of whom had settled in Corinth after their expulsion from Rome under the Claudian edict. They too followed the same trade as Paul, and he settled with them and took up his tent-making again. Aquila, Priscilla and Paulus, Tent-makers – it is not an impossible shop sign. Paul, like any rabbi, had been taught that the teacher or exponent of the Law must never be a burden on the community but must pay his own way, earn his own bread. A very proper aspiration, and one which has, unhappily for all concerned, been forgotten by too many sects of Christians in subsequent centuries.

Paul may often have seemed anathema to the Jews, but it was the iron core of Judaism in his nature that made him so successful a Christian revolutionary.

As usual he was given a hearing in the synagogue, where he 'argued every Sabbath, trying to convince both Jews and Greeks'. He was later to thank the people of Corinth for their treatment of him, and to confess that he had come to them 'nervous and shaken with fear'. The words are interesting, for they can hardly refer to his treatment in Athens where he had been heard with scepticism but not with violence. It is possibly right to assume that the cumulative effect of his treatment in other cities had prepared him for further beatings, stonings and mobbings. His courage and physical endurance, over hard roads, through mountain passes, on wet, wave-swept decks, in shipwrecks and storms at sea, as well as human storms in cities, never deserted him. Few 'soldiers' in the cult of Mithras, dedicated though they were to a belief in the value of courage, could have equalled the endurance of this small, balding Jew who was also often physically ill. Paul was a living proof that the weaknesses of the body are surmountable, and that there is in the power of the will some force which has still escaped medical or psychological analysis.

When Silas and Timothy rejoined him from Macedonia they brought disquieting news. First of all, the Christians were being persecuted by the orthodox Jews, who were saying that Paul was nothing more than a charlatan and that his whole message was a lie. This in itself was bad enough, although only to be expected. But what Paul possibly could not have expected was that his insistence that the Second Coming was imminent had led among some to a complete breakdown in morale. If the end of the world was at hand, why bother with attempting to get on with one's daily life? Why, indeed, work at all? Paul's first letter to the Thessalonians was one of encouragement. It was dictated by him, but very probably written by Timothy. It would have been on the standard papyrus sheets which were among Egypt's main contribution to the bureaucracy and the communications of the ancient world, written with a pen made out of reed and ink composed of gums and soot. The dialect is the colloquial demotic of the day with, very naturally, a sprinkling of Hebraisms. It opens in the normal style of ancient letters with a conveyance of greetings, proceeds then to the substance, and closes with a blessing. Very probably it was conveyed back to Thessalonica by Timothy in person. He seems to have been both amanuensis and courier to Paul.

It is significant that in his second letter to the Thessalonians he concludes with what might be termed a 'trade mark', a personal salutation which he takes care to put in his own hand, adding: 'This is my mark of identification in every letter. I write as follows: The grace of our Lord Jesus Christ be with you all.' It is quite clear that some spurious letters must have been in existence, letters which can only have been forged by enemies of this doctrine; orthodox Jews almost certainly. Why would pagans and others have cared in the slightest what one obscure foreigner was writing to another small group of foreigners?

But in Corinth as elsewhere it was inevitable that the vehemence of Paul's proselytizing would lead to trouble. The Jews denied that his arguments about Christ being the Messiah were convincing. As always, they were not going to have the Saviour of Israel compared to a man who had been crucified between two thieves, nor were they going to hear that this was the doing of the Jews themselves. Paul was no longer welcome in the synagogue, they abused him, called his so-called Messiah by evil names. Paul responded with the traditional gesture, shaking off the dust from his clothes, and saying, 'Your blood be upon your own head! I take no blame for it. From now on I will go to the Gentiles.' Yet, despite this, Paul had managed to convert Crispus, who is described as 'a leader of the synagogue'. He had baptized him and all his family, so it could hardly be said that he had entirely failed with his own race. He now took up residence with a certain Titius Justus, a Gentile whose house stood next to the synagogue. From his name he was presumably a Roman, possibly a descendant of one of the retired legionaries or freedmen with whom Julius Caesar had repopulated the city.

A sum of money now reached Paul from the community at Philippi. It is likely that he abandoned his tent-making at the same time as he moved into the house of Justus. Paul had over a year of more or less undistracted preaching and instruction in Corinth, and it seems almost certain that the majority of his converts were made among the Greeks and Romans. Despite his rejection by most of the Jews he was comforted by a vision in which Jesus spoke to him, telling him that he must carry on with his mission and that he would not be harmed, for 'I have many people in this city'. But in the summer of 52 there was a drastic change. In July that year a new proconsul of Achaia was appointed, Lucius Junius Annaeus Gallio. He was a man of some distinction, the brother of the philosopher Seneca, whom the poet Statius refers to as 'Sweet Gallio'. Seneca also wrote of him that no one was ever 'so pleasant as Gallio is to everyone'. This then was not the hard Roman proconsul of tradition, but a man of culture and sensitivity. The Jewish community now made a grave mistake. They thought that with the change of government, they might find a Roman new to the office who would be willing to accede to their request. And the request was very simple – remove Paul from Corinth.

'The Jews got together, seized Paul, and took him to court. . . .' These are the brief words of Acts. There is no mention of Silas, no mention of Timothy. It was always Paul who caused the dissension. Because of his formidable power of argument he could upset the elders of any community, and make them feel inferior in front of all the others. If they would not believe, then let them perish! Such confidence does indeed move and inspire many of the people in this world – most of whom in any case do not know what their true opinions are – but it is certain to make enemies. Once again, no doubt beaten and mauled, this indomitable, ageing man was dragged in front of the ruling authority.

The charge laid against him was that he was trying to persuade people to worship God in a manner that was against the law. What did this really mean? There were many gods, there were indeed myriads of gods, each and all with their different rituals and ceremonies. So how could it be possible to teach people to worship some Oriental god in a way that was against the law – and by the law, of course, was meant the law of Rome, not that of the Jewish Torah? The answer, which is often evaded, is simple enough: Paul was teaching what in effect, if not in reality, was subversion against Rome and against the Emperor. He was teaching the End of the World, the imminent arrival of a Jewish king, who was king above all kings, the destruction of Rome and all that it stood for, and the uprising of a small group of Jews and Gentiles who would create a new kind of state. This at any rate was how it appeared to many people, and certainly how the orthodox Jews always wanted to make it appear to the Roman authorities.

Unfortunately for them they met their match in the liberal and sensibly minded Gallio. Gallio has often been traduced as another Pontius Pilate, anxious only to wash his hands of the whole affair. This is far from true. Having listened to the charge that 'This man is trying to persuade people to worship God in a way that is contrary to the law', he came to the conclusion that the law of Rome was in no way being broken. Apparently it was all a matter of a different interpretation of some aspect of Jewish religion and history. It seemed to him to have no connection with any material offence. These Jews were the most troublesome people in the empire! The

Gaul, the German, the barbarous Briton even, were no trouble compared with this violent little race out of the East. The Emperor – and wisely, as it would seem – had just banished them from Rome. Yet here they were in Corinth indulging in exactly the same tedious disputes. Gallio's decision was simple. 'If,' he said, 'this was a matter about some wrongdoing or crime, I would be reasonably patient with you Jews. But, since it is simply an argument about words and names and your own law, see to it yourselves. I refuse to be a judge of such matters.'

After this he had them all removed from the court. The Jewish community felt that the whole affair had been mishandled by the leader of the synagogue, Sosthenes, who had clearly concentrated on offences against the Jewish Law. What he should have impressed upon the Roman was that Paul was proclaiming a doctrine that was a threat to Caesar. In their fury at the outcome of the issue they seized Sosthenes and beat him in front of the court. 'But that did not bother Gallio at all. . . .' 'These Jews!' he thought, no doubt. Well, that was clearly one of them who was not going to bother him any more. Paul went away free.

[30]

The Traveller Again

The proconsul's decision meant that Paul was able to continue uninterrupted in his activities. The Jews, no doubt chastened by their experience of the cool indifference of Gallio to their private feuds and disputes, kept themselves to themselves. In the spring of 53, when in early March the sailing season was officially declared open, Paul left Corinth. He had been there for at least a year and a half. He had seen the establishment of a strong core of believers and he can only have felt that his time there had been well spent. Corinth, like Alexandria (to which he never went), was by reason of its shipping activities one of the nerve-centres of the Roman world. Sailors and merchants who had been converted would spread the word through the blue arteries of the Mediterranean, taking it to other seaports all over the body of the empire. With Paul went Aquila and Priscilla.

Acts mentions laconically that 'before sailing he made a vow in Cenchreae and had his head shaved. . . .' This is extremely interesting, for it suggests that Paul had been ill. It was an ancient custom among the Jews, if they had been dangerously ill or in other ways distressed, to take a vow to go to the Temple in Jerusalem. As token of this they shaved their heads, kept the shorn hair, and then ceremonially burnt it at the altar. Now Corinth was notorious for being malarial. (Gallio himself contracted it during his office there and went off on a sea-voyage to restore his health.) Paul had no other reason, as far as is known, to feel distressed. His time in Corinth had been extremely fruitful. If, as some have assumed, he had already contracted malaria while in Asia Minor, a second attack would have been very serious. He also mentions in his letter to the Romans, written some four years after his visit to Corinth, a deaconess of the small Christian church established at Cenchreaen named Phoebe, 'who has nursed myself and many others'.

Ageing, most probably still shaken by terrible recurrent bouts of fever, Paul and his two friends now embarked on a coaster across the Aegean, headed for Ephesus. It will have been too early for the steady northerlies, the *Meltemi*, to have been blowing. But, assuming it was April when they finally got under way, the prodroms, the forerunners of the Etesian winds, will have started. Variable in strength and direction they are nevertheless handy for small boats, and one may assume that Paul was embarked on a typical Aegean coaster. She was probably taking manufactured goods from Corinth to sell in the great market of Ephesus. Salamis to the north of them, craggy Aegina to the south, past Athens shining in all its glory, they will then have raised Cape Suniun on their port bow. There, giving them its blessing, stood the great temple of Poseidon, the god himself with his trident promising them freedom from harm as they sailed across the Sea of the Kingdom. Very likely, if the wind permitted, they took the shortest route, going north of the island of Zea and then through the

Andros-Tinos channel. Paul's writings are full of music. It is impossible to believe that he was not moved on spring days and nights as they made their way through those lovely islands. They were far greener and more fertile then than now, although even by the first century many of them had been despoiled of their trees in the hunger for wood to build ships such as that in which Paul was travelling. Lonely, dolphin-shaped Ikaria they left to the south and then they were passing all the grandeur of Samos, with its two great mountains spinning up like tops out of the Aegean, and dominating the fertile plains below. Throughout their voyage they had hardly ever been out of sight of land, of islands which had furnished an imagery for generations of Greek poets – and it must never be forgotten that this Jew, like so many of his race, was a poet as well as a religious. Indeed, it is hardly possible to be one without the other.

Their stay in Ephesus was brief, Paul's intention being no more than to see that all was going well with the congregation before hastening on to Jerusalem. It was comforting and peaceful. His next visit to the city would be very different. Aquila and Priscilla stayed behind, presumably to set up their tent-making business again, and to provide at the heart of the Christian community a firm core that would make sure that the belief was not misinterpreted. Paul went on alone, days and nights in a merchantman along the Asian coast, north of Rhodes – where they probably stopped in the Sun God's island to unload merchandise and let passengers disembark and take on others – and so across the sea, south of Cyprus, to land at Caesarea. Paul's second great journey was over. The traveller stood in the Temple and fulfilled his vow.

He had said to the congregation at Ephesus that he hoped to return to see them 'if it is the will of God'. After leaving Jerusalem he made his way north again to Syrian Antioch. He was ending his second expedition in the place from which he had begun his first. After all, it was the community at Antioch that had first sent him out, and it was only right and fitting that he should come back to his emissaries and give them all the news in person. It is true that there were many other travellers on the roads and waterways of the

Roman world, but Paul's obsessional travelling is quite unique. He must often have 'slept rough', constantly sailed under the cheapest conditions, and more often than not, when he could not afford a mule or a horse, have travelled the roads of the eastern empire in sweat-stained cloak, with his knapsack on his back and staff in hand. Yet it is an astounding tribute to the organization of the empire that he and so many others could move so freely and easily through areas which for thousands of years had been the haunt of bandits and pirates, of warring tribes, of conflicting empires, and of danger, dirt and inefficiency. Everywhere he went the hand of Rome was visible.

R. H. Barrow in *The Romans* has commented that:

> The movement of men was as extensive as the movement of goods. Soldiers and traders, officials and civil servants, travellers for pleasure, students and wandering philosophers and preachers, commercial agents, the couriers of the imperial post and of banks and shipping offices – these and many more thronged the roads and the sea-routes. The great cities, especially on the coast, were cosmopolitan in their population. Syrians and Greeks, Spaniards and Africans and scores of other nationalities were mingled in the towns and served in the same offices and departments or factories or private households. The satirists are never tired of calling attention to the 'Orontes' – a river of Syria – 'pouring its waters into the Roman Tiber'. Men of alien origin brought with them their customs and superstitions and cults and moral standards; and Eastern religions spread far into the West. . . .

When one considers the size of the area controlled from Rome, and the millions of inhabitants, it is a tribute to the efficiency of Roman arms and communications that the armies which policed the frontiers can hardly ever have numbered more than half a million men. About 50 per cent of these were local auxiliaries. Paul's missionary activities, his rescue on more than one occasion from violence, indeed his continued life, were made possible by the Romans.

We know little or nothing about his stay in Antioch, so it is reasonable to presume that everything there was in good order. But it was probably during this period, when he had his sights set on a return to Ephesus, that he heard that all was not well in

Galatia. The Pharisaic 'circumcision' party had been at work again during his years of absence, saying that a man was not freed from the Law just because he had accepted the belief that Jesus had been the Messiah. Paul was furious. These people were undoing the very thing that he had set himself to proclaim – that beyond the Mosaic code there lay another law, one which freed all men who believed. His letter to the Galatians opens formally enough: 'Paul, an apostle, not from man nor by means of man, but from Jesus Christ and God the Father who raised him from the dead. . . .' He then admonishes them for their backsliding, but there is no doubt when Paul is enraged he never spares his enemies. 'Anathema' he pronounces them, going on to say that 'If anyone preaches a different gospel from that which I preached to you let him be anathema!' Although the word had not yet acquired the meaning that it would later in the history of the church, its meaning would be very familiar to people who were acquainted with pagan practices. It indicated the cursing of enemies by means of wax figurines in which the hair or nail-cuttings of the enemy had been inserted, as well as the use of inscribed lead tablets (a number of which have been found) designed to ensure that the curse would endure as long as the lead itself. Although he comforts the believers, although some of his noblest expressions are to be found in this letter, there can be no doubt after reading it about the temper of its writer. Paul could spit fire as well as any of the early prophets. He could descend also to good old earthy imagery – not so surprising from one who had travelled the hard way, lived among sailors, and in towns like Corinth. He has this to say about the people who have been contradicting him: 'I wish that those who are shaking your faith by insistence on circumcision would go all the way – and castrate themselves as well!'

From Antioch he set off again north and then west, headed for Galatia and Phrygia. He was absolutely determined that if there had been any backsliding, or any misinterpretation of the message which he had brought to these churches he had founded, he in person would make quite sure that error was corrected. His other aim was to ensure that the relief fund for the poor and for the church in Jerusalem was regularly collected and dispatched, and that every Christian should regularly put aside part of his income for this purpose. Back then again he went, on the long roads through Derbe and Lystra, Iconium and Pisidian Antioch. Older now, but still indomitable, alone and yet never lonely, he walked through all the familiar scenes, through the passes, along the uplands, past the lakes; the soldier with his face set firmly against all enemies but with his hand extended to all who believed. If Paul had not been what he was, a man blinded by God, he might have been one of the greatest generals the world has ever seen. But he was better than any Alexander the Great. He did not bring death and the sword, but a message of compassion and love that was to transform the whole of this empire – and empires that he can never even have dreamed of.

While Paul was on his way through these early congregations 'a certain Jew named Apollos, who had been born in Alexandria, came to Ephesus'. He was clearly a gifted man, an eloquent speaker, and a believer that the Messiah had come in the person of Jesus. However, as Acts puts it, 'he knew only the baptism of John'. That is to say that he (like Paul) preached that the kingdom of God was close at hand, but he clearly was ignorant of other facts such as the Resurrection and Pentecost. Aquila and Priscilla, those pillars of the early church whom Paul had left behind at Ephesus, assisted in instructing Apollos more correctly as to what 'the Way of God' really was. Before Paul reached Ephesus Apollos had already taken ship for Greece, carrying a letter from the Ephesian community to the churches in Greece. He preached in Corinth and was apparently a great help to the Christians, 'defeating the Jews in public arguments and proving from the prophets that Jesus was the Messiah'. An Alexandrian Jew, Apollos will have learned in that most cultured city all the twists and turns of argument. One would like to know more about him but unfortunately he disappears from the scene. The spotlight turns once more upon Paul.

[31]

The Great Goddess

He came into Ephesus, not on this occasion just as a passing visitor but as one who intended to stay for a long time, and to make this powerful and immensely rich city into a stronghold of belief. The city which he now grew to know well was, apart from being a major commercial centre, a home of occult studies. It was also proud to be known as *neocorus*, the servant of the goddess. It was here that the Roman governor of Asia always landed and assumed his office. Although both Smyrna and Pergamum strongly contested the claim, it was generally accepted that Ephesus was the first city of Asia. At a later date, long after Paul himself was dead, it was widely believed that Ephesus was the last home of the Virgin Mary, and that she had died there. This was after the triumph of the Christian Church. There can, however, be little doubt that Mariolatry was no more than an extension throughout the Mediterranean of the worship of the Great Goddess, the Mother of All Things, the goddess who had been dominant over this sea since the Stone Age.

'Diana of the Ephesians' was Artemis, the Greek virgin–huntress goddess, but she also combined the qualities of the Egyptian Isis. She was, to quote Dr R. E. Witt's *Isis in the Graeco-Roman World*, 'Thou who art worshipped in the shrine at Ephesus.' Throughout the novel by Xenophon of Ephesus it is tacitly assumed that Artemis and Isis perform interchangeable roles. Lastly, writing at the beginning of the fifth century A.D. Macrobius describes the figure of Isis as having 'the whole body thickly covered with nipples joined together'. . . . The total effect was that of Great Artemis–Isis as a fertility figure personifying birth and growth.'

Paul was to find that his doctrine of Christ as the Messiah of the Jews, and the Saviour of all mankind, met with considerable opposition here. The goddess who had largely given Ephesus its wealth and importance – so that it was a kind of Lourdes of the ancient world – was at the core of so much human thinking. She derived from those early manifestations of religious belief, the mother–goddess figures to be found from Asia Minor to the Cyclades, and westward to Sicily. The embodiment of the female principle, she represented not only fertility but resurrection in the shape of new birth, the eternal return of life to the earth and, as found in a number of early carvings (at Tarxien in Malta, for instance), the 'Tree of Life'. As Isis she bore the divine son, Horus; and as Artemis she was the Mother of Wild Things, the goddess of all animals. The Isis–Artemis conception embraced everything. It could be taken at any level; from the simple peasant's conception of the divinity who would ensure that his beasts and land were fruitful, to the intellectual idea of an all-creating mother who sustained the whole universe.

Her temple, one of the Seven Wonders of the World, was sited on the plain north of Mount Pion, near a small hill. It was over 400 feet long and 220 wide. It was surrounded by Ionic pillars, sixty feet high, each one of which had been erected by various monarchs as a token of their devotion. It was not the first temple that had been erected at this place for, starting from a small archaic shrine, there had been at least three or four previous temples. The one which Paul will have seen had taken over 100 years to complete. Much of the cost of its construction had been met by the famous Croesus, the last king of Lydia, whose wealth and power was a byword in the ancient world, as it still is today. It was of Croesus that the tale was told how one day he asked the great Athenian legislator Solon who was the happiest man in the world – expecting no doubt to be told that it was he. Solon's reply was that no man could be called happy unless he finished his life in a happy way. Some years later, when Croesus had lost a war against the Persian king Cyrus and was about to be burned to death, he remembered Solon's words and called out his name three times; Cyrus asked him whom he was invoking at the end of his life. On hearing the story he saw that there was also a moral in it for himself, and reprieved Croesus. But all this had taken place six centuries before Paul came into the city that was known as the Light of Asia, and saw the astounding temple which celebrated the female principle, fecundity, and the eternal rebirth of all living things. His basic doctrine was that a *man* had come into the world, who was also God, and that the end of the world was imminent. When that end came, everybody would be judged and the good and the bad would be separated. The chosen ones would inherit 'the Kingdom', some kind of world that was quite different from this one that was ruled by Emperors in Rome.

Why should anyone want to believe in the end of the world? People wanted to live happily, and enjoy all the pleasures of life as far as they could. Paul's doctrine could hardly appeal to the people of Ephesus, and it is noticeable that he seems only to have made a small number of converts in the city, among some of those who had been baptized in 'The Baptism of John'. These he carefully instructed, explaining that John's baptism had been only a token of repentance, but that the baptism of Jesus was that of the Holy Spirit. He took them down to the river Cayster, the source of the importance of Ephesus for it led to the Aegean only four miles away, and baptized them himself. '. . . The Holy Spirit came upon them: they spoke in strange tongues and proclaimed God's message.'

It has been said that Ephesus was the centre of occult studies, indeed it has been called 'The Home of Magic'. This prophesying or speaking in wild and whirling words was not something confined to the Christians. The followers of Dionysus and the followers of Isis and Cybele, for instance, were prone, under the influence of wine or drugs, to glossolalia. It would be absurd to accept John M. Allegro's identification of Christianity with an ancient drug cult based on the properties of the mushroom *Amanita muscaria* (*The Sacred Mushroom and the Cross*). At the same time, it would be equally absurd to pretend that Christianity grew up completely untouched by the cults and mystery religions of the ancient world. Paul, like any other man, was influenced by his surroundings.

For three months he taught in the synagogue but, as usual, the majority of the Jews were hostile to this novel and unpalatable doctrine. So, at the invitation of a schoolmaster appositely named Tyrranus (the Tyrant), he took his small group of believers into the latter's lecture-hall, presumably at the end of the day when lessons were over. Soon, and how natural it was in a city like Ephesus, the rumour grew about that this man teaching a strange mystic doctrine was possessed of supernatural powers. There was nothing new in the idea. Ephesus was full of wizards, sorcerers, witches, astrologers, diviners of the entrails of animals and people who could read one's fortune by the palm of the hand or the fall of knucklebones.

Paul, it was said, was a powerful magician, and it was well known that anything associated with a magician was full of power. Power was transferred automatically into anything which had been worn or touched by the one who possessed this mysterious gift. Accordingly, coarse handkerchiefs which he had used or aprons which he had worn at his tent-making business were eagerly seized and – so it was claimed – amazing cures were effected by these efficacious pieces of cloth. The core of the matter here, as always, is the question of belief. It is only in recent years that the power of the mind in relation to matter has been scientifically investigated. Already it has been proved that some people do have the ability to influence, for instance, the roll of dice, or to read a sequence of hidden cards in a manner quite beyond the laws of probability. In the case of the 'miracles' performed by Paul in the course of his life it is noticeable always that those to whom they have happened believed in him implicitly. It is clear that belief is the necessary switch which turns on the current.

There were others apart from Paul, many others who, whether charlatans or not, were said to have magic powers. The ability to cure diseases or, in the phraseology of the time, 'to cast out evil spirits' was claimed by a number of other Jews, among them seven who are described in Acts as 'the sons of a High Priest, named Sceva'. Sceva can presumably only have been a rabbi, if that. He and his sons were clearly part of the general throng of nomad–mystics who moved from one town to another (like the quack doctors of later ages), handing out their potions or their pieces of papyrus, on which a scribble in Aramaic would seem both strange and powerful to a Greek or Roman or one of the indigenous natives. Hearing about Paul, and the supposed efficacy of this, to them unknown, 'Lord Jesus', they tried to use what they imagined was the mystic formula on a man who was clearly a violent lunatic. Upon their saying to him, 'I command you in the name of Jesus, whom Paul preaches', enjoining the evil spirit to leave him, the man replied: 'I know Jesus and I know about Paul. But you – who are you?' He then attacked them, tore off their clothes, and drove them out of the house. The logical sequence to this story is that Paul should have come and cured the man, but there is no mention of it. And it surely would have been recorded. The point again is the same one: the sick man had no belief or faith in these so-called healers.

The consequence of this episode was that many Jews and Gentiles who heard about it – and the news would have gone round Ephesus in a few hours – were convinced that this God, about whom Paul spoke, was indeed the true and veritable Saviour. In the climate of mind where Attis, Osiris, Artemis and Isis were all confused, and where men and women were dedicated to so many mythic and mystical concepts, it was hardly surprising that Paul's version of a resurrected God-Man was acceptable. 'They were all filled with fear . . .' says Acts, 'and many of those who had practised magic brought their books and burned them openly.' It is evidence of the extraordinary power of Paul's personality that these books of magic which were burned in Ephesus are said to have been worth many thousands of pounds. It was hardly likely that this episode, somewhat reminiscent of the effects of Savonarola's teachings in fifteenth-century Florence, would have been popular with the majority of people, let alone with those who had a vested interest in the cult of the Great Goddess. It was to lead to the famous riot in Ephesus.

[32]

Of Human Beings

The riot was only to be expected. It is a proof of the success of Paul's work that he had the effect of drawing large numbers of people away from the worship of the Great Goddess. Since this worship had been in existence for untold centuries, and since Artemis–Isis seemed to contain within her legend most of the aspirations of human beings, it is important to ask the question, what exactly did Paul, and his fellow workers like Aquila and Priscilla, have to give that was not given by the goddess? The answer to this is the reason why the great temple in Ephesus is in ruins to this day. The goddess was the whole cosmos, but she did not hold out any hope for human beings beyond the renewal of earthly life. Paul preached a doctrine that – apart from his belief in the imminent end of the world – still stands firm. He taught that goodness (by which he meant the Jewish and Mosaic idea of right behaviour towards one's fellows – quite apart from loving the Creator) was the most important thing in the conduct of human life. But, above this even, came the concept of 'loving-kindness'. If one understands this then one can see why his revolutionary doctrine was ultimately to change the whole of the Roman empire. One hears, perhaps, the words of Mithraism in: 'Stand watch, stand steadfast in the faith, act like men, be strong.' But in the following sentence one hears the unique statement: 'Let everything you do be done with loving-kindness.' This message, contained in none of the mystery religions, nor in the worship of 'Diana of the Ephesians', was the essential yeast in Paul's teaching.

The riot was sparked off by 'a certain silversmith named Demetrius'. He was almost certainly the head of the silversmiths' guild, for it is recorded that it was he who brought all the other members of the trade to a general meeting. The complaint of Demetrius and his fellow craftsmen was that the teachings of Paul were causing people to lose faith in Artemis. Now the silversmiths, as in any tourist area in the world, lived largely by making souvenirs. Thousands of people came to Ephesus every year to visit the great temple, and they took away with them small silver models of the temple and of Artemis. Demetrius declared:

> Men, you know that our livelihood depends on this trade. You can see and hear what this fellow Paul is doing. He says gods made by human hands are not gods at all. Not only here in Ephesus, but

> all over Asia, he has managed to convince people that this is the case. Now there's a great danger that our trade will come into disrepute. More than that, there is also the danger that the temple of the great goddess Artemis will itself come to be despised and even She, Artemis – whom not only Asia but all the world reveres – will be stripped of her greatness and come to mean nothing!

The appeal to the religious sensibilities of his hearers as well as to their self-interest had an immediate effect. Guilds throughout the Roman empire were, like modern trade unions, extremely touchy, and hostile towards any outsiders – let alone to some foreigner who was trying to take away their livelihood! Out came the banners that were borne in the processions, out came the drums and the clashing cymbals. The cry went up, 'Great is Artemis of Ephesus!' As always, it was Paul whom the crowds wanted. But on this occasion he happened to be in the house of some friends, who wisely refused to allow him to leave. Paul asked to go and answer the charges, but by that time the whole city was in a state of riot. Everywhere people were shouting and screaming that the goddess was affronted by these foreigners, that Artemis was the Mother of the World, and that Ephesus was the home of the greatest divinity, the only one who had all-embracing power. The mob finally converged on the great theatre, having seized *en route* two Macedonian companions of Paul, Caius and Aristarchus. Most of the crowd, as is usual on such occasions, had no idea what the disturbance was all about except, perhaps, that some visitors had insulted their goddess.

As always, the Jews were the most apprehensive. That was the reason why they inevitably hated Paul. Although they thought that all Gentiles were destined for Gehenna, they managed to keep up reasonable relationships with them. Then along came these maniacs, and particularly this one Saul, who invariably managed to cause an uproar. They knew perfectly well that Artemis of Ephesus was an evil idol, the kind of image that all their prophets had warned them against, but they kept that knowledge to themselves.

A Jew called Alexander, who was clearly one of the leading men in the community, was asked by the others to try and explain that it was not they who were to blame, but only a dissident handful, for whom they themselves had no respect. (This Alexander may well have been the metal-worker to whom Paul refers in harsh terms in his second letter to Timothy.) In any case, he was a brave enough man to face the howling crowd in the theatre, all of whom must certainly have known that the Jews did not believe in their goddess. He was not to get a hearing. As soon as he stepped out to speak and they recognized him as a well-known Jew they all began to chant, 'Great is Artemis of Ephesus!' The uproar went on for two hours. It was only quelled in the end by the arrival of the clerk of the city, a man who clearly knew how to handle a crowd. First of all he soothed them by pointing out that everyone knew that Ephesus was the keeper of the temple of great Artemis, 'and of the sacred stone that fell down from heaven'. (The reference is interesting; the whole origin of the cult on this site had derived from centuries past through a meteorite having fallen here.) He then went on to warn them not to do anything reckless. He added that if the guild of silversmiths had any justifiable complaint then they knew well enough that there were regularly constituted courts where such issues could be heard. He pointed out that for all the citizens of Ephesus there was a danger that they would be accused of rioting (and everyone knew that the Romans had a heavy hand when it came to any serious disturbances of the peace). That was quite enough to send them all away silent and subdued to their homes.

Paul was the root cause of the whole affair. There can also be no doubt that, had he been permitted, he would have been the first to stand up and address the crowd. The likelihood is that he would have been torn to pieces. It is significant that immediately after the episode he left the city. Indeed, some of the provincial authorities who liked him, and may well have become converts, had warned him not to show himself in the theatre. It was they too, most probably, who advised him to leave. He had been in Ephesus for two years. Even though it ended – as usual – in a storm, he could feel confident that, confronted by one of the greatest strongholds of pagan belief, he had managed to establish an active cell of Christians, and to have caused a number of others to doubt the whole concept of their fertility goddess. It seems perhaps strange that a message of peace and love should constantly have ended in violence, but the fact was that Paul was challenging thousands of years of accepted beliefs. People are unwilling to rethink their emotional heritage. For one thing, it requires a considerable intellectual effort.

While Paul was in Ephesus something that mattered very greatly to the whole of the empire had happened. The Emperor Claudius had died. Some said that he had been poisoned by his wife, the poison having been administered in a dish of mushrooms, his favourite food. 'Poisoned' was always a way of describing the death of anyone rich and powerful in the ancient world, when medical knowledge in any case was in its infancy. At the same time it is not unlikely that his wife Agrippina, a woman whom he had described as 'unchaste but unchastened', had a hand in his death. Despite his physical deficiencies, he had been a good ruler, a man who had tried to administer his vast empire with justice and commonsense. Paul, who possibly heard the news while in Ephesus, may not have realized that the death of this Roman was going to have an important bearing on his own life – not that he valued it very much, but he certainly wanted to use it to its fullest extent. Claudius was sixty-four when he died and he had been fourteen years on the throne of Rome. It has been remarked before that the great and successful years of Paul's activities occurred during the reign of this Emperor. This was not entirely a coincidence. The administration had been good, the highways, byways and seaways of the empire had been policed and made safe, and justice had been well administered. Paul owed his life on many more than one occasion to the impartial hand of Rome.

The man who succeeded Claudius had been adopted by him because he was the son of his wife Agrippina by a previous marriage to a certain Gnaeus Domitius Ahenobarbus (the latter name meaning 'Red Beard'). Tradition had it that the founder of their family had been blessed by the gods, who had turned his black beard to a bronze colour. The new emperor's name was, in full, Nero Claudius Caesar Drusus Germanicus. Of one of his ancestors it had been said, when he celebrated a Roman triumph riding on the back of an elephant: 'Why should his bronze beard surprise us? He has, after all, a face of iron and a heart of lead.' His great-great-great-grandson was to show similar characteristics, although in rather a different fashion. Suetonius says of Nero's father that

> His character was completely despicable. . . . On one occasion when driving through a village on the Appian Way he whipped up his horses and quite deliberately ran over a boy. When one of the knights criticized him frankly in the Forum he gouged out his eyes on the spot . . . Shortly before the death of Tiberius he was charged not only with treason, but adultery and incest [with his sister Domitia Lepida].

The Emperor under whom Paul as a Roman citizen was to live out the rest of his life had a disastrous genetic background. His mother Agrippina, the notoriously unfaithful wife of Claudius, was as violent, sadistic and temperamentally unstable as her first husband. Nero's father, on being congratulated on the birth of his son, had himself remarked that any child by him and Agrippina was certain to be a curse to the state, and a monster as well.

Otto Kiefer in his *Sexual Life in Ancient Rome* makes the following comment: 'It is certain that Nero was afflicted with a grave hereditary taint. . . . The young Nero developed sexual characteristics so numerous and so conflicting that it is astonishing to find them all in one and the same person. A preliminary summary would be this – Nero was a good husband, who nevertheless had strong homosexual tendencies; in addition, he had many extra-marital relations with women; his character also contained sadistic elements.' The fact remains that he was also an accomplished singer, poet, admirer of the opera and drama, and a great lover of architecture, who did much to beautify Rome and other cities of the empire. One of his ambitions, and a very sensible one, was to drive a canal through the isthmus of Corinth so as to connect the Aegean Sea with the Ionian and the western Mediterranean. This, in fact, was not achieved until the nineteenth century. The rocky nature of the terrain could not be mastered by the manpower and relatively primitive tools at the disposal of the Romans. At the same time, as a completely irresponsible master of the world, he was somewhat like Tiberius in his private life.

The following translation by Robert Graves is from *The Twelve Caesars* of Suetonius:

> Nero practised every kind of obscenity, and at last invented a novel game: he was released from a den dressed in the skins of wild animals, and attacked the private parts of men and women who stood bound to stakes. After working up sufficient excitement by this means, he was dispatched – shall we say? – by his freedman Doryphorus. Doryphorus now married him – just as he himself had married Sporus – and on the wedding night he imitated the screams and moans of a girl being deflowered.

Sporus was a beautiful boy whom Nero had (theoretically at any rate) turned into a girl by castration, and with whom he had gone through a formal wedding ceremony. Suetonius quotes a current Roman joke that if only Nero's father had married that kind of wife the world would have been a much better place.

His famous 'Golden House' in Rome contained a statue of himself over 100 feet high, with an immense swimming-pool surrounded by innumerable buildings – so that the whole edifice resembled a city more than a house or even a palace.

> All of the dining-room had ceilings of fretted ivory, the panels of which could slide back and let a rain of flowers, or of perfume from hidden sprinklers, shower upon his guests. The main dining-room was circular, and its roof revolved slowly, day and night, in time with the sky. Sea-water, or sulphur water, was always on tap in the baths. When the palace had been redecorated throughout in this lavish style, Nero dedicated it, and condescended to remark: 'Good, now I can at last begin to live like a human being!'

At about this time another human being, a balding, bearded little man, was about to set off with a few companions on a coaster bound for the port of Troas. He had been responsible for a great riot in the city of Ephesus. He was undoubtedly a troublemaker. Nero did not even know of his existence.

[33]

A Chosen Course

He was a traveller in time as well as in space. Paul's almost obsessional movement throughout eastern Europe cannot be compared to that of explorers in later centuries. Christopher Columbus, for instance, was inspired by a dream – at the back of which lay the hope of a large fortune. Francis Drake was inspired by a desire for revenge on his enemies – at the back of which lay the hope of a large fortune. Paul was seeking no fortune in the worldly sense. His activities over these years can only be interpreted in the light of that blinding light which had struck him on the Damascus road.

From Troas he went on to Macedonia again. In Macedonia he found the inevitable trouble of false readings of his message. And it was always *his* message. When it came to other interpretations being put upon it his fury knew no bounds. His energy, as shown both in his letters and in his life, is astounding, especially when one remembers that he was often very ill. From Macedonia he went south into Greece, 'where he stayed three months'.

All this, done on foot, on muleback or on the unsteady decks of small sailing vessels, would have taxed any man. If in his heart he was a dreamer, a romantic, a poet, yet he was always the practical businessman. The success of the organization that he managed to create in his travels might well be compared with that of a brilliant travelling sales-manager. Paul was the embodiment of energy, yet none of this was directed towards worldly advancement. In the final analysis one can only say that practically no one except of a desert race could have concentrated so much vitality and power towards a goal that seemed impossible. Paul had known the desert in his early years after his conversion, but he had been born in slothful and sleazy Tarsus. His extraordinary ability for concentration upon abstract thought can only be traced to his Semitic ancestry. The Semites – good men of commerce – have at the same time always possessed the ability to devote themselves to a dream.

Acts give the full pace of his travels in its usual succinct fashion: 'He was on the point of leaving [Greece] for Syria when he found out that there was a Jewish plot against him. He decided to go back through Macedonia.' With him went several of the companions. 'We sailed from Philippi after the Feast of Unleavened Bread. . . .' He went back again to Troas where he found Timothy among others waiting for him. Troas, relatively unimportant today, seemed then to have some significance which at first sight escapes one. And then one realizes that, apart from being quite a thriving port, it had this regular influx of Roman tourists bound for Troy, and Troy was the legendary home of Aeneas, in his turn the legendary founder of the Roman race. Paul liked seaports because there were no better disseminators of information than sailors. They travelled all over the empire, and a few converts made among their fraternity meant that in due course dozens of others would hear the word in places as far apart as Italy, France and Spain.

It was on this last visit to Troas that there occurred the famous episode involving the young man called Eutychus. On a Saturday evening Paul and all the other members of the community were gathered together for the communal fellowship meal. Afterwards Paul addressed all those in the room and 'kept speaking until midnight'. The room in which they met was probably in one of the typical tenements of the time, three storeys high, and all built around a central courtyard. Eutychus was sitting in one of the window embrasures and Paul's incessant monologue, probably coupled with the fact that Eutychus had had a skinful of the good local wine, made him nod off. Finally he went completely to sleep and fell out of the window. Everyone rushed down and pronounced him dead. Paul motioned them back, threw himself upon the supposed corpse, and told them not to worry, that there was still life in him. To their astonishment and vast relief they found that what he said was true and took the young man home.

Eutychus was a great deal more fortunate than the other young man, mentioned in Homer's *Odyssey*, who was named Elpenor. He got drunk on the night before Ulysses and his friends left Circe's island and went to sleep on the roof. Waking in the morning he forgot to 'take the right way down by the long ladder and fell headlong from the roof and was killed'. Ulysses unfortunately did not have Paul's healing gifts. The two stories, however, are so similar that one cannot help remarking a kind of resemblance between Homer's famous Greek wanderer and the Jewish wanderer described in Acts.

Paul knew in his heart that he had not much more time left. He could, as it were, see the end of the road lying not very far away. It is significant that when he, Luke, and the others left Troas, all except Paul went down the coast to the town of Assos by ship. Paul, at his own request, walked the twenty miles or so, alone. He had determined in due course to go back to Jerusalem and from there he was equally determined to go to Rome. He must first of all return to the sacred city, the place where Christ had died, but beyond that always lay the ultimate objective – Rome. He did not want the bustle and the squalor aboard the little coaster, even with his close friends. He needed a walk not this time with a view to making any converts, but to think out his position and the way ahead. All along his way over the years, whether in Corinth or Philippi, wherever he went, he had felt the hand of the Sanhedrin close at his shoulder. He knew that the return to Jerusalem would mean probably another scourging, almost certainly arrest, and quite definitely an attempt to have him put away altogether. But that, as he well knew – unless it was done by assassins – was something beyond the Sanhedrin's power. He knew also that he always had one recourse. As a Roman citizen he could take his appeal against whatever charges were laid against him to the highest court of all – to the Emperor in person. And that meant a voyage to Rome, at the government's expense.

He came to Assos, to that enormous rocky outcrop dominated by its temple to Athene. He had thought out his position and made his decision. Throughout Asia Minor, Macedonia and Greece, he had left thriving communities, and by his constant instruction in his letters he had done his best to ensure that his message was not corrupted and that each and all of these various cells paid their contributions to the mother church in Jerusalem. He had not failed James the Just in that. He joined the ship in Assos and they coasted down to lovely Mitylene, the capital and main harbour of Sappho's Lesbos. The poetess had been dead many centuries but they still sang her songs to the lyre in the island where the head of Orpheus had been washed ashore. The olive groves whirled like dancers. A day later they were at Chios, home of the mastic plant whose hard oval tears were highly prized for their supposed medicinal properties. From here they went on to Samos, birthplace of Aristarchus who, thousands of years before Copernicus, had come to the conclusion that the sun was the centre of the solar system and that the earth like the other planets moved around it in essentially circular orbits. One wonders what Paul would have made of that. . . . Another one of these ignorant Greeks?

Their next port of call was Miletus, city of the four harbours, whose inland territory was rich in sheep, from which the local craftsmen made the famous woollen fabric, the *Milesia vellera*. Once a great maritime state, it was still, at the time that Paul visited it, a thriving commercial port and city. It had been the birthplace of philosophers like Thales, who died in the sixth century B.C. (a man who had enough scientific knowledge to predict an eclipse of the sun), Anaximander, who had maintained that the Infinite is the source of all things, and such early Greek historians as Hecataeus. A city of culture as well as wealth then, but it was not for this reason that Paul visited it. He wanted to get in touch with the leaders of the church in Ephesus, some twenty miles away. The reason he did not leave the ship and go overland to see them is clear enough – he had been warned that the hostility towards him in Ephesus had not diminished and that his appearance would almost certainly provoke another riot.

He sent a message asking them to come and meet him. His famous address to them (Acts xx) should be read by everyone who in any way wants to understand something of the nature of this fiery, indomitable little man. It is his farewell to Asia, and in it he declares that he knows that they will never meet again. 'I go in obedience to the spirit of Jerusalem. . . .' Those words were certainly plain enough to his hearers. Stoned, scarred, lashed, scourged, the Slave of God was deliberately going to his death.

Somewhere on that walk to Assos he had come to the conclusion that, although he could probably stay in Asia or Greece for some years to come, he had to provoke the ultimate situation. The closing words of that master historian Luke are moving indeed: 'When Paul had finished, all of them kneeled down and prayed. Everyone was crying and they hugged him and kissed him farewell. They grieved above all because they knew that this was the last time they would ever see him. Then they went with him to the vessel. . . .' Paul has sometimes been portrayed – especially in Protestant circles – as an unattractive personality who corrupted Christianity. If one accepts the words of Nietzsche that 'There has only been one Christian, and he died on the Cross', then there is perhaps some argument that Paul changed the message. At the same time, any study of his own writings or of Acts will reveal a man who, though he could arouse intense hatred among the orthodox Jews, was both lovable and kind.

From Miletus they went due south to Cos, borne always by that favourable northerly wind which cools the Aegean and gives all the area that astounding pencil-sharp clarity to be found nowhere else in the Mediterranean. Hippocrates, the 'Father of Medicine', had been born in Cos some 500 years before, and at the time that Paul passed the island a Greek physician, Soranus, a native of Ephesus, was writing a biography of Hippocrates. Luke, if he had never been there, must have wanted to visit Cos, home of the man who had founded his healing profession. They passed it by and sailed on, leaving Rhodes on their starboard hand. It is curious perhaps that Paul never went to Rhodes, for the island's sailors were the backbone of the imperial navy and it was a busy and prosperous commercial port. If they sailed close to the city he would have seen the ruins of yet another of the Wonders of the World, the 100-feet-high Colossus of Rhodes, the bronze image of the Sun God Apollo. It had stood at the entrance to the harbour until thrown down in an earthquake about 200 years before Paul and his companions came this way.

They now headed west to Patara on the Asia Minor coast, one of the most important cities of Lycia, and the centre of a cult of Apollo. Here they transhipped from their coaster into a merchantman which was carrying a cargo down to Phoenicia. It was quite a long sea-voyage this time, some 400 miles over that beautiful summer sea, the dolphins leaping in the hushing rustle of the bow wave. Then they sighted Cyprus to port of them, and the shining temple of Aphrodite above the harbour of Paphos. Paul must have wondered what had become of that false prophet Bar-Jesus, and whether Sergius Paulus was still Proconsul, and whether he had remained true to his conversion. Then it was the open sea again until, after a run of about twenty-four hours, they sighted the bustling harbour and city of Tyre ahead of them. It is a tribute to their knowledge of winds and weather and the stars at night that the sea-captains of those days could so regularly make their landfalls, and could conduct a steady transport of merchandise all over this sea. Few modern sailors would care to take a vessel from Patara to Tyre without a compass.

After a week in Tyre, where he stayed with the local Christian community, waiting for the vessel to unload and take aboard Tyrian exports, Paul was on his way again. But before he left they implored that, whatever he did, he would not go to Jerusalem. He had made up his mind on that. Even the sight of all these believers, together with their wives and children, kneeling and praying on the beach, though it moved his heart as he knelt with them, could not break his inflexible resolve. From Tyre the ship sailed the few miles down the coast, called in for a day at Ptolemais, and then ran down to Caesarea. They were nearing the end of the journey. Paul's carefully chosen and deliberately set course was bringing him to the point of departure that he had long desired.

[34]

The Inevitable

It was not necessary to be a prophet or a soothsayer to foresee what Paul's intended visit to Jerusalem would mean. In Caesarea he stayed in the house of Philip the evangelist and his four unmarried daughters. They warned him not to proceed any further. This was reinforced when Agabus – the same man who had secured Paul's services years ago to take the famine relief to Jerusalem – came down to the city and implored him not to go. Agabus was well known as a prophet. In a symbolic gesture he took the cord of Paul's cloak, knelt at his feet, and swiftly tied up Paul's feet and wrists with it. 'In the words of the Holy Spirit,' he said, 'the owner of this girdle will be tied in just such a way by the Jews in Jerusalem and handed over to the Gentiles.' Paul had known this all along, and the reference to 'the Gentiles' meant of course the Roman authorities. This was exactly what he hoped for, and for no other reason would he have come back. At the same time he must have been well aware that he might suffer the same fate as Stephen had done. He had been stoned before, but this time it would certainly prove fatal, in which case he would expiate his acquiescence in Stephen's death. If, on the other hand, he was protected by the Roman authorities he would ultimately find his way to Rome.

When they heard the words of Agabus everyone implored Paul not to go. His reply indicated his resolve: 'What do you mean by crying like this and breaking my heart? I am prepared not only to be bound, but even to die in Jerusalem for the sake of the Lord Jesus.' He and his party now set off on muleback, taking the contributions from Caesarea for the mother church's relief fund. Apart from money, this no doubt included grain, dried fruits and salted fish – the latter a staple part of diet for the poor. They stayed a night *en route* at the house of a Cypriot convert and then pressed on up the winding road, which at this time of the year would have been crowded with pilgrims. The Feast of Pentecost was due in a few days' time and Paul was determined to be there for it. The curious fact is that Pentecost, which in the year 57 fell on 28 May, corresponded to an agricultural feast of Canaanite origin. It was celebrated fifty days after the Passover and is described as 'the Feast of Harvest', being held seven weeks after the beginning of the corn harvest. Apart from appropriate offerings being made in the Temple in thanks for the 'Harvest Home', it was a time when the wine went round in no uncertain manner.

As the Romans knew well, it was during this festival period that they might always expect trouble.

Paul's first objective was to see James and the elders of the church and to hand over the money for the general relief fund. He was well received and was encouraged to tell them all about his work in Asia, Macedonia and Greece. They were of course delighted at the success that had accompanied this extraordinary missionary who had been to so many places that they would never see, and who had managed to establish so many groups of believers so far afield. At the same time there were reservations. To judge from his account wherever he had been there had been trouble – and they remembered his previous record only too well. The church in Jerusalem had been quietly flourishing and they had managed to reach a kind of *modus vivendi* with orthodox Judaism. They urged Paul to go to the Temple with four other men who had taken a vow to go through the ceremony of purification. This entailed abstaining from wine for seven days, shaving the head and, at the end of the period, offering up a formal sacrifice. In this way they felt the orthodox Jews would accept the fact that Paul still followed the Law, and that reports about him which had filtered back that he had taught Gentiles and Jews things which were contrary to the Law would be discredited. Their intention was good and sensible, but in the heady atmosphere that always prevailed during the feast period it was unlikely to succeed.

Shortly before the seven days were up, Paul was seen in the Temple by some Jews from Asia who instantly recognized him. Here was the fellow who had caused trouble wherever he went. He had polluted their communities from Antioch to Lystra to Derbe, all over the place, even as far afield as Macedonia and Greece! They had also seen him in Jerusalem in the company of a Greek called Trophimus, and they assumed that he had even contradicted God's law by taking him into the Temple. This was most unlikely, for Paul knew as well as anyone that no Gentile might pass that barrier. He was dragged out of the Temple, the authorities in charge wisely closing the gates after him. At once mass hysteria swept the city. 'The people were doing their best to kill Paul. . . .'

The commander of the Roman garrison was immediately informed that Jerusalem was in a state of riot. Just the kind of thing he had expected! These Jews, outwardly so formal, so pompous, so smug – but let them get a few jars of wine under their belts and they were worse than any other race in the empire! The riot squad was immediately summoned. They came at the double, sweeping the crowd aside with the butts of their spears, smashing them back with their shields. No doubt they wished in their hearts that they were in some quiet corner of the empire, where the girls were more easily available, the wine better, and the people more tractable. Once again, Paul owed his life to the long arm of Rome. The man who was actively bent on disseminating a revolutionary doctrine throughout the territories administered by Rome owed his life on many more than one occasion to the laws of the empire, and to the Roman guardians of the peace. (One is inevitably reminded of the lives of many agitators and revolutionaries in the British empire. Their own peoples would often have killed them if it had not been for the protective hand of the very power that they were seeking to overthrow.)

Followed by the screaming mob, Paul was hustled away by the legionaries up to the fortress Antonia, overlooking the Temple and dominating all the city. The commander, Claudius Lysias – another man who no doubt wished that he had had a different appointment – had Paul arrested and chained. He then demanded of the ringleaders of the screaming crowd what charge they laid against this savaged and beaten man. Some were shouting one thing and some another, so that he could not understand what definite charge was preferred. He had Paul carried up to the garrison, while the mob continued to shout out: 'Kill him! Kill him!' As he was being taken into the fort Paul said to the commander in Greek, 'May I have a word with you?' The Roman recognized at once that this was an educated man, not some sneak-thief or ignorant peasant. 'You speak Greek then?' he asked with some surprise. 'Then you certainly aren't that Egyptian fellow who led some 4,000 men out into the desert – terrorists – and started a revolution?' He was referring to a comparatively recent occasion when there had been yet another of the practically perennial uprisings in the country, and the Procurator Felix had been forced to take action and kill most of them.

'I am not,' said Paul, 'I am a Jew, a citizen of Tarsus in Cilicia. May I please speak to these people?'

The Roman, wisely recognizing that the best way out of all this brouhaha was to let the prisoner address his own race – in the course of which he might possibly learn what the devil all the trouble was about – gave him the necessary permission. Shielded by the legionaries, standing on the steps of the great fortress, Paul (with that characteristic gesture) 'motioned with his hand to the people'. It is significant of his amazing personality that they fell silent to listen to a man whom a few minutes before they had been trying to tear to pieces. He spoke in Aramaic. This was proof enough that he was really a Jew, for what Greek or Roman had ever really learned to master the intricacies of their language? He was not a foreigner then but one who, whatever might have been said against him, belonged to their own blood. That fact won their silence and even their potential approval.

Paul went on to recount his Tarsian birth, the fact that he had been a student under Gamaliel, and that he had received strict instruction as to the Law. He told them how he had persecuted what he had then considered this dissident sect of Christ-believers in Damascus, and how he had been struck down on the way. He had been convinced that Jesus was indeed the true Messiah – the one so long promised – and that he, Paul, had a special mission to take this message to the Gentiles. That was enough. They had listened to him with attention and interest before, but here he was proclaiming that their special *Jewish* Messiah was for the Gentiles as well! Intolerable. Their fury mounted, they raved and screamed, and the still somewhat baffled Roman commander ordered the guard to take Paul into the fortress. This was not only to protect him from the people, but to find out exactly what he was saying that had provoked this riot – the last thing, he, like any garrison commander, wanted on his hands.

Torture was as widely used in the Roman world as it still is today to elicit information. It was slightly more primitive though (there were no electric contacts to apply to the genitals, for instance), but it was still extremely efficient. Paul was taken to the whipping-post, his shabby cloak stripped from him, and the lash was about to be applied. Over the years he had had enough of physical suffering, nearly always administered by his own race. He was, after all, a man now in his middle fifties. He appealed to the lieutenant in charge: 'I am a Roman citizen. Have you any right to whip a citizen who has not even been charged with any crime?'

The reaction was immediate. Panic. True citizenship was so valuable and rare that most probably the lieutenant, and few if any of the soldiers, were citizens. Word was immediately sent to Lysias that this Jew, whom they had been about to lash, was a 'Civis Romanus'. Nobody can possibly improve on the account in Acts: 'The commander went to Paul and said "Is it true that you are a Roman citizen?" '

'Yes,' was the answer. Claudius Lysias no doubt looked at this beaten-up ageing Jew with blood on his body (and every sign that he had been in many a brawl before) with some astonishment. Roman citizens, after all, were the rulers of the world – and there were few enough of them. He himself, after a distinguished military career, had managed to buy himself citizenship. But this man, whom he had been on the point of having whipped, had been – if he was to believe his words – born a citizen. Paul, as has been said before, no doubt had some documentary evidence, somewhat similar to a modern passport, which proved his status. The man was clearly highly educated, could speak Latin, Greek and this cursed Aramaic. Until his statement was proved, it was clearly unwise to treat him as if he was just another of these troublesome colonials who were always making some kind of fracas about their religion. Lysias had him freed at once but, in ordinary consideration of military security, kept him confined to barracks. The conclusion he came to, logically enough, was to allow him to meet his accusers the following morning. It was clearly, as far as he could see, not a political matter that infringed the laws of Rome, it was something to do with their infernal religion.

[35]

The Imprisoned Man

The confrontation next day between Paul and the assembled council of the Sanhedrin is one of the most dramatic events in history. Here he was at last then, the man who had done his utmost to overthrow their authority and who seemed also to be trying to overthrow the Roman empire. It was true enough that they hated being under foreign rule and treated as second-class citizens in their own land – but that had happened to their ancestors before them. One thing, though, that they had always clung to was the inevitable rightness of their faith. They had very reluctantly (rather less than more) accepted this offshoot of Messiah-believers headed by James the Just. It was difficult to fault James. He conformed impeccably to the Law in every respect and was as good a practising Jew as anyone living. There was only one thing wrong with James: he maintained that his brother had been the Messiah predicted by all the prophets. But this man Saul, or Paulus as he apparently preferred to call himself, this suspect Jew of Tarsus (probably a bastard of Roman stock for all they knew), he was something different altogether.

Paul infuriated them at once by addressing them as 'Brothers', whereas they should have been called 'Elders of Israel'. He then went on to say that he had lived a good life and had a clear conscience. A good life, a clear conscience? A man who had been spreading a corrupt version of the Jewish faith all over the world, living with Gentiles, probably eating 'the other thing', and for all they knew fornicating with heathen women in terrible temples. The High Priest, Ananias, very naturally ordered him to be struck on the mouth for blasphemy. Paul's reaction was to call the High Priest 'a whitewashed wall' for allowing him to be struck contrary to the Law. This was a terrible insult. Whitewash was used for the outside of tombs, for the mud houses of the poor, and for privies. He was accused of insulting God's High Priest, to which he replied that he did not know that he *was* the High Priest. He added in mock contrition that he was well aware from the prophets that 'Thou shalt not speak evil of the ruler of thy people'. Paul certainly knew who the High Priest was. He knew his name, he knew him from where he sat, and from his robes. Once again the revolutionary in his nature asserted itself. He then saw the chance to cause dissent among the members of the Sanhedrin. He was of course perfectly familiar with the bitter division that existed between the Pharisees and the Sadducees on the subject of resurrection from the dead. The Sadducees said that it did not exist. He now proclaimed himself a Pharisee, born of Pharisees, and that he believed in resurrection. Immediately tumult broke out, some shouting one thing and some another. The Roman commander, Lysias, who had brought Paul to the meeting, no doubt looked on with amused contempt. What could you do with such people? Here they all were shouting and screaming and tearing at one another's beards over some purely abstract matter. In any case, every man knew that when you were dead you were dead. He had seen enough of them in his life. He ordered his bodyguard to take Paul away before he got injured in the brawl. Paul was imprisoned once more in the great fortress of Antonia.

The whole thing was beyond the comprehension of Lysias. After all, he was only a *chiliarch*, the commander of a thousand men. This matter seemed to have reached a stage when it must be referred to higher authorities. At this point there was a very unexpected intervention. Paul's sister (whose name we do not even know) had married and settled in Jerusalem. Her son now came to Lysias and reported that he had heard of a plot to kill his uncle. It is almost certain that Paul's sister and her family were orthodox Jews. Had they been Christians, it is highly unlikely that her son would have been allowed to listen in on such a dangerous conversation. No doubt they disliked Paul's views, but the closeness of Jewish family relationships was such that a threat against any member of the family was a threat against all. Blood was much thicker than water – or even differences of religious belief.

Lysias, who must have been sick and tired of the whole matter, learned to his astonishment that over forty Jews, probably Zealots, or possibly Temple police, whom the Sanhedrin occasionally used to do a little discreet killing (quite contrary to Roman law) had taken a vow to murder Paul. They had declared that they would neither eat nor drink until they had accomplished their mission. Paul's nephew was brave. He took his life in his hands by reporting such a matter to a Roman. It is the first time that we hear either of him or his mother, but one must assume that in every respect there was a reconciliation, and that some part of the family patrimony must have been shortly afterwards handed over to Paul.

In the latter phases of his life there is no indication that he had to revert to his trade, or that he was ever desperately short of money. From his shipwreck journey, on to his years in Rome, there is no mention of tent-making or of poverty. It is almost equally certain that some of the churches which he had founded sent some part of their poor relief donations to this man who had brought them the news about the Messiah, and about the imminent end of the world. Lysias in any case wanted this man out of the city. Whether he was right or whether he was wrong, or whether all the Jews were mad (as he sometimes suspected), it was his duty to remove a troublemaker from a city that was fiery enough at the best of times. He wrote immediately to the Procurator of Judaea telling him that a Roman citizen by birth, though a Jew by blood, had been seized by the Jews in Jerusalem, who were screaming for him to be killed. It would appear in his view that this man Paulus had done nothing to contravene the laws of Rome. He thought, however, that for his protection it would be best to send him down to Caesarea with an escort, for there was a plot to murder him. Felix, the Procurator, must have received the news with melancholy resignation. Caesarea was pleasant enough in itself, his palace was extremely comfortable, the wine was drinkable (especially the imported Cyprus), but he was aware of the misfortune that had attended some of his predecessors. How much pleasanter it would have been to have been posted to Greece, to France – anywhere but Judaea!

In due course Paul arrived at Caesarea and was put in one of the dungeons of the palace that Herod the Great had built. Roman citizen or not, he must be securely locked up until Felix had heard exactly what were the charges preferred against him. Five days later the High Priest Ananias and some elders of the Sanhedrin came down from Jerusalem to see the Procurator. Intelligently enough, they had taken the trouble to bring a Roman lawyer named Tertullus with them. He could speak in the kind of rhetorical way that these Romans understood. They themselves could only talk about the Law and contraventions of their faith. These things, they knew perfectly well, were quite beyond the understanding of pagan Gentiles. Tertullus began in the usual manner by saying how wise the Procurator had been, and how well he had administered the area. He added that he did not want to take up too much of a busy man's time, but the fact was that the accused was a menace to society. Everywhere he went there was a riot.

Felix, who had been born a slave and had risen to his high position through his brother having been one of the Emperor Claudius's favourite freedmen, did not want trouble any more than Lysias did. He heard from this Roman lawyer that Lysias had removed Paul 'with great violence' [quite untrue] from the hands of the Sanhedrin. Paul's reply was logical – and absolutely in character. He had done nothing to contravene the Roman laws; his only argument had been with the Jews because he had said that he believed in the resurrection of the dead. Felix must have sighed. His wife was a Jewess: he had heard about all this dispute between the Pharisees and Sadducees. It seemed to him unimportant. He had a territory to administer for the Emperor Nero, and it had to be administered under the laws of Rome. He dismissed the case. But at the same time he gave orders that the prisoner, who had caused all this disturbance, should be held in custody until further notice.

Paul was well treated, allowed to receive friends, and to have his own food brought to him from outside. More than that, Felix and his wife Drusilla had this strange character brought up to them, and listened to his opinions concerning this man whom he maintained was the Saviour of the human race, and not just the promised Messiah of the Jews. Drusilla's position was a curious one. She was the third wife of Felix and, as a Jewess, should never have married a Gentile. It is more than possible that the interest shown in Paul's teachings stemmed from a feeling on her part that she should expiate her sins. She had, after all, previously been married to the King of Commagene whom she had divorced in order to marry a Roman. This certainly made her in Jewish eyes an adulteress. Felix, for his part, was a self-indulgent and rather lax administrator. He was in due course to be summoned back to Rome for an inquiry about a riot that broke out in Caesarea between the Jewish and Greek inhabitants of the city. Also, according to Acts, he hoped that this prisoner Paulus might give him a bribe in order to secure his release. Most Roman governors sent to distant parts of the empire expected that in return for their services to the state they would make themselves a small – or even a very large – private fortune. Paul was not interested. He must have known well enough that for a sum of money he could be released. He also knew that once outside the safety of the palace-prison the Jews would kill him. He saw his friends, he wrote his letters, he kept in touch with the communities, so why should he venture out?

Paul stayed in prison in Caesarea for close on two years. Then, in 59 when Felix was recalled to Rome, the new Procurator Porcius Festus had to consider among all his other problems the one of this unusual prisoner. After landing at Caesarea and being formally installed in his office, Festus left after three days to visit Jerusalem. That city, after all, was his principal charge and, as he knew from the records, the place where any trouble inevitably originated. It was his duty also to meet the Sanhedrin formally and hear their opinions about the state of things in Judaea. He heard soon enough about the prisoner in his palace. He was apparently a revolutionary, who had broken all the laws – those of Rome and those of the Jews. Festus was well briefed and he was no man's fool. He suspected at once, when these elderly Jews asked for the prisoner to be brought up to Jerusalem to stand trial, that an attempt would be made to murder him either on the way or in the city itself. He insisted that the accusers should themselves come down to Caesarea and put their case before him, where he would ensure that dispassionate justice would be administered.

The result was exactly as Paul had long ago foreseen. The charges that he had done 'anything wrong against Jewish Law, or the Temple, or the Emperor of Rome' did not hold water. Apparently he believed in some dead man – whom he maintained was still alive – and that this man was the Saviour of the world. He believed also that the world was soon to come to an end. To Festus all this meant very little. The world ended every minute of every day for someone or other. Men, women and children, they were dying all the time. Death was the only certainty. All Romans knew that.

As a Roman citizen Paul knew his rights, just as well as the Proconsul did. When asked if he was willing to go and stand trial in Jerusalem, he said 'No', he knew well enough that no trial there would be unbiased – if he ever arrived alive. He took the ultimate step. 'I appeal unto Caesar.' This was something that Festus certainly could not deny him. Paul's voyage to Rome was assured.

[36]

'Where two seas met . . .'

A few days after Paul had been granted the right of appeal to Caesar – which could not be denied him – the puppet king of Judaea, Herod Agrippa II, arrived in Caesarea to pay his first official call on the new Proconsul. He arrived in company with his sister Bernice, with whom he was living in incest. A man who owed his position to the Romans, and who was later to assist them in the capture of Jerusalem in the great siege of A.D. 70, he was one of those Jews who had become almost more Roman than the Romans. (Other and later colonial societies have witnessed many similar cases.) Festus, who was naturally preoccupied by the problems raised by his Jewish prisoner, asked this thirty-two-year-old son of Agrippa I if he would care to help him over this peculiar case. This king was Romanized, but he was after all still a Jew, and ought to be able to enlighten Festus on some of the points of their law. As far as he could see the prisoner had done nothing that contravened Roman law, and the Jews who had come down from the Sanhedrin had been unable to convince him that he had done anything contrary to their own.

Paul was brought in next day before the incestuous royals, Procurator Festus and an assembled crowd of local notables. He was chained to a soldier. He was not known as a man of violence, but only as a man who was constantly the victim of violence. In any case, he was a prisoner and the chain was symbolic more than anything else. It was a very formal occasion, the new Procurator, the King and his sister–Queen, the Roman soldiers, and the slaves waving peacock-feather fans over the assembled company. They had come to hear the opinions of a strange, balding, grey-bearded Jew about some event which he insisted had occurred within their lifetimes.

There can be small doubt that Luke himself was present, for the record in Acts is so vivid that only an eyewitness could have written it. If it was not Luke, then it was a reporter of great brilliance. Rather than recapitulate the whole scene, it is better to refer to Acts xxv–xxvii. He would be a daring man who would attempt to challenge the brevity and authority of that writer. In brief, Felix put before the assembled company the charges that had been laid against Paul, explaining also that when he had asked Paul if he was willing to go to Jerusalem the latter had appealed to the Emperor. He himself, he said, could not find that the man had done any wrong or any harm against either the Jews or the empire. Agrippa now said to Paul, 'You have our permission to speak on your own behalf.'

Paul made a characteristic gesture – 'he stretched out his hand'. He then recounted the whole of his history; born a Pharisee, became a persecutor of Christians, and then had his extraordinary vision on the road to Damascus. Since that moment he had devoted his whole life to setting up communities throughout Asia and Greece where both Jews and Gentiles had adopted the belief that a man called Joshua had indeed been not only the chosen of God, but the son of God. The world was soon to come to an end – at any rate the material world of the Roman empire – and then another kingdom would ensue, the one so long promised by the prophets of Israel. It would be the physical resurrection of this Messiah that became too much for the Roman. Festus shouted out: 'Paulus, you are mad!' He accepted the fact of Paul's considerable intelligence and knowledge of the Jewish prophets, but added the corollary. 'Too much learning has driven you insane!'

Bernice was uninterested, Agrippa was bored, and Festus for his part was infuriated with these maniacs he had been sent to govern. He had a couple next to him to whom he had to pay token respect, and he had this ragged-cloaked lunatic raving on about a crucified criminal who had apparently fulfilled all the prophets of the ancient Jews, which automatically made him the Saviour of all mankind. On the other hand, there was absolutely no reason why he should be jailed. Both Agrippa and his sister–wife agreed that he had broken no Jewish law, and he certainly had broken no Roman one. He could go free. But the trouble was that he had asserted his rights and appealed to Caesar. Agrippa remarked when he left the hall, 'This man could certainly have been released if he had not appealed to the Emperor.'

It was in this way that Paul, accompanied by Luke and Aristarchus, a Greek convert from Thessalonica, were dispatched on their way under the covering arm of Rome, in the shape of the Lieutenant Julius. Their voyage, which started from Myra, was to end in the most famous shipwreck in history on the island of Malta – or Melita as it was called by the Greeks, meaning 'Honey'. (The small island then as now was noted for the quality of the honey which its black bees made from the innumerable herbs that grew on its rocky slopes.) It was round about midnight on the fourteenth day of the *Gregale* that had driven them across the Mediterranean from Crete that the look-outs on the bows heard the sound of breakers ahead. They took a sound with a deep-sea lead and found that it was rapidly shallowing – first about 120 feet and then shortly afterwards only ninety. Quite apart from this tangible evidence, they knew by their sailors' instinct that they were rapidly approaching a shore. They could hear the boom and sizzle ahead of them and, although the night still seems to have been dark and cloudy, they could probably descry the outline of the coast.

There has been endless controversy about the exact site of this shipwreck, and for a time even the island of Meleda in the Adriatic was canvassed as the place where Paul came ashore. There can be absolutely no doubt that this was a complete misconception and later Papal pronouncements that it was undoubtedly the island of Malta are hardly necessary. I quote from a distinguished meteorological officer who formerly worked in Malta:

> The sequence of meteorological events encountered by St Paul after leaving Fair Havens, is consistent with an eastward-moving depression passing to the south of Crete. Southerly winds ahead of the depression would back to east or north-east and a strong northerly flow would be triggered down the Aegean; winds funnelling down the Cretan ravines and through the Kithera Channel would probably increase the natural wind-speed. Persistent strong winds from between east and north are normal in this area after the passage of a 'low'. The ship would thus be driven well to the west-south-west of Crete into the open sea, much as Ulysses was in the same general area centuries before.

The traditional site of the wreck is still called St Paul's Bay. It is usually unwise to query tradition. Words transmitted for generation after generation by a simple people who have little or no knowledge of books are often completely accurate. For instance, it took the genius of Heinrich Schliemann, acting solely on the basis of the Homeric poems and local legend, to find the city of Troy in the very place where all early accounts had said that it was. The only thing that can raise any controversy as to the site of Paul's shipwreck is Luke's very clear words that the ship came into a place 'where two seas met' (*Tropon diathalasson*). The bay concerned and the island on which a statue of Paul has been erected can hardly be called a place where two seas met. There are few of such in the whole Mediterranean. One is the Bosphorus where the Black Sea runs into the Mediterranean, another is at the Strait of Gibraltar, another is the Messina Strait where the Ionian and the Tyrrhenian Seas meet, yet another is the Bonifacio Strait between Corsica and Sardinia. In the small

Maltese archipelago there is only one other place where 'two seas meet' and that is in the channel between Malta itself and its sister-island Gozo to the north. At this point the eastern Mediterranean does indeed meet the western. Homer rightly called Malta 'the navel of the sea', and such it is, being almost equidistant between Cyprus to the east, Gibraltar to the west, and roughly half-way between Italy and North Africa. One might opt for the north-easternmost point of Malta called L'-Ahrax ('Fierce, cruel, rough and uneven'), for at this point the two seas meet. In any case, the exact location is relatively unimportant, some scholars having argued for one place and some for another. In the final analysis it is perhaps better to stick to tradition. Recent archaeological investigations have disclosed that the villa of an important Roman official (possibly Publius, the chief magistrate of the island) was at a place long called San Pawl Milqghi, 'St Paul welcomed'. This is comparatively close to the traditional site of the shipwreck and there is interesting evidence that a very early Christian church was built on the site of the villa. Furthermore, graffiti depicting a bearded man with the inscription 'Paul' below, in Greek letters, as well as what appears to be a shipwreck scene, would seem to confirm what the Maltese themselves have long believed.

As the ship drew in on that dark November night towards the rocks, 'they lowered four anchors from the stern and prayed for the daylight'. Some have found it strange that they should have dropped the anchors from the stern. There is no room for any confusion here. Ships of this period always carried a number of anchors both fore and aft, usually with stocks of wood and flukes or iron or lead. In some ports the ships came in to the jetty bows-on – thus necessitating stern anchors. Today in the Mediterranean it is customary for sailing vessels to lie stern-to, that is, dropping an anchor or anchors from the bow, and then backing up to the quay or jetty. But practically all modern sailing yachts or small cargo boats have engines, which means that this operation is not too difficult. In the times when Paul was sailing about this sea it was always necessary for a ship to be able to anchor either bows-on or stern-to. In any case, the master of the ship was eminently practical. He was driving on to the rocks of some unknown shore with a strong wind and following sea behind him. Had he dropped his forward anchors the ship would inevitably have swung around and her stern would have struck.

The sailors now attempted to abandon ship and began lowering the longboat – the same which they had hoisted aboard off the island of Clauda. Paul, practical as ever, spotted what they were up to and pointed out to Julius that, if the sailors went, the ship was certainly doomed. The passengers were all seasick and terrified, and in any case did not know the trade of the sea, and their only hope of salvation was to see that the professionals remained aboard. Julius gave the necessary orders to his soldiers. They cut the rope securing the longboat and let it wash ashore. St Paul's Bay can be a terrifying place when the *Gregale* blows for, although a good anchorage in summer, it is wide open to the north-east. (Only a few years ago dozens of yachts, some of considerable size, were wrecked here under just such conditions as Luke describes.) Paul, again showing that commonsense which never deserted him, and fully aware that they would all probably have to swim ashore, urged everyone to eat some bread. Acts can hardly be accurate in making him say that for the whole fourteen days none of them 'had eaten a thing'. They would not have survived. The expression is metaphorical. The bread must have been old and wet, for the galley fire would have been doused many days before, but at least it was some form of sustenance for the ordeal that lay ahead of them.

After everyone had eaten something they set to along with the sailors and threw the rest of the wheat cargo into the sea. The captain of the ship – if he was also the owner – must have been in a very sad frame of mind. He had lost the whole cargo with which he had been hoping to catch the winter wheat-market and the high prices that then prevailed in Italy. Now he was about to lose his ship as well. When dawn broke they saw that they were just off a bay with a beach (this does indeed sound like the traditional site of the wreck), so they cut the hawsers to their stern anchors, let go the two big steering paddles, and hoisted the small fore-sail. There was nothing else for them to do, with the *Gregale* still blowing, but to run the ship aground. From the shore the Maltese villagers watched them. They would have been fishermen mostly, and it is quite certain that this would not have been the first merchantman that they had seen swept upon their shore. Malta is an ideal sailing area for about eight months of the year but in the late autumn or winter, if a north-easter makes up, it presents its hard limestone rocks to the unlucky visitor.

Acts says that the bows hit a sandbank and got stuck. It was equally probably a rock-shoal such as are common on the east coast of the island. At any rate the bows were held fast while the thundering swell behind them was gradually pounding the stern to pieces. Looking back with the benefit of hindsight, if their stern anchors were holding, they would have been better to have stayed where they were, and sit it out. But they had been under extremely unusual conditions of bad weather for a fortnight (*Gregales* usually do not last much more than four days) and the sight of land proved too much for the captain and the crew. Comparatively few ships are lost at sea, it is the land that destroys them – as the evidence of ancient wrecks all round the Mediterranean littoral testify.

At this point, as the ship was breaking up, the military escort decided that it would be better to kill the prisoners under their charge than give them the opportunity of escaping. This was natural enough, for to lose a prisoner meant forfeiting your life. Julius, their commander, intervened. It is clear that he had become fascinated with Paul's character – possibly even with the doctrine that he preached? He could not make an exception just for one prisoner, so he ordered that none of them were to be harmed. Those passengers who could swim he ordered to jump overboard and make for the shore first, the rest would follow on planks or pieces of the ship's broken timbers. There was no loss of life, and all reached the shore safely. It was exactly as Paul had forecast. They would be wrecked on an island, but everyone would be saved.

[37]

Winter and Spring

The friendly islanders welcomed them, and they learned that the island was called Melita. Some of the people possibly spoke a version of demotic Greek but most of them spoke a Semitic tongue derived from their occupation in earlier centuries by the Phoenicians. The Maltese had already started to gather sticks and brushwood together and had got a fire going even before the salt-stained survivors from the wreck reached the shore. 'The natives there were very friendly to us. . . .' They still are to this day, hospitality being a very noticeable characteristic of their race.

Paul, undaunted as ever, was one of the first to start helping with gathering sticks for the fire. It was at this point that the famous episode with the snake occurred. As he was about to throw on his contribution a snake, which had no doubt been hibernating in the brushwood, jumped out and fastened on his hand. When the Maltese saw the snake hanging from his hand they assumed that he must be a murderer, a man whom their god – or goddess – had allowed to escape from the sea, but would not allow to escape from justice. Paul merely shook it off into the fire. They expected him to die but, when he carried on quite normally, they decided that he must be a god. His reputation was established from the very beginning.

The fact of the matter is that the snake was almost certainly not poisonous. To quote the *Encyclopedia Britannica* on the subject of the fauna of Malta: 'There are four species of lizard and three non-venomous snakes. . . .' The legend in the island to this day is that Paul removed the venom from all the snakes there – just as St Patrick is credited with having done in Ireland some four centuries later. Occasionally, but only rarely, a poisonous snake may be met with in Malta – despite the *Encyclopedia*'s dictum – but these have probably come in on cargo-boats from other countries such as Lybia. F. A. Spencer in *Beyond Damascus* quotes the interesting fact that 'To this day in southern Italy there are persons called Sanpaulari, who by virtue of being born on St Paul's night (24–5 January) can, according to popular belief, kill poisonous beasts with their spittle....'

One unusual thing emerges from any consideration of Paul's stay in Malta. Luke takes a disparaging view of these kindly people and calls them 'barbarians'. This was because he was a Greek. The term in his language for non-Greek-speakers had long been – indeed since the days of Homer – *barbaroi*, people who went 'bar-bar-bar' and were not civilized enough to speak Greek. Paul on the other hand, quite apart from his friendship with Publius, the 'head-man' or chief magistrate of the islands, had the considerable advantage over his two Greek companions of being able to speak Aramaic. Now the Punic dialect the islanders spoke had descended from the same roots as Hebrew, and there can be little doubt that Paul would have been able to communicate with them in their own tongue comparatively easily. To this day, indeed, Maltese who visit Syria and the Lebanon, homes of their distant ancestors, do not find it so difficult to do the same. This might well account for the success of Paul's winter months in Malta, where it would seem certain that he left behind the nucleus of a flourishing church. Publius is traditionally credited with having been the first 'Bishop' or Elder of the church in Malta.

The principal cause of Paul's success was that he managed to heal Publius's father, who had fever and dysentery, by the traditional 'laying on of hands'. Again there can be little doubt that the all-important element of faith and belief came into play. Here came a man who could speak not only Latin and Greek, but even a version of the Maltese tongue. He had been wrecked and saved, bitten by a snake and taken no harm – all the elements requisite to implicit trust were present. Julius, Paul and his two attendants stayed three days in the house of the chief magistrate and then left, no doubt to rent a room in the capital city, which was sited on a rocky ridge almost in the centre of the island. It is very unlikely, contrary to local tradition, that Paul was imprisoned in a cave or dungeon. Julius by now had come to trust his prisoner completely and, in any case, it was Paul who of his own volition was taking his case to the Emperor in Rome. No doubt the other unfortunate convicted criminals were so immured, which must have been very unpleasant for them. The winters in the island, although not very cold, can be extremely windy and damp. But from the viewpoint of Julius they were expendable – they were probably going to be expended in any case in the arena – and the only thing that he had to see to was that they did not escape. And a small island, only eighteen miles long by nine wide, was prison enough in itself, once the sailing season had closed and no ships were available. If any of them had escaped by boat they could not have got any further than the even smaller sister-island of Gozo, where they would have been still more marooned.

Luke records that after the sensational recovery of Publius's father numerous islanders 'came to Paul and were healed'. One may possibly suspect that some of Luke's medical knowledge came into all this. He records that 'they gave *us* [my italics] many gifts. . . .' Some of the low-lying areas of Malta would certainly have been malarial, and indeed have been so right into the twentieth century until brought under control by modern science. Luke is very brief about the winter in Malta; no doubt, for the reason given above, that he could not speak the language. He concludes his account with the words: 'After three months we sailed off on a ship from Alexandria called *The Twin Gods* which had been wintering in the island.' A ship from Alexandria was certainly a grain-ship which had probably been lying in that great limestone cleft in Malta's eastern side which is now known as Grand Harbour. The 'Twin Gods' under whose protection Paul and all the others sailed were Castor and Pollux, sons of Zeus, to whom he awarded immortality by placing them in the sky as the constellation still known as Gemini (The Twins).

They had been wrecked in November, so, as they were only in Malta for three months, they must have left before the official opening of the sailing season – probably in early February 62. Paul was now in his middle or even late fifties, a man who had suffered all things, but who had remained consistently faithful to his dream for many years. He had set up his network of communities throughout the Levant, Cyprus, Asia Minor, Macedonia and Greece, and now he had even added the island of Malta to his list. Rome lay ahead and, quite apart from the city itself, he was eager to see what remained of the Christians there – if any – after the Claudian expulsions. One of the reasons that the captain of the ship left so early was undoubtedly that he wanted to catch the grain market as early as possible to get a high price just after the winter, and before the other big grain-carriers began to move up from Alexandria. The other reason was that at this time of the year there are a great many southerly winds. Sicily, his next landfall, lay only seventy miles to the north. They passed Cape Passero, the southernmost cape of Sicily. Then, presumably, their favourable wind failed them for they put into Syracuse for three days. It was there that the Athenian fleet had been destroyed during the Peloponnesian War over four centuries before, and the fate of the Athenian empire had been sealed. Luke may have known this, but it is doubtful if old dead history meant anything to Paul. Once the greatest port in the central Mediterranean, indeed one of the greatest cities ever created by the Greek genius, Syracuse was now no more than just another big commercial port in the communications network of the empire.

When the wind shifted they headed on up north, passing under the giant bulk of Mount Aetna which at this time of the year would have been covered with snow. It cannot have been warm in February going up the Sicilian coast, but the travellers of those days were a hardy lot – they had to be. But in a large ship of this type there would have been a good galley, hot soup and bread, and no doubt many of them would have brought fresh provisions with them. The ship called in at Rhegium, the city and port on the toe of Italy. Possibly some of the travellers had to disembark here, but it seems more likely that the current which pours through the Messina Strait was against them. This strait connects the Ionian and Tyrrhenian seas, and twice daily the current reverses from north to south. The captain would have given a wide berth to the whirlpool Charybdis on the Sicilian side, not so fearsome to his large vessel as it had been to the open craft of Ulysses, and the monster Scylla no longer leaned from her rock on the Italian side to seize sailors from passing ships. The Romans had very largely tamed this sea – as far as any sea is tameable.

They got a favourable southerly again and were on their way up the coast of Italy, passing Capri which Tiberius had made so infamous – that beautiful rocky island with its sweet vines which would still have been in their winter sleep. They were now in the Bay of Naples with the great mountainous peak of Vesuvius on their starboard hand. At the moment it was dormant, and the citizens of Stabiae, Herculaneum and Pompeii, those resort towns which nestled at its feet, were happy in their market places, their village bars and brothels, unsuspecting that the mountain was potentially active. One year later, in 63, the giant began to stir, and there was a severe earthquake which did considerable damage. Then it went to sleep again. Everyone forgot about it until, on 24 August, 79, for the first recorded time, it exploded in that violent eruption which destroyed all the towns in the area. No doubt, if Paul had known the manners and mores of the Pompeians and others, he would have said that it was the just judgement of God. But by then he had been dead for fifteen years.

On their starboard bow there now lay the city of Neapolis, gleaming white in the sun. One of the earliest Greek settlements in this area and long a great centre of culture and commerce, Neapolis (the modern Naples, now disfigured by high-rise buildings and international architectural sub-standardization) was at that time one of the pearls of the Tyrrhenian Sea. Its wonderful scenery and luxurious life had long attracted Roman residents, although it still remained basically a Greek city. Paul's ship was not bound for it, however. The excellent harbour of Puteoli, which lay some miles to the west, was the principal emporium for the Alexandrian grain trade. The town had a better harbour than that of Neapolis, partly resulting from the extravagance of Caligula, whose floating bridge of boats, extending as far as the spa of Baiae, had in part been extended into the mole behind which all the merchantmen were berthed. The whole place was a seething cosmopolitan hotchpotch from all over the empire. There were traders and sailors from every nation, mountebanks, flute-players, barkeepers and whores – everything that can be found in a great international port. Paul was nearing the end of his journey – of all his journeys.

[38]

A Roman End

Paul was permitted by his escorting officer Julius to spend a week in a private house in Puteoli. The latter no doubt had a number of official tasks to execute, such as getting his condemned prisoners on the road to Rome. Probably, like any soldier, he also wanted some days and nights ashore in a cheerful place where there was plenty of entertainment. He knew in any case that Paul would not, as it were, desert. Paul himself was undoubtedly highly encouraged to find that there was a small Christian community already established in Puteoli. He heard about a similar one thriving in Rome. Messages were sent ahead to tell the members to expect the imminent arrival of the man who had done more than almost anyone else to promote their cause. Clearly the Claudian expulsions had not proved entirely effective or had been rescinded by Nero or, which is far more likely, had just been allowed to lapse. A change of emperor in Rome was somewhat similar to a change of government in a modern state. The previous administration was almost invariably discredited. A new set of administrators took over, and many previous edicts were abolished – or quietly forgotten.

From Puteoli, Paul, his two friends and his escort made their way up to Formia, an ancient town from which the great Appian Way marched all of forty miles to Rome. Many Roman nobles had their villas near Formia, for the area produced good wine and the climate was considerably better than that of Rome in midsummer. Paul at last was nearing his destination, the one for which he had fought so hard over so many years. He was nearing the heart of the matter, the place from which one man alone, the Emperor, proclaimed that he was God.

What did Rome mean to Paul? It was certainly the largest city he had ever seen. It made Tarsus, Jerusalem, Corinth and even Athens look provincial. Its population at that time was over a million Roman citizens, and probably about the same number of slaves. It was the same Rome which the great satirist

Juvenal was to write about not very many years after Paul's death:

> The wagons thundering past
> Through those narrow twisting streets, the oaths of draymen
> Caught in a traffic jam . . .
> If a business appointment
> Summons the tycoon, he gets there fast, by litter,
> Tacking above the crowd. There's plenty of room inside:
> He can read, or take notes, or snooze as he jogs along –
> Those drawn blinds are most soporific. Even so
> He outstrips us: however fast we pedestrians hurry
> We're blocked by the crowds ahead, while those behind us
> Tread on our heels. Sharp elbows buffet my ribs,
> Poles poke into me; one lout swings a crossbeam
> Down on my skull, another scores with a barrel.
> My legs are mud-encrusted, big feet kick me, a hobnailed
> Soldier's boot lands squarely on my toe. Do you see
> All that steam and bustle? The great man's hangers-on
> Are getting their free dinner, each with his own
> Kitchen-boy in attendance. Those outsize dixies,
> And all the rest of the gear one poor little slave
> Must balance on his head, while he trots along
> To keep the charcoal glowing, would tax the strength
> Of a muscle-bound general. Here's the great trunk of a fir-tree
> Swaying along on its wagon, and look, another dray
> Behind it, stacked high with pine-logs, a nodding threat
> Over the heads of the crowd.
>
> (Translated by Peter Green)

This was the world that Paul was to get to know during the years that he spent in Rome awaiting trial. Undoubtedly he lived in his own quarters, part of a tenement rented and paid for by himself and his supporters. It was possibly in the vicinity of a barracks, for day and night a soldier on duty would have been chained to him. It was from here that he wrote some of those magnificent letters to the Philippians, the Ephesians, Colossians, to Philemon, Titus and Timothy, and doubtless others which have since been lost. Rome stimulated him, and how could it not? At long last, after years of travel and constant ill-health and much physical ill-treatment, he had reached the seat of power. He talked with the Christians, he talked with the Jews, he talked with anyone who would come and listen to him. He established in Rome a centre of believers that, despite all the later submergence of the Roman empire, would never die. Acts concludes with the words: 'For two years Paul lived there in a place that he rented himself. He welcomed all who came to see him. He told them about the Kingdom of God and about the Lord Jesus Christ, speaking with complete boldness and freedom.' It is evidence of Roman liberalism that, even under the reign of Nero, he was allowed such liberty of speech.

Paul was also to get to know the Rome described so brilliantly by J. W. Mackail centuries later:

> The drip of water from the aqueduct that passed over the gate from which the dusty, squalid Appian Way stretched its long suburb; the garret under the tiles where, just as now, the pigeons sleeked themselves in the sun and the rain drummed on the roof; the narrow, crowded streets, half-choked with the builders' carts, and the pavements ringing under the heavy military boots of guardsmen; the tavern waiters trotting along with a pyramid of hot dishes on their heads; the flower-pots falling from high window-ledges; night, with the shuttered shops, the silence broken by some sudden street brawl, the darkness shaken by a flare of torches as some great man, wrapped in his scarlet cloak, passes along from a dinner-party with his long train of clients and slaves.

There is no evidence that both Peter and Paul were in Rome at the same time, or that Peter had preceded him. All rests on tradition which, as has been seen, is very often right. Despite later tales that Paul extended his missionary voyages as far as Spain after an acquittal, it seems highly unlikely that he or Peter survived the Neronian persecution of the Christians which followed on the Great Fire of Rome in 64. The story that Nero himself instigated this is, as Tacitus remarks, uncertain. It is highly unlikely. Even some of the Emperor's possessions, including the palace he had built to link the Palatine Hill with the famous gardens of Maecenas, were destroyed. Nero, unstable though he was, was hardly the man to instigate a fire that destroyed two thirds of his capital city.

The people could not be compensated even by the wise measures that Nero took in ensuring that, in the rebuilding of the Capital of the World, only a small percentage of the new buildings might be of wood. The major part had to be of stone from Gabinum or Albano, which was fireproof. The fire no doubt, like the Great Fire of London, started entirely accidentally. As Rome was composed largely of wooden tenements it would have spread swiftly from house to house if a wind was blowing. The fire-fighting services were inefficient. Nero had them considerably improved, ordering that in future every household should have its own fire-fighting apparatus. People had also been illicitly tapping the water-supply so that sufficient pressure was not available at certain key points.

Prayers were offered up at various shrines, and the famous Sibylline books – the supposed repository of all wisdom – were consulted in attempts to discover how to appease the gods. 'But,' to quote Tacitus, 'no human aid, no bounty from the Emperor, no prayers to heaven, did anything to erase the popular impression that the fire had been started deliberately.' Nero looked around for a scapegoat, and found an easy one in the most unpopular sect in Rome – the Christians. The Jews with their arrogance, their extraordinary god, and their strange eating and social habits were bad enough – but even the Jews hated the Christians! Another good political reason for getting rid of them was that they denied the divinity of the Emperor. They would make no formal concession on this score, as even the Jews were prepared to do. 'Their founder,' as Tacitus tells us, 'was one Christus who had been put to death in the reign of Tiberius by the procurator Pontius Pilate.' Infanticide, incest and cannibalism (because of a misunderstanding of the Eucharist) were among the charges laid against them. '. . . This abominable superstition was held in check for a time, but then it spread not only throughout Judaea, where it had started, but even to Rome itself, that enormous reservoir and natural home for every kind of filth and depravity.' Tacitus, greatest of Roman historians, was an aristocrat by nature. He hated this slave-religion, just as much as he detested the Roman mob.

The Christians were put to death 'amid every kind of mockery'. Dressed in the skins of wild beasts they were torn to pieces by dogs. They were crucified or burned to death. By night they were strung up and set on fire. They were used as human torches to illuminate Nero's gardens, which he threw open to the public for their entertainment. Even Tacitus concludes his assessment of their treatment with the words: 'Although they were guilty and deserved their fate, a kind of compassion for them spread among the people. They were being killed to satisfy the cruelty of one man and were serving no public end.'

It is almost certain that, amid this holocaust, Paul would have been one of the first to go. Whatever the fate of Peter, whether crucified upside down as tradition has it, Paul would to the last have been able to insist on the rights of a Roman citizen. There can be little doubt that he was beheaded. His dust, long since sifted with that of Caesars and of peasants, trembles somewhere beneath the roaring traffic of Rome. The Kingdom still has not come.

The words remain for ever:

> Though I speak with the tongues of men and of angels, and have not charity, I am become as sounding brass, or a tinkling cymbal.
> And though I have the gift of prophecy, and understand all mysteries, and all knowledge; and though I have all faith, so that I could remove mountains, and have not charity, I am nothing.
> And though I bestow all my goods to feed the poor, and though I give my body to be burned, and have not charity, it profiteth me nothing.
> Charity suffereth long, and is kind; charity envieth not; charity vaunteth not itself, is not puffed up,
> Doth not behave itself unseemly, seeketh not her own, is not easily provoked, thinketh no evil;
> Rejoiceth not in iniquity, but rejoiceth in the truth;
> Beareth all things, believeth all things, hopeth all things, endureth all things.
> Charity never faileth: but whether there be prophecies, they shall fail; whether there be tongues, they shall cease; whether there be knowledge, it shall vanish away.
> For we know in part, and we prophesy in part.
> But when that which is perfect is come, then that which is in part shall be done away.
> When I was a child, I spake as a child, I understood as a child, I thought as a child: but when I became a man, I put away childish things.

For now we see through a glass, darkly; but then face to face: now I know in part; but then shall I know even as also I am known. And now abideth faith, hope, charity, these three; but the greatest of these is charity.

EXPLICIT

Index